Stereophonics

Just Enough Evidence to Print

Stereophonics

Just Enough Evidence to Print
The Official Inside Story

Danny O'Connor

Danny O'Connor is a respected music journalist with the BBC who has made programmes on subjects ranging from the Beat Writers to the Nu Skool Punk scene. For the last four years he has been one of the voices of Entertainment News on Radio One and is currently responsible for journalistic output across the network's flagship *Lamacq Live* and *Evening Session* programmes. He has been responsible for documentaries on U2, Travis, Gomez, Coldplay and Stereophonics, to name but a few.

Danny began his career in news in 1990 but soon his lifelong passion for pop culture took over and he moved to GLR where he became daytime editor. He has also worked in TV, notably on the Channel 4 music show *The White Room,* and has written for magazines and newspapers including the *Irish Post* and *Melody Maker*.

Danny has recently produced a TV series called *Play Loud* for the BBC digital channel PlayUK. This is his first book.

In memory of Patrick Kevin Murphy

First published in Great Britain in 2001 by
Virgin Publishing Ltd
Thames Wharf Studios
Rainville Road
London
W6 9HA

A catalogue record for the book is available from the British Library.

ISBN 0-7535-0527-4

Typeset by TW Typesetting, Plymouth, Devon
Printed and bound by Mackays of Chatham PLC

Contents

All that old road of the past unreeling dizzily as if the cup of life had been overturned and everything gone mad. My eyes ached in nightmare day.

Jack Kerouac
On The Road

Acknowledgments

As you would imagine, chronicling a band over a period of four years is a task that is impossible without the help and kind hearts of lots of people. Likewise chronicling a band from their infancy is a privilege not afforded to many because of the degree of trust involved. So, first off, a heartfelt thank you to Kelly, Richard and Stuart for inviting me into their worlds and making me part of their great adventure. It has to be said that none of this would have been possible without John Brand who, in his role as manager, has been an invaluable help. There have been many great nights, many great conversations and lots of smiles. Thank you also to Natalie Seymour at Marsupial for dealing with several hundred enquiries!

When I first went to Cwmaman I wandered into the Ivy Bush not knowing a soul. That night I met Kelly's parents, Oscar and Beryl, and Stuart's mother, Mabel, for the first time. All I can say is thanks for not running me out of town! Since then our paths have continued to cross, so particular thanks to Oscar for sharing his infectious love of music and to Mabel for those 'setting the world to rights' phone conversations. Thank you also to Richard's folks, Richie and Mairwen and to Graham Davies and Mervyn 'The Mop' Owen.

The Ivy Bush may be firmly rooted in South Wales but I could swear sometimes it has four wheels and twelve bunk beds. A big thank you to the crew for making my little 'holidays' more than memorable. From V97 to Reading 2000 Julian 'The Cap' Castaldi has given me more abuse than I've had in a lifetime and that from a man who looks like Murdoch from the A-Team! He has also provided most of the photos for this book and has, from the beginning, been a great support and a font of information. As ever I am forever in his debt. Likewise thanks to Dave Roden, Stephen 'Rooster' Davies, Simon Collier and Chris 'Swampy' Stone for upholding the Welsh constitution wherever you roam. Come on down Mick Brown and Abbiss and Arturo take a bow. Thanks also to Terry Jones for being 'the star' of the Reading weekend. Hearty thanks too to Neil McDonald, tour manager extraordinaire and all round top man, for looking after me like a parent.

The Stereo family has of course grown and taken on international dimensions over the years so a big thank you to 'the main men', Marshall Bird and Steve Bush, for their support and help along the way. Thank you too to Marco Migliari and everyone at Real World. I raise a glass also to Jeremy Pearce and David Steele from V2 Records for their repeated hospitality. Thank you too to Pier Reid for smiles and tears and to Pinko for inspiration and beers. To Julia Connolly in London and Sharon Lord in New York – thanks for sorting out the Crowes interview. Thanks also to Richard Branson for taking the time and to Jackie McQuillan for making it happen. Likewise much love to Scott Thomas at ITB, Emyr and Eilian at Avanti, Cath Goldby at Rima Travel and Julian Carrera and everyone at Hall or Nothing.

Special thanks to Scott Piering who ran the company responsible for, among other things, Stereophonics' Radio and TV Promotions. Scott is no longer with us. He was an inspiring individual and a very good friend and mentor. He is sorely missed. Scott surrounded himself with some great people too, so a big thank you to the entire former cast of Appearing. At this stage I have to thank Nicky Sussex in particular because she has worked hand in hand with me over the years on many many radio interviews with the band. More importantly she's done it with enthusiasm and great efficiency – even when confronted with a gaggle of virtually naked men, so thank you Nicky!

Thank you, too, to the people who have given up their time to be interviewed for this book – the aforementioned families surrounding the band plus Gil Goldberg, Noel Gallagher and Gem from Oasis, Chris Robinson from the Black Crowes, Owen and Cerys from Catatonia, the Charlatans and Tom Jones. Thanks to Caroline Lewis from Gut Records and Tom's management, Mark and Donna Woodward, for making things 'flow' in Los Angeles. A special thank you also to keyboard impresario Tony Kirkham for being a top geezer and to Steve Lamacq from Radio One for his contribution, advice and unfailing support.

So to the team that worked on the book. Respect to Ian Gittins for getting things up and running and thanks to James Bennett at Virgin Publishing for picking up the torch. A big thank you to Scarlet Page for her inspired cover photo.

Thank you also to Chloe Buswell for helping me out in a time of need. Special, special thanks to my No 2 on this adventure, Rachel McHalroy – without your hours and hours of hard work this wouldn't have happened and for that there aren't words and there wouldn't have been words!

Last but not least, thank you to the family and many friends who have unknowingly helped out. To Izzy, Jimbo, Rosaleen, and Eileen, your love and support is everything. Thanks to Paulo Hewitt and Steve Turner for their professional advice and to the powers that be at Radio One for giving me the go-ahead. Thanks also to Sean Collins for my rough guide to Wales, not to mention an unforgettable day at Morfa. Likewise a big thank you to Mark, Eileen, Sheila, Robert, Aidan, Helen, James, Roger, Leesy, Sali, Karen, Murray, Muttley and Spencer for their interest/concern. Before I go, cheers to the gang at 'the O'Conor Don', Marylebone Lane, W1 and to the fine people behind and in front of the bar at 'the Ship' on New Cavendish St, W1. I couldn't conclude without tipping my cap to the good people of Loughanure, Co. Donegal, especially Sean McFadden who was a big part of my American adventures. Finally thank you to Joanie for all her love, laughter and unfailing support.

Prologue – The Big Chill

THE WIND BLOWS IN HARD and cold from the Bay, drowning out the sounds of Christmas revellers in the city nearby. Looking out there, over the water and beyond the horizon, it seems like we're on the edge of forever. Turn the other way however and there's a thousand different stories unfolding every moment. Cardiff is no longer the port that time forgot; quite the opposite in fact. It's now one of Europe's youngest and most vibrant capital cities.

The St David's Hotel stands centre stage in the heart of the Cardiff Bay area, towering like a monument to a new world. Millions of pounds are being invested all around. Offices, leisure facilities and housing now stand where the docks used to be. Gone are the mudflats, replaced instead by a freshwater lake leading out to the rivers Taff and Ely. There's an eight-mile boardwalk on top of the barrage that encircles the Bay, but tonight it's too dark to see anything out there.

It's 7 December 1999, and tonight from the St David's Hotel you can almost hear the ghosts of Christmas past. You can imagine a century ago when this area was awash with ships ready to set sail with their loads of coal, steel and tin-plate brought in from the surrounding valleys. You can imagine the cross-cultural melting pot that it must have been, with sailors from all over the world waiting to pick up the minerals that fuelled the industrial revolution. You can imagine the steam, the noise and the smells of the busiest port in the world.

What's harder to dream up is what happened when the place began to wind down. It's thought that Cardiff's docklands, or Tiger Bay as it became known, went into decline in the early 1900s. From the beginning, the dockers' fortunes were inextricably linked to those of their contemporaries at the nearby steelworks and collieries. While the World Wars brought a perverse prosperity due to the need for armaments, the post-war eras saw a slow reduction in trade. Coal was cheaper elsewhere, where there were no unions or wage structures, and so the British coal industry soon began to lose out to cheap foreign imports. However, it wasn't until the 1980s that business in the Docklands ground to a bitter and messy halt. By the late twentieth century there was only a fraction of the pits and steelworks still operating, so the docks were virtually redundant. Market forces had conspired against them.

So here we are, almost 100 years after the boomtown era, and Wales is, for the first time ever, partly self-governing. In fact the seat of that government, the new National Assembly is due, rather aptly, to move into a building nearby. Welcome to new South Wales!

There's one subject on everyone's lips this evening. Immediately after I got off the train at Cardiff I noticed the cab drivers at the station's rank. They were standing around in groups of two or three, blowing through their hands to keep warm, swapping anecdotes and talking up the night in prospect. A few hours later they would be rubbing their hands together as it became apparent that they were in for a good night's business.

The newspaper seller kept shouting 'CIA Sell Out', as if advertising some grand tale of espionage and shady dealings. En route to the hotel I wandered into a pub and it was obvious that the same topic was being discussed there.

At the hotel the two receptionists disappeared down the other end of the desk when I tried to check in. A minute later one of them came back and shyly enquired whether I was a member of the Stereophonics party. I said I was and she grimaced in embarrassment before asking if I knew of any way of getting tickets for the Cardiff International Arena, or the

CIA as it's better known: 'You see, my friend is a big fan and the show sold out within minutes.' Her friend, it transpired, was the other girl on reception. I could tell because she was scarlet. I collected my room card and said I would do whatever I could.

Things had changed quite radically from Stereophonics' days of playing to twelve people in the Y Club in Cheltenham.

The Cardiff International Arena is much like the NEC and the SECC, or Wembley Arena for that matter. The huge stage is flanked on either side by large video screens. True, there are several bars dotted on either side of the main standing area, but in the main the place resembles a giant school gymnasium or an aircraft hangar. That's not to suggest that the atmosphere is subdued or downbeat – quite the opposite in fact. Arenas, without exception, are pretty soulless places, but tonight the crowd is loud and colourful. There are lots of Santa hats, lots of Stereophonics T-shirts and lots of Christmas party spirit.

Since the band played here for the first time last December, they've sold over a million records, picked up several awards and become national pin-ups. In doing so, they, along with the Manic Street Preachers, Catatonia and the Super Furry Animals, have come to symbolise a new-found confidence in South Wales. Tonight 7,000 people have turned up to acknowledge that, including the two receptionists from the St David's Hotel!

The gig is more than just a bunch of songs. Like the band's Morfa spectacle some months earlier, which drew 50,000 people to a stadium in Swansea, it's a heady celebration of a place that has once again found its own heroes and villains. The kids here don't need to look to America, or even to England, for inspiring stories or role models. Welsh sporting life is once again all over the back pages, courtesy of Joe Calzaghe, Ryan Giggs, Neil Jenkins, Mark Williams and the Quinnell brothers, among others.

Welsh cinema has also emerged from total obscurity largely due to the success of *Twin Town*. In the same way that Welsh music has moved beyond the mammoth talents of Tom Jones and Shirley Bassey, it was important that Welsh cinema did likewise and produced some contemporary stars to rival

3

legends like Richard Burton and Anthony Hopkins. *Twin Town* took a tentative first step along that road while introducing the many talents of Rhys Ifans. Before *Twin Town*, not too many films had been shot in Wales using Welsh talent. *Twin Town* turned that on its head and opened the floodgates. It was no surprise, then, that a year or so later the much-hyped club culture flick *Human Traffic* was set in Cardiff, giving the city the official seal of approval from the style *cognoscenti*.

Anyway, back to the CIA. Outside there's a fleet of parents waiting to ferry their offspring home safely. Inside their beloved sons and daughters party with ruthless abandon, aware that this is a defining moment on their journey into adulthood. Talking to them afterwards it's it clear why they're here. Songs like 'Local Boy in the Photograph', 'A Thousand Trees', 'Traffic' and 'Just Looking' aren't simply raucous anthemic stomps or searing ballads: they're real soul records. The songs relay experiences that resonate, and because of that they are tunes these sweat-drenched fans will take home with them, tunes they'll hold dear for a very long time.

The band's looks and origins are also an attraction, but it's that ability to connect with their audience that seems to make the difference.

Everyone has had a party tonight, and it's a party that they won't forget too soon. Time has shown that the artists who define a generation are often those who have something to say. Tonight as the crowds sing along word-perfect to 'Billy Davey's Daughter', no one can deny that this band provides more that just the soundtrack to a simple Christmas piss-up.

Back with the band at the hotel the mood is understandably celebratory. The bar area is packed and the evening has a seasonal feel, complemented by the view. Through the window hundreds of lights flicker across the bay and you can see why, at night anyway, Cardiff is likened to that rather more established Bay area, San Francisco. The scene couldn't be more festive – the place is lit up like a Christmas tree.

Closer to hand there are lots of familiar faces from the band's home town of Cwmaman. In addition there's John Brand and Natalie Seymour from the management company,

David Steelefrom V2 records, Neil McDonald the tour manager and dozens of other well-wishers milling around.

The band are getting cleaned up after the show so it's perhaps a timely opportunity to explain who the hell I am and what I'm doing in the middle of all of this.

Three years ago on a dismal Sunday morning in November 1996 I went along to interview a new band called Stereophonics at Battery Studios in Willesden, North London. It was raining heavily and, you've got to admit, 11 a.m. on a Sunday is a bad time by anyone's standards, unless you're a priest. They were there recording a couple of tunes which would eventually see the light of day, almost a year later, on their debut album, *Word Gets Around*.

At the time, I was a freelance music reporter for BBC Radio, doing interviews and features for programmes on Radio 1, Radio 5 and the BBC World Service. The idea was to do an interview that could be used, in some form, on all three networks the following week. Interest was high because their limited edition debut single was the first ever record on Richard Branson's much-hyped new label, V2 records. The record, 'Looks Like Chaplin C/W More Life in a Tramps Vest', was due for release the following day.

The interview went well despite my opening quip about the previous day's footy. Holland had hammered Wales 7-1 in a World Cup Qualifier twenty-four hours earlier. Bergkamp got a hat-trick. Kelly Jones, Stuart Cable and Richard Jones weren't impressed.

We talked about Cwmaman, which I'd never heard of. I talked about my family home in the northwest of Ireland. They'd never heard of it either, but the conversation naturally moved on to the pros and cons of small working-class communities.

An hour or so later, after chatting further about the music, we said our goodbyes and I emerged into the grey glare of a wet Sunday lunchtime and drove home armed with a demo tape. As my endearing but crappy little grey car wound its way through North London, I repeatedly listened to 'A Thousand Trees' on its tinny stereo system. If this was how it sounded coming through something with a street value of fifteen quid, how would it sound on some proper gear? I was intrigued.

Some months later I moved to Radio 1 on a full-time basis and our paths continued to cross regularly. There was a particularly memorable weekend at V97 during which Kelly unveiled his fleeting love of Hawaiian shirts. Cardiff Castle was probably the stand-out moment of the following year, although Stuart's Afro-like barnet for the NME Brats tour came a close second. This year (1999) has had too many highs to mention but a particularly messy night in Cannes is up there (chairs in hotel pools, Kelly skinny dipping) and then there's tonight.

So right now, fifty-odd gigs and almost as many interviews later, I'm at the St David's Hotel to talk books. The boys have been asked if they'd like to co-operate with me on an authorised biography of the band. They're reluctant but agree that the book should tell not simply the story of the last three years, but the two decades that went before as well. They're also aware that there are various cut-and-paste jobs out there riddled with misinformation – one writer even suggested that Kelly and Richard were brothers!

The meeting is characteristically brief and to the point and, once all parties are in agreement, everyone returns to the party. That is, everyone except Kelly and myself, who retire to a quiet corner to do an interview for a Radio 1 documentary called 'A Kick up the Nineties', talking about the previous decade in music.

Ten years earlier, Kelly was about to start college to pursue his interest in scriptwriting. I, on the other hand, was just finishing college and entering the wonderful world of paid employment as a journalist:

DANNY: One of my lasting memories of the early part of the 1990s was one of my first big rock interviews. I was at Rock City in Nottingham to talk to Nirvana. Unfortunately Kurt Cobain had had better days and decided to lie on the floor for the duration of the interview. A brilliant songwriter but a deeply disturbed human being.

KELLY: When I went to college I was really into Nirvana, Pearl Jam and the Black Crowes. I went to college because I didn't know what to do when I left school. I didn't want to get a job because I thought, if I get a job I'll end up being stuck in a rut, so I thought I'd bluff my way through college for a few years. When I was there Nirvana were nearing their peak. I'd obviously heard of bands like Mudhoney and all the Subpop stuff. There was the Pixies and then Nirvana came out and did it in a way that everybody could kind of relate to ... I'd say it was the songs. 'Smells Like Teen Spirit' was completely different to anything else we'd heard. Before that we'd had stuff like Bon Jovi and Def Leppard. I think *Nevermind* was, and still is, a brilliant album.

DANNY: I remember that time obviously being dominated by grunge. There were so many great tours coming to the UK. Sonic Youth with Pavement, Nirvana, Pearl Jam, the Pixies and, later on, the Breeders. At the same time, though, I remember watching a lot of MTV and it was championing bands as diverse as En Vogue and the Red Hot Chili Peppers, Arrested Development and the Black Crowes. It was also the time when U2 released *Achtung Baby* and started that whole *Zoo TV* concept which, love 'em or hate 'em, was genius.

KELLY: It just seemed to get bigger without being part of any particular scene. Somebody bought me the *Popmart* video for Christmas last year and we were planning this Morfa stadium thing. I looked at *Popmart* and it really depressed me. I thought, how are we going to follow that? They're from Dublin and here they were on the other side of the world, in Mexico City, in front of all these people with big lemons and mock McDonald's signs. The sound of the video was incredible as well, and the way they perform – Bono chasing the cameramen and stuff. I've never seen a band play as well as that live. I've watched people like Beck and he's been incredible. I watched Beck on the side of a stage at a festival and I thought he was inspiring. David Lee Roth once said, 'If you can't do it in a pair of jeans and a light bulb then you're crap' – but if you've got the money, there's nothing wrong with giant lemons.

DANNY: I suppose the other thing the nineties will be remembered for is the birth of the boy-band. It was a decade when record companies really focused on getting them young. It just seemed to be quite blatant. Target twelve-year-olds and create disposable bands to suit their tastes.

KELLY: It's really disappointing, to be honest. Once, pop music 'for the kids' was made by people like the Supremes, who actually could sing, people like Elvis Presley, who actually could play, and people like the Beatles, who could write songs. I find it a bit disappointing that there are so many bands out there who have got talent and never get to that level because kids are buying that other stuff. It's a bit weird how the whole thing works. There's not many people out there just writing stuff which is changing things. People like Lauryn Hill I think are brilliant but there's not much creative stuff going on any more. It's just people bringing out records to chart and make money. They might as well be making soap.

That's why Kurt Cobain shot through the middle because he came along and he did do something different. All of a sudden somebody goes completely against the grain and everything changes.

DANNY: So, ten years ago in Wales there was the dying embers of the Alarm. Shaky and Bonnie had had their day and the Manics were just kicking off really. Their story straddles the nineties. They came in inspired by punk rock, Public Enemy and Guns N' Roses and are ending the decade in three weeks' time as one of the biggest bands in the land.

KELLY: I think the thing is that there's always been talent here but there's always been a major misunderstanding that, as a nation, Wales was somehow backward. People in England forget that when you go abroad they actually call Great Britain England, and unless you're Welsh you don't know how frustrating that is. The great thing about the Manics, Catatonia, the Superfurries and ourselves is that, hopefully, the image of Wales is changing. At the same time, local attitudes have changed. When we started playing here in Cardiff it was dire. Unless you were a tribute band, nobody would give you any decent gigs. We were going to become a Jimi Hendrix tribute band at one point. That's true. We were going to have two bands and then the money from the tribute band would pay for us to go to London to play in front of people who allegedly knew about music – record companies, I think they call them.

Things are changing here. There are more and more things out there, drama-wise, writing-wise and music-wise. Everybody seems to be doing something now whether it's new media, magazines, whatever. Cardiff has got a buzz about it now. I've been to a lot of cities and I still think Cardiff is one of the better cities in the world to be honest. It's quite small but it's got everything that you want, including hotel bars – and it's your round!

Since then there have been many adventures and many conversations. The midnight oil has been well and truly burned and, hopefully, the result is a real insight into the worlds of Kelly, Richard and Stuart.

Their critics accuse them of being pedestrian, even ordinary. The phrase 'meat and two veg' is thrown around by journalists and record company people who don't get it.

On the flipside, their fans are among the most loyal and passionate around, and in keeping they've emerged as one of the biggest bands in the UK.

There's no denying Kelly is a small-town raconteur with a universal tongue. His words have impacted upon millions and doubtless will continue to do so. There's also no denying that when Stuart and Richard are added to the mix then you have that rarest of things – a genuine band who are friends first and musicians beyond that. They share the same heritage and culture and that, in the fickle world of rock'n'roll, makes them a very special entity indeed.

This book is by no means definitive but it's as close as we're going to get, for the time being anyway. It's more of a 'story so far' than a complete biography. Stereophonics don't pretend to be anything other than what they are. That's why this whole experience has been challenging and intriguing.

Their story is not a rock'n'roll cliché. There are no overdoses or visits to rehab. There are few slanging matches. Instead there's the tale of three dreamers who were brought up on a diet of music; three dreamers who now revel in living the life of a real rock'n'roll band; three dreamers who realise how lucky they are; three dreamers who have no intention of fucking it up. There are too many new songs to write, too many untapped territories to play and too many fascinating people to meet. For now, though, there is just enough evidence to print.

1

Wake Up and Smell the Rain

Standing at the bus stop with my shopping
in my hands when I'm overhearing elder
ladies as the rumours start to fly you can
hear them in the school yard scrap yard
chip shop phone box in the pool hall at
the shoe stall every corner turned around

it started with a school girl who was
running running home to her mam and
dad told them she was playing in the
change room of her local football side
they said tell us again so she told them again
they said tell us the truth they found it hard
to believe cause he taught our steve he
even trained me taught uncle john who's
father of three

but it only takes one tree to make

a thousand matches
only takes one match to burn

a thousand trees

you see it in the class room in the
swimming pool where the match stick men
are made at the scouts hall at the football
where the wise we trust are paid they all
honour his name he did a lot for the game

he got his name knocked up above the
sports ground gates but now they are
ripping them down stamping the ground
picture gathers dust behind the bar in the
lounge it takes one tree to make

a thousand matches
only takes one match to burn

a thousand trees

wake up and smell the rain shake up he's
back to stay he hasn't been on a holiday
his growing seeds don't believe why he's
been away in the school yard change room
playing fields bathroom phonebox office
blocks corner turned around they keep
doubting the flame tossing the blame got
his name knocked up above the sports
ground gates but now they're
ripping them down stamping the ground
picture gathers dust in the bar in the
lounge it takes one tree to make

a thousand matches
it only takes one match to burn

a thousand trees

1 LA Confidential

'THAT'S BLOODY WHATSISNAME!'

The words trail off, discouraged by the lack of interest from the assembled throng. It's 27 January 2000, and Stereophonics are in Los Angeles to shoot a video for 'Mama Told Me Not To Come' with Tom Jones. The flight was a lengthy one, and everyone is a little dazed and confused. Half of the gang has arrived from the UK, the others from Las Vegas, where they partied hard with Tom last night. Still, Pinko (video director and band confidant) persists.

'It is, it's Johnny Depp sitting over there by the plants near the door!'

He's not wrong. Edward Scissorhands, Gilbert Grape, Cry Baby, Ed Wood – he's just yards away. Kelly admits that Depp is an actor he really admires but when encouraged to go over and say hello, he's reluctant.

'I was watching *Donnie Brasco* on the plane the other day and now he's sat over there and I'm supposed to go and say hello? He's probably never heard of Stereophonics and I'll end up making a prize dick out of myself.'

As everyone checks in, Depp's musical dalliances become the topic of conversation. He had a brief spell playing guitar with Shane MacGowan, and more recently he spent time with Noel Gallagher while Noel was writing *Be Here Now*.

Suddenly Kelly is walking towards the seated area where Depp is chatting to some guy. There's a brief moment of uncomfortable silence, but seconds later the two are talking.

Kelly is trying to explain who he is and why he's interrupting. Gradually the quizzical expression on the actor's face gives way to a broad smile, and minutes later Kelly's back, grinning like the cat that got the cream.

'I thought, he's just a bloke. That other guy is the director of *Backbeat* and they're having a meeting about a Hunter S. Thompson adaptation. Anyway I said, "Sorry to interrupt, but, er, my name's Kelly and I play in a band called Stereophonics." He stood up and shook my hand. I said, "You know Noel, right?" He said, "Yeah." I said, "He's just had a baby girl this week." He stood up and shook my hand again and said, "What was your name again, man?" I told him. He said, "Fuck, man, she's had it, are they OK? What's the name?" I told him I didn't know the details but he was like, "Thanks man, thanks; fuck, I'd better call him." I said, "It's good to meet you, see you later!"'

The Mondrian is the place to be in Los Angeles, or so they say. It's a multi-storey complex towering over Sunset Boulevard with a room-rate to make your eyes water. The legendary rock'n'roll hotel, the Chateau Marmont, is across the road (comedian John Belushi was found dead there in 1982 of a drugs overdose), and the Sunset Marquis is a stone's throw away.

This is it – the city of angels, Tinseltown, the beautiful place for the beautiful people, LA – the self-professed capital of pop culture, the place where the only currency is dreams. Here the screens are always big . . . and silver, of course. Granted, it has a seedy underbelly, a sick soul and as much sincerity as a TV evangelist, but tonight that is of no concern; tonight the town needs a paint job and the decorators are on hand. Reality is on standby ready to be summoned in 48 hours, but for now it's cocktails in the Star Bar (where else on Earth would have the sheer brass to call its watering hole the Star Bar?).

The Vegas contingent has had a shorter trip but has got off to a bad start. Kelly, Tony Kirkham (keyboard player), John Brand (manager), Julian Castaldi (friend, photographer) and Pinko had three hours' sleep the night before and are uncharacteristically subdued. Stuart, Richard and myself have, to use

Kelly's phrase, 'camping eyes'. It's 6 p.m. local time, 2 a.m. body-clock time, and the eleven-hour flight from London has left us in need of immediate distraction. Everyone has hit the adrenaline reserve and there's an air of mischief hovering over proceedings.

So, as the dusk settles, the sky does that beautiful scarlet thing and a massive neon Tommy Hilfiger sign lights up the encroaching darkness. It features Lenny Kravitz decked out in black Raybans, posing with the American flag as a backdrop. Perfect!

The candles suddenly come alive on the poolside tables and a sound system starts pumping out 'Gypsy' by Fleetwood Mac.

To make life even more surreal, upon arrival at the Mondrian there's a message waiting for Kelly from Rhys Ifans (he of the suspect underwear in *Notting Hill*). Rhys is out here shooting a movie with Harvey Keitel in which he plays the devil's son, or something. More immediately, though, Kelly has been summoned to the phone. It's Rhys on the line. They make tentative plans to meet up and Kelly returns to the table by the pool.

'We've never actually spoken before, but we hit it off straight away. We've both gone through the same changes. One minute you're one thing, the next it's all turned upside down. He's on call shooting nights, so he's got to wait until ten to find out whether they need him or not, but he's invited us round to his hotel for a quick beer!'

Rhys Ifans is a born entertainer. There are stories of dinner with Ozzy Osborne (a big fan of *Notting Hill*, apparently) and of course about making *Twin Town*. The tales of his first ever US visit with his co-star and brother are seriously colourful, to say the least. Rhys had also been based at the Mondrian until a few weeks ago, when he decided the all-white minimalist décor made it feel like waking up in an asylum ('Four hundred dollars a night to wake up in the nuthouse!').

Anyway, over at his current hotel he's just happy to get out of his room and hang out with some boys from back home, though the threat of a certain phone call is definitely hanging over proceedings.

'Fuck it. I'm going to ring them.' And with that, Rhys disappears to his room.

He's barely gone before the door into the bar area swings open and there's the bedraggled Welsh film star standing with his arms raised like he's just lifted the FA Cup.

'Enter the Dragon, lads – I've got the night off!'

More drinks are ordered, and Kelly stands up and makes an announcement. 'Boys, we are on the pop! We are well and truly on the pop!'

A few beers later and its time to consult the local listings. By an amazing twist of fate the El Rey Theatre boasts Brit hopefuls Catatonia, and ten minutes away the Troubadour has some outfit called Travis playing.

Catatonia are doing an early doors, invite-only gig for press and radio but, despite the fact that we're closer to the San Fernando Valley than the Rhondda, the assembled 'Taffia' easily sort out tickets upon arrival.

Cerys and the boys play a collection of tunes from *Equally Cursed and Blessed* to a packed hall of Bon Jovi lookalikes, many of whom are led into the dressing room afterwards to do that quintessentially American thing – the meet and greet. Owen from the band, meanwhile, is taking a trip down memory lane.

'I remember when we were on a bill with Stereophonics at the Coliseum in Aberdare. They were billed as the Tragic Love Company and there was a lot of talk about them at the time. I think that was the night they met their manager. The other band on the bill, the Pocket Devils, also met their manager that night. I wonder how he feels!

'I think Kelly had a bit of a football hooligan mullet and baggy jeans but we didn't really spend a lot of time with them. Stuart said hello but the other two seemed quite shy. Anyway, on the night they were blinding and we were terrible. My amp went down and it was all a bit grim.

'Still, here we are just over three years later in Los Angeles. It's a bit mad really.'

Cerys joins the conversation. 'I remember Kelly had a fur coat on and Stuart wasn't quite as loud as he is now I've got to know them. The stand-out moment with these fellas for me was in Amsterdam just over a year ago. We were sharing a bill at this gig at the Paradiso called "London Calling" and I went on and lost my voice after about four songs. They were gorgeous. They were there telling me not to worry about it and I really needed that at that time. It was just fantastic having people who share the same experience and come from a similar background. They were so comforting.'

It finally gets too much when the twelfth unknowing soul asks Richard what it's like to be in Catatonia. Everyone says their goodbyes and plans an escape. Within minutes the dressing room is full of pseudo-Richie Samboras, wondering where the band is. Cerys is outside looking for a cab with Stuart and Richard. They're all heading back to the Mondrian, but Kelly and Rhys are on a roll. A breakaway party, including John, Julian and myself, has decided to accompany them to see Travis.

The Troubadour is a legendary Los Angeles venue. It's hosted some seminal gigs by the likes of the Doors, Guns N' Roses and Nirvana, to name but a few. As you walk into the venue the side of the stage is right in front of you. This hasn't escaped Kelly's attention as he grabs Rhys and proceeds towards the stage where Travis are doing their thing. Frontman Fran is talking in between songs, when suddenly up pop two beaming faces on to the stage. He nearly jumps out of his skin but when he realises what's going on he throws his arms around Kelly, who grabs the mike and, in the worst Irish accent imaginable, does an impression of Eamonn Andrews.

'Fran Healy, you thought you were just playing a gig in Los Angeles but tonight, Fran Healy, this is your life!'

Fran recovers to play out the rest of the set, which culminates with a crowd-pleasing version of Britney Spears's '. . . Baby One More Time'.

Travis are nothing if not the best of hosts, and the after-show party is a friendly and intimate affair. As is the way with small get-togethers, it's hard to ignore familiar faces – especially when you don't know them. It's forgivable, then, that our entire party has clocked the fact that Billy Connolly has walked over and is currently chatting to Rhys.

If the truth be told, Kelly has very few heroes in this world, but the Scottish comedian is definitely one of them. You can sense that he's looking on in the same way he did when, as a 10-year-old, he was crouched inconspicuously in the Ivy Bush pub in South Wales listening to the grown-ups and their stories of small-town scandal.

Kelly grew up on a diet of storytelling, whether it was based around local folklore or tales from the silver screen courtesy of Jack Nicholson or Steve McQueen. Tonight there are similarities, but major differences as well – Kelly is no longer sitting quietly in the background. At 25 he's quite worldly for his years, but that doesn't prevent his sense of boyish wonder at what's happening around him. He still likes the same things, except the line between what happens on and off the screen is becoming increasingly blurred.

Suddenly Rhys summons his new best friend. The rest of the room carries on regardless but Kelly looks focused, as if everything is happening in slow motion and he can't hear anything around him. Billy Connolly says hello and starts talking about a friend of his, Eric, who runs a cigar place in Beverly Hills. Eric is a big 'Phonics fan. Kelly accepts the compliment graciously but all he can think of is the massive impact this guy has had on his life. After all, he owns every Billy Connolly video known to man and rates him as a storyteller in the same league as someone like Bob Dylan.

Meeting heroes is never easy, but Kelly is warming to the challenge. He tells Billy how surreal it is to come face to face with a man who has been making him laugh for as long as he can remember, adding that he has written him several letters (which he's never posted). The conversation then turns to their mutual love of Dylan and Neil Young before they trade numbers and Kelly returns to the gang.

A few yards away, Rhys has convinced a couple from Birmingham that he used to be an artexer in South Wales, and he got to know Kelly because he was his local milkman. God knows how, but they seem to swallow it, probably because Kelly is hell-bent on discussing the impact of huge superstores on small-town milkmen.

'People don't know what its like any more to wake up in the morning and go to the front door only to find that some bird has stuck its beak through the foil bottle top. That's real life!'

Tonight, on the other hand, is proving to be a long way from real life – as Rhys concludes, 'People believe anything when they think you're famous.'

Travis are congenial hosts but even they, after a couple of hours, fancy a change of scenery, so everyone decides, in true LA rock-star tradition, to retire to the Viper Room. The name alone conjures up images of wealth, fame and Bacchanalia, of Johnny Depp and his pals and of poor old River Phoenix, who died of a drug overdose on the pavement outside.

Kelly hitches a ride there with Billy Connolly's pal Eric, the aforementioned cigar man from Beverly Hills. Eric has a laptop in the back of his jeep and proceeds to put on a DVD. It's the Morfa Stadium show, which, as you would imagine, blows Kelly's mind. 'It's totally mad watching scenes from a gig you've done in Swansea as you're driving down Sunset Boulevard with a mate of one of your heroes!'

The Viper Room looks much like any traditional American bar, except smaller, a lot smaller. It's a lot more basic than you would expect, with simple wooden tables on a spit-and-sawdust floor. Dougie Payne from Travis is there, accompanied by fellow Scot Kelly MacDonald, of *Trainspotting* fame, but the posse is mainly drunken boys. But tonight it's only a quick drink and back to the Mondrian to join the others. The lethal combination of booze, jetlag and the fact that it's 2 a.m. local time has seen off plenty of casualties, and within a few minutes the party has ground to a snoozy conclusion. Just as well really, because tomorrow is the video shoot for 'Mama Told Me Not To Come'.

As the cab pulls out of the Mondrian on to Sunset Boulevard, Friday lunchtime is in full swing. There are dozens of groomed, beige-looking people on the terrace at the hotel trying to out-salad each other, but this side of the car window there's nothing but tired eyes and mumbled directions. The cab winds its way along Sunset, past Santa Monica Boulevard and Golden

Gate Avenue before hanging a left up Micheltorena Street. The automatic engine audibly groans as it begins its ascent up towards Silvertop House, which towers over the city and, from a distance, resembles the Thunderbirds HQ.

This is the location for the video shoot. Work started on the house in 1955 and was completed in 1977. In the process, the interior designers came up with a pad to rival Gracelands for sheer kitsch. It's owned by an ageing surgeon, who apparently has turned down offers from the likes of Leonardo Di Caprio. He's not daft – he's getting a small fortune for making it available for just one day. The place has a very cinematic feel to it, redolent of the movie *Boogie Nights* and most of the Bond films. It's not surprising to find out that the architect responsible, John Lautner, also designed homes that featured in *Diamonds Are Forever* and *Die Hard*.

The main room, where the party scene will be shot, has an abundance of toffee-coloured leather sofas, a perspex chess table with matching chairs and several animal-skin rugs, but the *pièce de résistance* has to be the cocktail bar in the corner of the room. As far as lounges go it's huge, with a floor-to-ceiling window providing an awesome view over nearby Silverlake, which is glistening in the afternoon sun. Closer to hand is the outdoor swimming pool, which looks idyllic; deep turquoise-blue water and pristine white tiling. Later it will come into its own, but for now all eyes are focused on the extras.

The idea is that Tom and the boys are the house band at an extravagant and downright extraordinary party peopled by a wide variety of weirdos and hosted by an elderly woman, who is transformed into a young, sexy model as the video progresses. The casting agent has definitely done the job on the freakshow front, not that you would expect anything else from Ridley Scott's production company. *Bladerunner* may have had mutinous androids, but this lot seems to be more extraterrestrial than human. The woman with the body of Elle McPherson and the face of Marilyn Manson particularly stands out. She, like the other twenty or so extras, is of course an actress who is forced to take on bit parts until Spielberg calls. One thing's for sure: no one in their right mind would dare question her on the subject.

Time for the turn! The 'Phonics wander in dressed in their wedding-band best. Kelly is sporting a black frilly dinner shirt, Richard has the same thing in maroon and Stuart neatly complements the picture with a black shirt and maroon shiny jacket. No one in the room bats an eyelid. The assembled cast aren't being nasty; it's just that, despite over two million album sales in Europe, the 'Phonics have yet to make a real impression Stateside.

Tom Jones, however, most definitely has, and when he enters the room decked out in a black shirt and tie and grey suit, he oozes star appeal and the room dutifully shuts up and stares.

The camaraderie between the four artists is tangible as they set about hamming it up for the cameras. They can't stop laughing at the antics of the supporting cast. The extras are going for it big time, dancing like amphetamine-fuelled loons who are having some kind of fit. It's part S Club 7, part *Rocky Horror Picture Show*, but the amazing thing is that they manage to reproduce it all day, much to the amusement of all present.

Tom Jones first met Stereophonics when they came along to see one of his shows in Cardiff in 1998. He returned the compliment, checking them out at Wembley Arena the following year, but the relationship is something more than professional opportunism. During one break in filming, Tom tries to pinpoint why a man of 59 years of age, a contemporary and confidant of Elvis Presley, is so enamoured of the Cwmaman contingent.

'There's some great young talent coming out of South Wales,' he reflects. 'When I came out of the same area in the sixties there were no local rock bands. I wanted to know what Stereophonics sounded like, what Catatonia sounded like, and what the Manics sounded like, so I bought the CDs and I was thrilled because it's new music. They're coming up with some great songs, and that's what I like about Stereophonics. They're a live band and they write their own stuff. They do it the old-fashioned way, and I feel at home with them.

'For instance, just two nights ago I wound up a fifteen-day stint at the MGM in Las Vegas. The boys turned up late on Tuesday night after I'd had my post-show dinner, so we started drinking in the bar. The chat was good so we went up to Studio 54, which is the discotheque in the MGM. We were in there until about 6 a.m., and then I decided to go to bed – but the lads hit the 24-hour bar. I had to walk past this bar to get to the lift and, after a split-second's deliberation, I thought we might as well finish it off, so we did! We didn't get to bed until about ten o'clock in the morning.

'I had to do a show that night, the last one of the run, and obviously the trouble with drinking all night is that you get dehydrated. Usually on stage I have a tray with six glasses of water on it and usually I'll drink one, maybe two, but the other night I drank the whole six. My voice was working, thank God, and the boys came to the show and seemed to enjoy it, so it was worth it in the end.'

Tom is interrupted by Rhys, who has arrived in the twilight and is greeting the Voice like a long-lost friend. If you're from Wales, you feel like you know Tom Jones, even if you don't.

Given that everyone has taken a reality bypass and entered a world where there are no hangovers, beers are once again the order of the evening. The director, Laurence Dunmore, is keen for Rhys to do a cameo in the video and suggests an Austin Powers-style 'parting of the waves' dance. Rhys refuses point blank. He's more than happy to be in the video but isn't so keen on coming across like a wanker. Eventually a compromise is reached. Rhys is to wriggle around the floor trying to look up girls' skirts. Not quite *Twin Town* but it's the lesser of two evils. One take later and it's all in the can.

Back at the Mondrian there's the small matter of Friday night at the Star Bar to deal with. It's nigh on impossible to get in unless you're at the very least a Baldwin brother, but all problems disappear into the warm winter night with the magic words 'Tom Jones will be joining us later'. A special table is hastily erected and we are ushered to a prime spot by the pool. What they don't know is that Tom has no intention of showing up. He's got a Disney soundtrack to do tomorrow.

Anyway, within minutes cocktails are being raised in his honour and, as the intrigued stares from the wider bar area turn away, Kelly is still trying to take the whole thing in . . .

'We're flying to Chicago in the morning and I don't think there'll ever be three days like this again. Tom Jones is the man. Where I'm from he's the stuff of legend, and we've been on the pop with him in Vegas! And Rhys – what a funny guy. If someone told me this was going to happen when we were doing Black Crowes' cover versions in the Ivy Bush I'd have told them to fuck off.' His voice trails away. 'These last three days have been the best I've ever had!'

2 Stand By Me

CWMAMAN TRANSLATES INTO ENGLISH as the Aman Valley. The River Aman is one of the tributaries that run into the Rhondda, which in turn cuts through the heart of South Wales. The town is one of the many small former pit communities that grew up along the sides of the valleys as the industrial revolution took hold in the second half of the nineteenth century.

Cwmaman lies to the northeast of the Rhondda Valley area close to Aberdare. Nearby Merthyr Tydfil is the biggest conurbation in the area. It acts as the northern vertex of a triangle that runs southwest to Swansea and southeast to Cardiff. During the boom years of the early twentieth century the area within that triangle was producing 57 million tons of coal per year. South Wales had a population of over a quarter of a million people, two-thirds of whom were living in the various communities that had sprung up alongside or close to the River Rhondda.

The local pits were linked by rail to Cardiff's docks, providing an easy route to the rest of the world. Coal was plentiful and the export trade was lucrative. In Cwmaman, like everywhere else in the area, life rotated around the local colliery. It did have one difference though. It was close to Aberdare. Aberdare didn't have any pits but it was well established as a market town and as such it played the party host to the area's good times. In later years it would be called the Las Vegas of the valleys.

The area also witnessed its fair share of mining disasters as poor working conditions and unscrupulous entrepreneurs combined to condemn hundreds of miners to an early grave. There were many more who didn't realise the side effects of working underground in substandard conditions and died of ailments brought about as a result.

By the 1980s a combination of cheap coal coming out of poorer countries such as Poland and parts of South America had meant that the South Wales coalfield couldn't afford to compete, and it fell into decline. That decline, though, accelerated at an unthinkable pace when the British electorate voted for a shopkeeper's daughter from Grantham. Margaret Thatcher's loathing of the unions and in particular the NUM resulted, ultimately, in the total demise of the coal industry throughout Britain. It left areas decimated and jobless. The population migrated and by the mid eighties the Rhondda Valley area and its satellites were home to 81,000. Sixty years earlier that figure had been 160,000. It's strange to think that the coal and iron mines came and went in just 150 years.

The early seventies was a tumultuous time for the Jones family in Cwmaman. Oscar and Beryl had two boys and would soon be expecting their third when Oscar's father, Godwin, passed away. He'd been suffering from the lung disease emphysema, brought about by years spent down the local pit, Fforchaman Colliery, or Brown's pit as it was more commonly known.

Oscar explains the situation. 'My father was a miner. He worked at the local pit practically all his life but he died quite young at the age of fifty-two. He died through working in the colliery. He'd contracted emphysema so he didn't have much of a life after about the age of forty-five. He was pretty much bedridden.

'My father and his generation had a very different life to what we know now. Most of their time was spent at work. My mother was a housewife and she also worked in a works canteen at a site where they were developing opencast mining.

'Beryl's father was a miner as well. He was a bit of a boy, Frank. He liked to drink, he liked a good song and he was quite a good footballer at one time. Apparently he was on the books for Wolves at the time Billy Wright was playing. Still, he too ended up spending most of his adult life underground.'

At the turn of the century there were two collieries in Cwmaman but it was Brown's pit that survived. Almost everyone living locally worked there. In fact the town was built almost as a labour camp to the pits, so when times got tough it was hard to find alternative ways of earning a crust.

During the sixties and seventies, as production at the pits was winding down, some businesses moved into the Aberdare area, attracted by reasonable running costs and a cheap labour force. Oscar's generation, who were leaving school in the early 1960s, were caught in the midst of considerable social and economic change.

Oscar further explains: 'From my era, when I left school at fifteen, a lot of lads my age did go to the collieries but most of them went to the factories.

'I think Brown's pit lasted until around 1970. I think that started the decline of Cwmaman village then. Before that there must have been at least six grocers' shops in the village plus a newsagent, a Co-operative and various other little shops – shoe shops, clothes shops. There aren't any shops left now. It wasn't just the people who worked in the pit who suffered. It was also the little businesses, which relied on the miners.

'A lot of the miners moved from Brown's and went to work at the other pits elsewhere in the valleys until they all started shutting down. It was a devastating blow to a little village, not just for Cwmaman but for other little villages throughout Wales which were in the same predicament.'

Oscar, however, had always harboured an ambition to succeed with his singing. From his youth, when he'd sung in variety shows in the social clubs peppered throughout the valleys, he'd always been keen to emulate his heroes, Stevie Wonder and Randy Newman. He started performing regularly in one of the pubs in Cwmaman, the Ivy Bush, which would later play a pivotal role in his son's development as well. The 'Bush' was run by a guy called Cliff Chips (so-named because his family once ran a fish 'n' chip shop), who soon joined Oscar on piano. Eventually Cliff went back to running the pub full-time and Oscar recruited a band. Oscar and the Kingfishers specialised in cover versions and soon became a top turn on the burgeoning early seventies circuit in South Wales.

Oscar picks up the story: 'One of my mates sent off a tape to Ron Richards, who was producing the Hollies at the time. Ron was in partnership with three other guys including Sir George Martin. He liked what he heard and came down to Wales with one or two other people from Polydor Records. They decided that I could have a future in it, so I started recording in Air Studios on Oxford Street in London. I recorded a song that Graham Nash wrote called "Simple Man". I also recorded a song George Harrison had written, which was called "It Won't Always Be This Way". On one of the sessions Dudley Moore was playing piano. Things were looking quite good for me at the time because Tom Jones had broken on to the scene. I think he had a number one with "It's Not Unusual".

'My biggest claim to fame was that I supported Roy Orbison back in the early seventies in a place called the Batley Variety Club, near Leeds. It was a big thrill for me then and is still a big thrill for me now. I really enjoyed that experience because I never ever thought I'd meet anyone like that. To work with a rock legend was out of this world for me.'

In April 1974 it seemed Oscar Jones was closer than ever to succeeding in his chosen profession. Since leaving school he'd worked in a series of factory jobs while singing in pubs and clubs on the weekend. Singing was his real passion and now he was booked to support the man Elvis Presley had described as 'the greatest voice on earth'.

'After I did that, I started doing other big venues around England, in places like Birmingham and Newcastle.

'It didn't work out for a number of reasons. When I first went to London I took the band with me, but the record company soon got rid of them, so I was on my own. When you're alone London is a big, frightening place. It got to the point that if I had a song to do and I didn't actually like it or I wanted to do something different with it, I couldn't actually tell anyone because I didn't have anyone to talk to. I got disillusioned with it all – being on my own and not having anyone to discuss anything with. It just went downhill after that.'

Oscar and Beryl's third son, Kelly, was born on 3 June 1974. They already had two boys, Kevin and Lee, who at the time were nine and six years old respectively. It soon became clear to his father that the baby of the family had a fertile imagination.

'He was always an inventive kid, trying different things and dressing up, being somebody else or whatever. I think he must have watched Clint Eastwood in *Two Mules for Sister Sara* about a thousand times. He'd disappear upstairs for a while and then come back down with a torn blanket draped over him that he'd made into a poncho. He was a handful but he didn't express any real regard for music until later on.'

Kelly, though, remembers an early childhood fraught with the usual traumas.

'The earliest memories I think I've got is my mother taking me to the nursery. I was three years old and I can remember her walking down the yard and me being on the doorstep crying. After that the next clear memory really is my annual trip to hospital for stitches. Every summer I managed to cut something that needed repairing.

'We spent most of our time as kids in the park opposite my mother's house. Then they built an outdoor swimming pool right next to the park and everybody just used to hang around the swimming pool. There was a shop opposite there called Booth's, which was basically a terraced house in the same street where I lived. We used to hang around there with a ghetto blaster listening to old tapes of bands like AC/DC, the Eagles and Deep Purple. From there we moved on to spending our lives making compilation tapes. It's ridiculous when you think about it – that's what you did all day! Then you'd go out on a night and play a mix tape and try to find some girls.

'I was a mad football fan from about the age of five. The first World Cup I can remember is the 82 tournament in Spain – that's one of my earliest memories. It was a really hot summer and we'd play football for hours while the World Cup was going on on the TV in the house. I just remember running back to check on the results. We were big Brazil fans. I think it's because they had the same colour kit as Cwmaman – or maybe that should be, we had the same colour kit as them.

'At about the age of ten I started getting interested in boxing because my uncle Cyril was a boxing referee. I ended up going training with him at the boxing club three nights a week. At one stage I was fighting five fights a season. Thing was I couldn't see the point in sparring with my mates and so after about three years I went back to football. Of course I became football crazy again and played U12s, U14s, U16s and U18s. The boxing, though, stood me in good stead when I went to Blaengwawr Comprehensive School because people thought I might be a hard nut. I pretended I was for a year but I never grew any higher so it didn't really wash.'

Sport aside, Kelly's love of making compilation tapes and listening to music was beginning to take over. He soon became fascinated with people who played live music, in particular his father, who was actually christened Arwyn but was better known by his stage alter-ego Oscar. Oscar was sympathetic to Kelly's musical leanings and tried to encourage him without being too overbearing.

'We used to take Kelly down to the Mount Pleasant pub in Cwmaman when he was about twelve years old. They used to have blues bands playing in there and he used to be fascinated watching these bands. I think that's where his musical influences really started. At the same time he used to come to the clubs and watch me sing most weekends and it wasn't long before he was doing it himself. I think he came to see me because we always used to stop off for a Chinese take-away on the way home.'

It was true. Kelly liked nothing better than a sweet and sour but, at the same time, he was paying close attention to his father's performance, perhaps more attention than anyone else realised.

'He used to do a lot of stuff like "Killing Me Softly". There were several Neil Sedaka songs there like "Going Nowhere" and "Solitaire". He had a big range on him – "Help Me Make It Through The Night" by Gladys Knight and stuff like that. That's probably how I knew a lot more about music than other boys my age. I'd grown up with my old man playing stuff like Randy Newman, Otis Reading and Stevie Wonder. My brothers had loads of rock stuff and then there was the music you'd hear through school like PIL, the Specials or Madness.'

Kelly was also getting interested in learning about the music world. He'd started to read *Kerrang!* magazine and, more importantly, started visiting the local second-hand record shop.

'I remember making a Christmas list for my gran and my mother and it was always AC/DC records. This second-hand record shop in Aberdare used to display vinyl releases in the window so as you'd pass on the bus you'd always see the AC/DC records there. I've still got those vinyl copies, complete with the £5.90 price tag on the back.

'I started getting *Kerrang!* because they gave away free patches and we used to get them sewn on to our Wrangler jackets. Sometimes you didn't know who the bands were but, generally, I probably knew a bit more than other kids. I think that went for Richard and Stuart too because we all had older brothers. From about the age of ten onwards I was always trying to hang around with older boys who were fourteen or fifteen, probably because I was into all my stuff and they were into it, I don't know.'

Oscar explains: 'He was spoiled rotten, especially by his eldest brother. Kevin's mates used to come round the house and Kelly was always in among it. More often than not Kevin would send Kel down the pub to get a video from the landlord. Kevin was supposed to be babysitting but he was probably getting pissed downstairs while Kelly watched the film in his bedroom. He was always around older people.'

Angus Young and Clint Eastwood had emerged as his first two real heroes. Kelly, though, didn't really differentiate between on and off screen. He was as fascinated and impressed by what was going on around him as he was when he watched the TV and listened to records. Kelly admits that Angus and Clint shared the limelight with his two older brothers.

'Lee was always the really quiet one. I wanted to walk like Lee because he walked really slow. I also wanted to be like Kevin because he could chat up all the girls, so I stole bits from both of them. In fact if you take both the beginning of Kevin's name and the end of Lee's you get Kelly, which is weird. I can't remember any of us having major rows. It was always a close family, but . . . it wasn't like you were telling each other you love them. It was never like that but it was always like how we are. Straightforward and loyal.

'Life eventually began to circulate around the local pub, the Ivy Bush, because that's where my brothers were, usually playing on the bandit or shooting pool. Everybody used to sit outside the pub in the summer and I'd just go down and listen to all these old geezers telling stories with their pint glasses with their names on. There'd be kids around trying to sniff lighter fluid but there was nobody smoking blow. There were no drugs around, just pure Strongbow and lager.'

Back at home, though, his imagination was running riot. The natural next step was to start trying to emulate his heroes: he was a bit young for trying out Kevin's chat-up lines; Lee's walk was a work in progress and Clint Eastwood had inspired the fascination with dressing up. However, it was Angus's school uniform and Chuck Berry-esque onstage 'duck walk' stomp that really impressed him.

Kelly went to a few school fancy dress parties dressed as Angus, and he was getting precariously close to perfecting the art of the air guitar – which is all well and good as long as no one catches you in the act!

'I remember singing into the mirror in my bedroom one day like a complete dick to Rainbow. I didn't realise my mother and my brothers were listening to me downstairs and they all took the piss out of me. I think I was probably emulating my old man because I'd seen him in a working men's club.

'I've got to admit I was always dressing up, whether it was as Spiderman, R2D2 or of course Clint Eastwood. I was always drawing or playing with cars or something like that. Spiderman, the Lone Ranger, Star Wars – I was really into all that sort of stuff and then, as I got older, I got into Leeds

United. I had all the kit handed down from my brothers so it was the vintage Admiral kit.

'Then there was my first record! I went to Woolworths in Aberdare with my father to buy *Flick of the Switch* by AC/DC. I remember him saying as we walked away, "Aren't you going to make them play it to check it's not scratched?" and I said, "No, I don't think so."'

It was Oscar too who bought Kelly his first guitar.

'It was this acoustic thing, which wasn't very good. The following Christmas, though, I bought him an electric one and he started going into the garage then with one or two other boys. That's when he joined his first band, Zephyr. I saw them perform. To be honest they were quite good for boys of their age. Kelly must have only been about twelve when he did his first gig. As they got a little older they of course got a bit better and so they started looking to play outside Cwmaman.'

'I opened my presents one Christmas morning,' Kelly remembers, 'and my father said there's one other thing under the settee. It was this £10 nylon-string guitar from the catalogue and he said, "If you want it, you can have it – but if you don't want to learn, don't worry about it." I probably had it for about a year before I asked if I could have some lessons off this local guy called Iuan Davies who used to play guitar with Oscar and the Kingfishers. I used to go down there for about four years.

'I started a band when I was about eleven because Stuart had a drum kit. He was fifteen. I could hear him playing and so we got together and then he asked this woman who lived on our street if it was OK to use the youth club for practice.

'I knew Stuart anyway. He used to hang around with another boy called Hugh Hughes. Him and Hugh were always around the park. I remember hanging on to them a lot. I can't remember us first meeting at all but when I started knocking on his door with the band thing we already knew each other.

'I never told anyone I was having guitar lessons because of the inevitable reaction. Some lads would say, "What are you doing having guitar lessons?" and they'd laugh at you. I've got to say it's the best feeling in the world now, looking back. I can remember my old man saying, "Perhaps you should learn to play the piano or something. You could stick it in the corner and if it's pissing outside you could come in and have a go." He was always kind of hinting at it, the old man, without forcing it.'

So, in the summer of 1985, 11-year-old Kelly and his 15-year-old mate Stuart named their first band Zephyr. It was the summer of Live Aid; Echo and the Bunnymen headlined Glastonbury that summer; ZZ Top, Metallica and Marillion played the Monsters of Rock festival at Castle Donington; David Lee Roth left Van Halen and the A&R world was getting very excited over Curiosity Killed the Cat, the Pet Shop Boys and Simply Red. Back in Cwmaman, Kelly was learning the basics of playing live.

'Our first gig as Zephyr was at the Top Club in Cwmaman. There were about 250 people there so it was a baptism of fire. After that though, we just played a few gigs in the local pub. My old man gave us his PA and lots of good advice, whether we wanted it or not. There was another boy in the band called Nicholas Geek, who was kind of making it his own band. It was a five-piece basically. The other two lads, Paul Rosser and Chris Davies, ended up being in another band with me when Zephyr split.

'I went away to Corfu with my mother and father but when I came back they'd done a gig without me in this big hall. So, when I came home I thought, sod this, I'm going to knock this band on the head. I'm the singer. What's going on?'

If only he'd had David Lee Roth's phone number.

'I never wanted to be the singer in the first place but Stuart wanted me to sing. He said, "Your old man can sing, so you must be able to sing!" So I was pushed into doing the singing. Anyway, after Zephyr split, me and Stuart didn't see each other for the best part of two and a half years.

'In retrospect a lot of it was to do with Nicholas Geek. He was the leader of the band I suppose. We were all growing up and Nicky was writing most of the songs. I didn't write any songs. I was just singing and playing whatever he told me to play. At the same time, my old man was putting in his twopenn'orth. I can't remember exactly what happened but it was an argument between me, my old man and him, and we all kind of split up. Stuart stuck with Nicky, so me, Paul Rosser and Chris started another band, Silent Runner.

'My cousin Gene had a drum kit. We gave him a tape of some of the covers we wanted him to learn, like "Hotel California", and we just started practising in the Mount Pleasant pub. We asked around for gigs and before we knew it we were in demand. The pubs used to sell out of lager because there were so many people turning up. In a way we were one of the first bands to do the pub thing locally. Before us it was mainly solo singers doing cover versions.'

The majority of Silent Runner's gigs took place in the newly revamped Ivy Bush, under the careful eye of landlord Morgan Jones and later, when Silent Runner became Tragic Love Company, Graham Davies.

'When they started playing in the Bush they were raw. You could see there was talent there but they were a raw, nervous sort of band. But a band with potential. They had their own particular following. People who were friends of theirs, same sort of age, and then people like myself who were a bit older who appreciated the music. Their parents and family would go along as well and wherever they went you could guarantee a half-decent crowd, whether it was the Bush or the local institute down the road. They always had a good following.'

Things may have looked buoyant enough to the punters in the Ivy Bush but, offstage, it wasn't long before Silent Runner began to fall apart. Kelly says it was simply a case of too many cooks.

'We ended up with six people in the band. We were like the Eagles by the end of it! I can remember an argument about equipment because I'd written a letter to the Prince's Trust to get money for gear. I'd had the money and bought the gear and kept the gear and then, when we split up, there was a big argument that they wanted some of the gear. I was like, "Well you didn't pay for it!" So we haven't really spoken much to any of them since. The bottom line is that we all got bored and we all tried to do different stuff in different bands. It basically disintegrated in the end.'

Outside of music, Kelly's school life flourished despite a few early teething problems.

'I developed psoriasis just around the time I went to comprehensive school, which was not good. PE became an ordeal, so I started doing games with tracksuits on. It got to the stage that I started growing my hair over the top of my ear because I had some of the rash there as well. It used to do my head in because I didn't know what it was, and then we went to the doctor and tried to get all the different stuff to sort it out, but it wasn't responding. In the end my mother started writing me notes to excuse me from gym, but her signature wasn't always consistent. I remember the teacher accusing me of forging the note and hitting me with this hockey stick in this box cupboard.

'I've got to say, though, hockey sticks aside, I loved school. There was always loads of girls there and it was a good *craic*. I had loads of good mates. As far as lessons went, I was really into art. I liked English because it involved writing plays. Our English teacher used to ask us to write episodes of *Fawlty Towers*, which I thought was brilliant. I hated maths and I hated physics. I left there with an "A" grade in graphic design, a "B" in art, "C" in history – I think I had six proper O-level qualifications: English language, English literature, history, graphics, art and craft design technology.

'If I was to pinpoint a teacher who had a major impact on me it would be this guy at primary school. There was one teacher, John Oliver, who used to finish the lessons early and tell us ghost stories. It was like being taken away into this scary mythical world and, to cap it all, at the end of term you could bring in tapes. I brought in *Led Zeppelin II* and I remember him telling me that Jimmy Page was using a bottleneck. It's not what you expect from your teacher.

'There are certain people throughout your life that you remember, and he's one of them definitely. I remember him telling a story that was like that film *Stand By Me*. When he told it, it made a real impression on me. It was easy to relate to because it was so like our own lives. The story's about these young kids who set out on a big adventure along old railway lines and by the sides of rivers. It was like a coming of age movie where it showed how the boys' early lives shaped what happened when they became men.

Stereophonics

'That's what our life was like growing up in Cwmaman –
just a bunch of young lads going on treks down by the river
and along the railway line, making it up as we went along.'

3 Angels With Dirty Faces

'ONE NIGHT, I'D BEEN DRINKING and this mate of mine pulls up in a stolen car and asks me if I fancy a spin. There were five of us in this car and we were racing round Aberdare and Aberaman and then, behind us, suddenly there it was – the blue flashing light and the siren. We legged it but on the way back down the side of the valley the road was cordoned off with police cars and vans and everything.

'I told one of the lads in the car that I was going to pretend I was asleep. Not surprisingly the police didn't believe me, so later that night my mother and father came up to the police station. My father wanted to leave me there but my mother insisted on taking me home. At least I thought I was going home!

'It was 4 a.m. when we left but, instead of punishment, my father decided to take me to work with him there and then. He'd had a call out from the steelworks so I went to work with him in the steelworks down in Cardiff. I was weeks away from my sixteenth birthday, hungover and en route straight from a police cell to the steelworks in the middle of the night.'

Richard's mother Mairwen wasn't impressed. 'I did give him a clip across the ear in the police cell,' she admitted. 'I gave him a firm talking to and he was grounded. Having said that, Richard wasn't a villain in any way at all. It was a one-off thing with him. He didn't have anything to do with stealing after that.

'He was in a cell once or twice after that for drunk and disorderly but it was out of character for Richard. He's always been very laid back.'

It wasn't that Richard Jones was bad, far from it. But he's the first to admit that he lost the plot a bit during his early teens.

'That was a turning point. I'd been running wild for a few years and I learned a big lesson that night. It's a simple enough lesson: if you want anything, you've got to work for it. So that's what I did. I started work, started getting a bit of money in my pocket and went down the straight and narrow.'

There is one road in and out of Cwmaman so the police had a relatively simple task working out where to erect a roadblock. It would have been trickier had the thieves been on foot, because the village straddles the River Aman with rolling countryside in every direction. It has one main road which branches off the B4275 and crawls up the side of the mountain, coming to an abrupt end close to where the pit used to be. On the way up there are numerous turnings leading into other similar streets with terraced housing laid out in an almost symmetrical formation.

The tightly knit houses on the valley slopes give the impression of a community huddled together for mutual protection against the elements. On all sides there are mountains, which guide harsh winds down through the valley and along the winding river. It can be a bleak place, but when the sun comes out, it is, as one person described it to me, 'God's little acre'. With its wheelie bins, its rows of chimneys and looming mountains, it's like *Coronation Street* with scenery!

In among the housing there's a few pubs and, as you approach the top of the village, there's the newly refurbished social club. In a way, this place offers the two polar opposite views of Cwmaman. Looking out of the club's main doors, you are confronted by the narrow claustrophobic streets of the village. However, if you walk into the main lounge bar, the huge windows reveal a green and lush wonderland descending the side of the mountain until it reaches the river. Looking down the valley you can see the river wind its way south for miles. It's not dissimilar to parts of the Scottish Highlands, the west coast of Ireland or even the northwest coast of the USA. It's a great place for the imagination to run riot. Especially if you happen to be a small child.

'We spent a lot of time up the mountain having fern fights,' Richard explains. 'We just used to rip the ferns out of the ground, clean the dirt off them and just throw them at each other; just stupid childish things like that. Peashooters were a big thing as well. We used to go down the local greengrocers and buy the old hard packs of peas, so that was the ammunition. The weapon, the shooter itself, was usually a plastic piece of tubing from somewhere. We used to make water guns out of squeezy Fairy Liquid bottles and we used to have big water fights in the village.

'We lived across the river from the main bit of Cwmaman, in a place that was not surprisingly referred to locally as "over the river". The river runs straight through Cwmaman and we live on the right-hand side of it as you're looking down the valley. It seemed like almost everybody else was on the other side of the river, so there was always a bit of a feud between "over the river" and downtown Cwmaman.'

Richard Jones was born on 23 May 1974. His parents, Richie and Mairwen, already had four other children, three boys and a girl. Richie tried his hand at several things, including pit work and building, before settling at a local firm, UBM Scaffolding. Since then he's set up his own enterprise, OK Scaffolding, which employs about twenty people and is based in Ynysbwl (also the birthplace of the popular entertainer Michael Ball). Mairwen looked after the children, which was no easy task, as Richard explains.

'My mother only had three bedrooms so, as I was growing up, we always used to share rooms. First of all there were my two oldest brothers: Jimmy, who's eleven years older than me, and Terry, who was eight when I was born. Next were Louise, who was five, and Jason, who was three. I can't really remember Jimmy living in the house because he was a lot older but there was a time when Louise, Terry, Jason and myself were all in the same room. Once Jimmy and Terry moved out,

Louise had her own bedroom and Jason and myself shared. By the time Louise left, my mother had given birth to my little sister Andrea, so it was always full in the house. There were always people there.

'I shared a room with Jason for all of my youth, so there was a lot of fighting. When you're growing up a lot of things that seem daft become very important, like whether he's wearing your socks or whatever. Every time I used to pinch his socks we used to end up having a fight, and they weren't mellow fights. There was always bleeding knuckles or noses.'

Mairwen confirms this. 'That was a very upsetting time for me. They did share a room at home and they were always bickering. There was one particular night where they had a nasty fight in a club in Aberdare. That was really upsetting. It was upsetting for me, Richard and Jason. Richard wouldn't go to bed. He didn't go up to the bedroom for weeks because he wouldn't sleep in the same bedroom as his brother and I really felt like knocking their heads together.'

'My mother and father thought we just couldn't stand the sight of each other but then once you reach a certain age it's like nothing happened,' Richard explains. 'When I was sixteen Jason would have been nineteen. It was about then we started drinking together so, basically, I'm closer to Jason than anyone else, just because of the age. Louise is close to him too. She's only two years older than him. And then Terry and Jimmy have always been close because there's three years between them too. In turn we all look after each other and they all look after me because I'm their little baby brother.'

Richard attended Cwmaman Infants, which was the local nursery, before graduating to Glynhafod Primary where he befriended another local lad who was in his class. His name was Kelly Jones.

'We just used to have a little gang on the go. There was me and Kel and a lad called Beanie (Darren Evans), who lived two doors down from Stuart on the same street as Kelly. Then there was a boy called Ian Jones. Beanie, Ian and Kelly were all about the same height and so they looked like the Three Stooges. The other lad who knocked around with us was called

Johnny Toghill. We were the tall ones. It was just a good laugh, playing football in the schoolyard or just pretending we were Angus Young, running around with your trousers rolled up like shorts, pretending to be in a band. Actually it was around that time that I went on holiday with Kelly to Barry, down near Cardiff. It was a big caravan park with a fair close by. It was great fun.

'Back in Cwmaman, there was a carnival every May Day bank holiday. They'd set up a big tent opposite the street where Kelly lived, so we used to go up there and try and knock the coconuts over and win a goldfish – stuff like that. It was always a good laugh growing up in the village because there were always plenty of things to do. There was a local pool up opposite Kelly's as well. Every summer it was open from early May until September and we used to go up there to hang around the older kids who were playing their Black Sabbath and Rainbow tapes on a ghetto blaster.

'I thought primary school was excellent. The teachers weren't into caning people when you'd done something wrong. It was like they'd rather teach you that that's not the right way rather than slap you into place. I loved art and I loved English then because they used to encourage us to write stories. It was usually what you want to do at the weekend or what you did last weekend, but I just made up nonsense stories all the time. It was like after the summer holidays you've got to write a four-page story of what you've done for the last six weeks. I just used to let my imagination go wild and say I went up to London to see the Pope or something like that. My father would always say he'd take me to London to see the Trooping of the Colour or the Changing of the Guards. So that's what I enjoyed about primary school. It was just the freedom to do whatever you wanted to do. That all changed with comprehensive school. There they told you exactly what to do and that's what I hated about comprehensive school.'

Richard, Kelly, Beanie, Johnny and Ian all went to Blaengwawr Comprehensive, but times were changing. School was no longer a laid-back affair and the days of carnivals and funfairs were about to be replaced by tattoos, heavy metal music, drinking and truancy. In one fell swoop, the eleven-plus exam broke the five friends up, placing them in different classes. Richard reacted like most eleven-year-olds – with a shrug of the shoulders.

'They made us do the eleven-plus before Blaengwawr, and as soon as that happens you split up automatically. Beanie and myself ended up together and Kelly and Johnny were in the same class. Ian was in a different class again. We just all split up. It's only natural at that age that you find different mates and I didn't really bother with Kelly all the way through comprehensive school because he was just in different classes. I didn't really hang out with him again until about five years later when we left school.'

While Kelly immersed himself in pastimes like football, music, art, English and history, Richard took the opposite road through his teens. Once again he was 'over the river' and soon earned himself a reputation as a bit of a rebel. It's no surprise, then, that education fell by the wayside.

'If you wanted to learn then you could learn, but after the third year I'd had a gut full. I wasn't doing the right subjects because I took the wrong options, so from then on I didn't go to school a lot. Truancy was my art. Always going on the mitch, as we used to say. Just up the mountain playing cards or down the local cafe playing the bandits down there or up in town drinking. I never had a full school uniform; I just used to wear black jeans, white trainers and a Fred Perry shirt. The official school uniform used to be black trousers, blue shirt and tie and a blazer, so we just stripped it down to the bare minimum. I think I just went a little bit down the path my brother went as well because he was a bit of a tearaway at school.

'There was always somebody who would say they were the hardest person in school and they'd go around bullying people. Then one day they'd try to bully the wrong person and they'd have a hiding. Then the person that gave them a hiding got labelled the hardest man in school. It was just all that childish stuff. I was never into it but if anybody asked, I never used to back down. I used to give it a twirl. If anybody started picking on me, I wouldn't hesitate to either put the head on them or jump straight on them. This all went on from about the age of thirteen until fifteen and a half, until we left school.

'I met a couple of other friends then who were the wrong type of friends, so it was an interesting time. We just used to go out on Friday nights and try to get booze. I was close to six foot when I was in form four – so I could get served in all the pubs and all the supermarkets for beers.

'One of the funnier episodes was when we nicked a Pentecostal van. I was about twelve or thirteen and still hanging out with Johnny Toghill. His mother went to the Pentecostal church. She used to be the one singing and dancing down the front of the church and everything like that. Don't get me wrong – she was a lovely woman. Anyway, they used to have an old double-axle transit van parked outside the house just to take the kids back and forth to Sunday school. The door was always open and the keyhole to start the ignition was easy to get at. Somebody had shoved a screwdriver in it so you could basically put anything in there and start it – so we just picked up a lollipop stick and started the engine. We drove it down the street, got scared and then reversed it back, and parked it in exactly the same position. That's how daring we were!'

The only thing that really inspired Richard around this time was music. He'd grown up in a household full of it and wasted no time in trying to master the bass guitar.

'My eldest brother Jimmy was really into the British ska thing – Two Tone records, Madness and Bad Manners. Ever since I can remember, we've had a stereo in the house and every other day we'd take it in turns just to listen to our records. Terry was into Genesis; Louise liked Bob Marley and then Jason was into punk. He had a lot of the post-punk stuff as well: bands like PIL and Talking Heads.

'I was into that a little bit. I was into the Sex Pistols, the Exploited, but then I started listening to heavy metal. I always liked bands like Rainbow, Metallica and all the Bay Area thrash bands like Exodus and Testament. I was a bit of a hard rocker. We used to go to a local disco called Flintstones on

Monday nights when I was about sixteen, take the records up there and headbang all night.

'I started growing my hair about three years before. All the people at school used to call me the Dulux dog because it was in my eyes. I really liked all the harder music because nobody else was listening to it – it was something new that nobody had heard of. That's when I started getting tattoos as well. I had my first one when I was at school at the age of fifteen. The tattooist I went to wasn't the world's greatest. He had this little motto, which was the size of a fifty pence piece, and if you let him put it on you, he'd give you another free tattoo. It was his way of advertising.

'That's when I got into guitars as well. I had a milk round when I was about twelve. It was tough working from 4 a.m. to 7 a.m. before school, but at Christmas the tips were good – so I bought my first guitar. I bought a fretless bass guitar and my father bought me the amp. I knew if I bought a bass somebody would need a bass player eventually. There were plenty of guitarists around but not many bassists.'

It was at this time that Mairwen realised her son was serious about music. 'I just let him carry on but my husband was like, "What a lot of noise. Don't give up the day job, boy!" and all the usual things a father tells a son I suppose. Because he was up in the bedroom and he had his amp up there as well, there was this noise for hours, but I just left him alone. I knew where he was; he was behaving himself and he was happy – so I let him be.'

In the meantime Richard had re-established his friendship with Kelly and now had his eye on any opportunities going.

Richard and Kelly had got in touch again through a series of coincidences. Richard was friendly with Kelly's cousin Leighton, who was also a good friend of Stuart. Leighton was a regular at the rock night at Bogie's nightclub in Cardiff and soon Stuart and Richard started accompanying him. They became friends and not too long afterwards Stuart and Kelly asked Richard to join them. For those about to rock . . .!

4 The Cable Guy

In the second minute of the game, Brian Williams gets the ball from Ian Kirkpatrick and kicks it deep inside the Barbarian 22. Phil Bennett picks up the ball around his own ten-yard line and makes three successive steps to elude the opposition before passing it on to JPR Williams. JPR gets tackled high, but still manages to pass to one of the few Englishmen in the side, John Pullin. He in turn gives the ball to John Dawes, who sells a dummy, covers ground and passes inside to Pontypridd's Tom David. Tom David is now inside the All Black half. He makes a one-handed throw inside to Derrik Quinnell. Quinnell throws another one-handed pass inside again. Gareth Edwards appears from nowhere and runs through the middle to pick the pass. Edwards runs the last thirty-or-so yards, weaving around what looks like half of the All Blacks side, before diving in to the left-hand corner flag at the River Taff end to score what is now known as 'That Try'. (Anon.)

I N THE SPRING OF 1973, Welsh rugby was at the height of its powers. The national side had established a stranglehold on the annual celebrated Five Nations tournament that would last for most of the decade and the biggest names in the game invariably wore red shirts, among them Gareth Edwards and JPR Williams. They had continued a tradition passed on from other greats such as Barry John and Gerald Davies and, as you would expect, they were the country's most celebrated sons.

So, when the Barbarians lined up against the All Blacks that year, it was no surprise to the rugby world that almost half the side was Welsh. The Ba-Bas, as they're known, are an invitation side which is usually made up of the cream of world rugby, so when seven of their fifteen-strong side are picked from one nation, it is extraordinary.

The game itself has gone down in history for a number of reasons. Firstly, within the opening two minutes Gareth Edwards scored what has been referred to ever since as 'That Try'. Secondly, he was joined on the score-sheet that day by his countrymen Phil Bennett, John Bevan and JPR Williams and, thirdly, the Barbarians ran out victors by a twelve-point margin in one of their most famous victories over New Zealand's finest.

Welsh rugby was not only enjoying its finest hour but its role, as a primary source of national pride, was also more important than it ever had been and ever would be again. The fact that Wales enjoyed a 26-year unbeaten home record against the English was priceless for a nation so used to being the underdog in every other walk of life.

To say that rugby permeated every aspect of growing up in Wales in the seventies is an understatement. You had to be spectacularly out of touch not to get caught up in the excitement of every key occasion at the Arms Park. While the rest of the world was idolising George Best, the Bay City Rollers, Elvis, Muhammad Ali and Starsky and Hutch, in Cwmaman people like Tom David (from nearby Pontypridd) and Gareth Edwards were 'the Boys'.

Stuart Cable was no exception. Born in Aberdare Hospital on 19 May 1970, he grew up fascinated by the legendary status of the Welsh rugby team. This interest was inspired in the main by his father, Arthur, who travelled the length and breadth of Britain following the exploits of the Welsh side in the Triple Crown. His passion was infectious to all who came into contact with him. Stuart's mother, Mabel, smiled, shrugged her shoulders and enjoyed every minute of it.

'Arthur ate, slept, walked and drank rugby. When the Welsh side would come on the TV he'd call us all over and say, "Sit there and watch these ballerinas." That was because the side was so good, they played rugby with an ease that reminded you of *Swan Lake*. His real pride and joy was his Grand Slam tie and blazer, which he bought after Wales had achieved the ultimate – beating everyone in the Five Nations. The rest of us couldn't help but be influenced by his love of the game.'

Mabel has two children, both of them boys. The first, Paul, is seven years older than Stuart, who came along unexpectedly when his mother was forty years old.

'Both my boys were little beauties. Paul really got into sport and is still one of the fittest people I've ever known. He runs every day in whatever weather. Stuart is a bit more of a charmer. In fact, when he was little he had such lovely curly hair that he was sometimes mistaken for a girl.'

Arthur Cable did a stint with the air force before finding work in a local factory that made car components, but it was sport and music that made his world tick.

'My husband was really into all the old big band stuff. He loved his Glen Miller records and there was always music in the house. I remember when they advertised the new stereo systems and he insisted on buying one. Beforehand, everything was in mono.'

Tragically Arthur died of a heart attack in 1980, when Stuart was only ten years old.

'Obviously it affected him like it would affect anyone that age. Stuart was very close to his father. Arthur had always seen the unexpected pregnancy as a gift and he spent a lot of time with Stuart. [When Arthur passed away] Paul became a father figure to Stuart because he was seventeen at the time. I couldn't have got through without him. He supported the family during that difficult time.'

'He must have been about fifty-three when he died, so he was quite young,' Stuart continues. 'I suppose, looking back, maybe it wasn't that young for people of that generation. You know – drinking, smoking, eating fatty foods – it's bound to kill you in the end really, isn't it? It was a heart attack.'

Although his father's untimely death scarred his early life, Stuart still remembers his childhood fondly.

'There was an outdoor swimming pool opposite the house. That's where everyone hung out, especially during the summer holidays. Kelly lived eight doors away on the same street, Glanaman Road, so we knew each other from an early age. In fact his father and my father worked in the same factory as well. There are no houses on one side of Glanaman Road, just playing fields and this outdoor pool. I just remember spending summers by that pool listening to music. Everything revolved around listening to music really, far more than anything to do with school because I hated school. I used to listen to music before I went to school; I used to listen to music when I got home from school, but at the end of the day I didn't particularly like school. I didn't want to study, I didn't want to do homework and I just thought school was the worst place in the world to be.'

While he may not have applied himself in the classroom, Stuart was no slacker, but it wasn't until he started playing drums that he was able to channel his energy and talent.

'I was in the last year of school. I was fifteen going on sixteen and I went to see this band that one of my mate's brothers was in. Afterwards I was talking to the guy who played drums and he said, "I know a bloke who's selling a drum kit." So there's me, fifteen years old with no money going, "I'll have it!" He phones me up two days later and says, "Do you want this drum kit, it's £60?" and I says, "Aye I'll have it, no problem. Give me a couple of days to get the money." At the time my older brother was working at Radio Rentals, so I said to him, "Can you lend me £60?" He said, "What for?" I daren't tell my mother 'cos she would have gone up the wall! I told him, "A drum kit," and he said, "Aye, no problem." The next thing he gave me the money; I went, got the kit and came back. Then my old girl comes home from work and there's this drum kit in the living room! She's going, "What?" I said, "Paul bought it." So, that was that and the strange thing is – we were talking about this recently – I still owe him that £60!'

Glanaman Road is a terraced street and terraced streets, by their very nature, are not ideal environments for an aspiring Cozy Powell. Stuart's neighbours, though, were understanding and, as his mother Mabel explains, they came to an agreement.

'I talked to the neighbours and they suggested a curfew. It was something like he couldn't play before ten or eleven o'clock in the morning and after eight o'clock at night.'

Stuart was delighted. 'I didn't mind because people have got to get up and go to work. You've got to respect your neighbours because you're living in a close-knit community, so that was that really.

'I played drums in my bedroom for about a year, just playing along to tapes. Kelly got a guitar for Christmas that year. He knocked at the door one day and he said, "Do you fancy going for a jam in my dad's garage?" and I said, "Why not? We can make a noise together rather than individually." We practised a few times in his garage and then we went up to the community centre up the road. They built this thing so the old biddies could have coffee mornings and the kids could have little Friday night discos. We went up and asked the woman running it, "Could we go and practise there?" and she said, "Yeah, fine." Twelve years later, we were still there!'

Stuart left school with one O level in metalwork ('We had to make a door latch or something') and a load of CSEs. He decided to take up a carpentry apprenticeship at Aberdare College, but six months later the appeal of actually earning a wage became too much to resist.

'I had a friend of mine who was working in a PVC factory making windows and doors and he said there was a job going. It was something like £35 a week, so I was an apprentice carpenter for six months and then I went to work in a window factory called PCR Windows. I stayed there for six years! Fucking awful when I look back at it now.'

The mid-eighties were in full swing. Thatcher's Britain was enjoying unprecedented prosperity – Thatcher's Britain, of course, being the southeast of England. Elsewhere the miners dispute had brought most of the Rhondda Valley to its knees, so 'yuppie' remained a phrase that existed in the papers and on TV and not in reality. Aspirational Athena prints of red Ferraris may have been all the rage with the new jazz-loving 'loadsamoney' set, but for Stuart it was becoming increasingly obvious that music was his only hope. His mother had already sensed her son's blinkered ambition.

'When Kelly started coming to play music with Stuart, you sensed that he was impressed by Stuart's confidence and charm. Kelly would always be mumbling whereas Stuart had the charm and the push. It was like they were opposites and that's why they got on. Stuart was very, very confident that one day they were going to make it. It was his dream – no, it was more than a dream – it was something that he knew was going to happen. I don't know why, but he did. He used to say to me, "We'll get there one day, we will."

'I knew that they would get somewhere one day because they got on so well together. They were comrades as well as being in a band.'

Stuart's dream, however, was met with derision in certain quarters.

'I can still remember people saying to us, "You'll never be anything, coming from Cwmaman. Nothing's ever come out of Cwmaman." To be honest, I think that drove me on more than anything else in the world. When I used to go down the pub and they used to say, "Oh, are you still playing in the band?" and I'd say, "Yeah." Then the advice would come, "Oh don't bother, get yourself a decent job because nobody wants to bother with people from Cwmaman. You live too far away from London." From then on I was determined to put Cwmaman on the map.

'I always wanted to do something a little bit different to everybody else. Everybody else was going to work in banks and going to university. Unfortunately I didn't have enough qualifications to do that. I had to fall back on music. I had a great love of music from a very young age. I grew up listening to bands like Black Sabbath, Deep Purple, AC/DC and Zeppelin. When you get interested in those types of bands, you read about things that happened on tour involving all these women. They seemed to have an endless supply of entertainment and booze and you think, what an amazing lifestyle that must be.'

There was only one problem – Zephyr. The band that Stuart and Kelly had formed was falling apart.

'It was something to do with Kelly's father being a singer. Obviously, looking back now, we wanted him to give us advice, but it didn't feel like advice when you're that age. He used to do it with everybody in the band, not only me, not only Kelly, and we used to be like, "Oh fucking hell!" It got to the point where I thought I'd rather do something else.

'I went and played a couple of gigs in a glam band – King Catwalk. We did a demo but we only played about five gigs. It was all right. It wasn't fantastic. I think we were just jumping on a bandwagon. Motley Crüe were huge at the time. Poison were big in Britain and you just do that kind of thing and then think this ain't for me.'

Things also began to go sour at PCR, when Stuart decided to approach his union over pay. He became a shop steward, which, in the spirit of the times, wasn't quite the route to promotion.

'At the end of the day Thatcher made it simple for small businesses to just walk all over people. That's a sad thing really, and it still happens to this day 'cos the power of the unions has totally gone. We asked for more money, so I just got made redundant because I brought the union in! Basically I went in there and kicked up a bit of dust and got my fucking wrists slapped for it and got made redundant. The union was powerless to do anything for me so I thought, fuck it, I'll be a man of leisure.'

5 The Outsiders

WHILE STUART HAD LEARNED A THING or two about eyeliner in King Catwalk, it was clear that the band were going nowhere rapidly. The eighties were coming to a close, signalling the end for big hair, headbands and spandex. Motley Crüe had enjoyed their glory days and bands like Poison had already been consigned to a life of eternal ridicule. The seminal mid-eighties cult film *This is Spinal Tap* had satirised the prog/glam eras so brilliantly that rock bands simply couldn't get away with it any more. King Catwalk were no exception.

It was also about this time that a three-piece from Aberdeen in Washington State on the northwest coast of the States were to release their debut album. *Bleach* by Nirvana was a sign of what lay ahead.

Back in Cwmaman, Kelly's fascination with American bar-room blues-rock was a little more in keeping with the times. By 1992 the Black Crowes had become a worldwide success. Singer-songwriters like Lenny Kravitz were prospering and, of course, Nirvana, Pearl Jam and a host of other bands from Seattle were rewriting rock history. Silent Runner's limited repertoire of covers wasn't setting Kelly's world alight, so one day, when he spotted Stuart on a passing bus, he knew the time was right for reconciliation.

'I was in the park at the bottom of Cwmaman, down the bottom of Bush Hill, and he went past on a bus and he waved and I waved back. It was probably the first time that we had acknowledged each other for well over a year. I don't know, I suppose I was messing about with different bands; he was fucking about with different bands and then one night we were pissed in the Ivy Bush and Julian was there. We were watching a band called the Moon Dogs and we said, "Shall we get the band back together?" I think Julian was going to sing at that time, I don't know.'

Julian Castaldi, as he's known to the registrar, declined the frontman role, opting instead to utilise his talents in other ways. He's since become responsible for a lot of Stereophonics' cover art and has been photographing and videoing the boys from the beginning. There was still some way to go before the band came to resemble its current line-up, as Stuart explains:

'First of all we wanted to be a four-piece, so there was myself, Kelly and two other lads. We went up and we started doing stuff like "Let Love Rule" by Lenny Kravitz and Black Crowesy kind of things: "Hard To Handle" and shit like that. Then Kelly decided one of the lads wasn't a very good guitar player, so we got rid of him. Then the other fella, Mark Everett, he went on holiday for two weeks and me and Kelly were sitting round.

'We knew Richard through Kelly's cousin Leighton, who was playing in a band. Leighton asked me to play drums with them. They used to practise in a pub called the Mount Pleasant, so I went down. I knew Richard anyway, but I didn't know he played bass. I saw him and was really impressed and asked him if he wanted to come and practise with us for a couple of weeks. I just thought, God he's pretty good really, and he was the coolest-looking bastard I'd ever seen in my life to be honest with you. He looked like Axl Rose. He was tall, he had this long blond hair and he's a good-looking guy and you just thought to yourself that's a statement in itself.

'So, Mark Everett came back off holiday and he never came back to practise. No one ever told him that he was sacked. That was that really. We had the nucleus of the band then, which was Richard, Kelly and me.'

Richard, however, was a little confused as to why they kept him in the band:

'Either they were too scared to tell me that they didn't want me to play or we did genuinely click. As soon as they asked me to play, I thought, now's my chance to learn the instrument inside out. They gave me a couple of songs to learn, so we started doing Tragically Hip and Neil Young cover versions. We did a song called "Baby Loves You" by Enuff Z Nuff. That was probably the first song I learned with them. "Ain't No Fun" and "Waiting Around To Be A Millionaire" by AC/DC followed soon after. There was "Little Bones" by the Tragically Hip. I don't think anybody in Wales knew who the Tragically Hip were. They're a Canadian band and so we thought, we'll start playing their songs. People will think they're our songs and we'll slip our own songs in as well.'

At this stage they were still keen to be a four-piece, so Kelly asked his friend Simon to join, but Simon hadn't fully appreciated the power of the video camera.

'We had Simon to play guitar and that ended up going pear shaped,' Kelly explains. 'We were playing a gig in a beer garden and we were doing "Purple Haze" by Hendrix when my guitar string snapped. Simon was supposed to be backing me up but when we watched the show back on home video he was actually buying a can from the bar. We thought, that's not right, so we ended up sacking Simon. [Incidentally, Simon has been Kelly's guitar tech for the last four years.]

'After Simon, we nicked the guitar player from the Moon Dogs. His name was also Richard Jones. The Moon Dogs were basically the Black Crowes and they were probably *the* band locally at the time. Richard was a good guitar player, but we didn't need a guitar player. We ended up befriending these people and because we liked them so much we used to ask them to join the band. We knew in six months we'd have to sack them because it never worked out. We did it again with another guy called Glen Hyde. He just walked away eight months or so before we got signed. We never really knew why.'

Glen's departure was bittersweet for Stuart. He had a lot of time for the guy but at the same time he was happy that they'd finally decided to be a three-piece.

'We couldn't bother with anyone else. We'd tried three different guitar players and it wasn't working, so we thought we'd just stick as a three-piece. I was happy because I was into Rush. I thought three-pieces looked better on stage anyway.'

Kelly, meanwhile, had started writing songs in earnest. His mini-plays chronicling the dramas he saw and heard around him were beginning to take shape and Graham Davies, who ran the local boozer, was more than happy to cock an attentive ear.

'Perhaps I'd say to him that he could have done this differently or done that a bit better. Then he started bringing his tapes to me and asking me to have a listen. What I liked I told him and what I didn't like I'd tell him as well and, in all honesty, he took criticism well. Kelly took everything in and, whether or not he decided to take the advice, he would still listen.

'I liked the fact that he was a storyteller. I'm a fan of Bob Dylan, Leonard Cohen and Neil Young. Kelly reminds me a lot of Dylan, not in songwriting ways, but because he's a storyteller.'

They made their first tentative attempts to send out demos to record companies, but it was a painful experience. Oscar takes up the story:

'Stuart was the pushy one. He always wanted to get on; he always wanted to be a superstar. They bought a four-track recorder, so that they could record themselves when they were playing, and they started sending tapes away to different record companies. They didn't have a lot of success at that. A lot of the answers came back "Thanks but no thanks," which was a bit disappointing for them. Kelly had just gone into art college.'

So Kelly, Richard and Stuart set about lining up their first gig as a three-piece. Before that, though, they practised as much as possible, which involved sacrifices on everybody's part, especially Richard's.

'Stuart wasn't working at the time and Kelly was in college, so he'd finish at five. I was working with my dad and giving him excuses so I could get to practise. My old man had me working what seemed like seven days a week, twenty-four hours a day for fifteen quid a day. I was seventeen.

'It was probably about four or five weeks after I'd joined that we did our first show. We were billed as Blind Faith, but then someone told us Eric Clapton had had a band called Blind Faith. The gig was a charity thing up in Aberdare at the Michael Sorbles Sports Centre. It was just a big marquee. There was about a hundred to a hundred and fifty people in there and three other bands on the bill as well. We thought we had to be good because of the other bands. They'd all played together before. The Moon Dogs were playing so we thought we'd go head to head with them. Our set was full-on rock. I think "Purple Haze" by Hendrix was in there but there were a few diverse covers now and again like Tracy Chapman's "Fast Car".'

'Blind Faith' soon became Tragic Love Company. The name was chosen in homage to three of their favourite bands, the Tragically Hip, Mother Love Bone and Bad Company. So, TLC continued to gig in and around Cwmaman and nearby Aberdare, but the name was beginning to get in the way of them moving further afield.

At this time they'd started travelling to London to do 'pay to play' gigs at the Rock Garden in Covent Garden. They'd also struck up a loose management arrangement with a 21-year-old Londoner called Gil Goldberg.

Gil admits, 'At the time I had no contacts in the music industry and didn't even know the hot venues, so I used to check the back pages of *Melody Maker*. Bands would advertise there if they were looking for management. Stuart placed an advert in one of the November '95 issues and so I got hold of a demo. The quality was poor but I liked the songs and loved the vocals.

'I called them up and Stuart was so happy to hear from me, a guy called Goldberg with a W1 address. They probably thought I was Mr Music Biz. They agreed to drive down the following weekend and meet me. They arrived in this yellow BT van with the BT logo painted over. The first thing I noticed was Richard's name tattooed on his neck. I thought he was very intimidating and he didn't say a word all day. Kelly, on the other hand, struck me as a very serious guy. He meant business and was determined to succeed.

'I wrote to them the following week to confirm it all and I put together a six-month plan, which was basically to gig and do some demos before I approached the industry.

'The first gig I booked was in the Falcon in Camden on a Friday night. They spent the next two months gigging in London every fortnight. They drove down in their ex-BT van and slept in my old office in the West End. I think we all knew their name was bloody awful.'

Kelly takes up the story: 'The name change started with this guy Gil Goldberg. He sort of managed us but in real terms he got us gigs in London. We put an advert in *Melody Maker* and he got in touch and started getting us gigs at places like the Kings Head in Fulham, the Bull and Gate in Kentish Town and the Dublin Castle in Camden. After a while he kept saying that the name was no good. We were like, "Fuck off, what do you know? It's a fucking great name!" So we didn't take any notice.

'That was until this guy, Wayne Coleman, was organising a gig in Aberdare as part of the Splash tour with recently signed bands like Catatonia and the Super Furries. The support slots were going to unsigned bands and we got on the bill at Aberdare supporting Catatonia. Part of the deal was that there was going to be a compilation album featuring everyone involved with the tour. Wayne was dealing with it and he said, "Look we've got to put this song on the record but the name is shit!" And we said, "It's fucking great!" Then we sat down and finally accepted that maybe the name wasn't great.'

The Ivy Bush once again became the HQ for a band in crisis, with Kelly at the strategy board (in this case a beer mat), armed with a pencil.

'We sat in the Bush and we changed the name first to the Applejacks, after the sweets, but we worked out that there was another band called the Applejacks. We must have gone through about fifty names that week: the Mabel Cables (in honour of Stuart's mum), the Stillborn Lambs . . . all sorts of stupid names.'

Irritated and confused, Kelly, Richard and Stuart were four days into their mental hell when Stuart had a bit of an epiphany, witnessed by his mum Mabel.

'One Sunday afternoon, Stuart was upstairs in his bedroom and he came running down the stairs and said, "Listen to this: Stereophonic." "That's good," I said. "That's really good. Where did you get that from?" He said, "Off Dad's radiogram." You see, my late husband loved the big bands and we bought a stereophonic radiogram when they first came out. He used to put all the big bands on to play, with the clarinets and the trombones and the sax and everything. It's like a mini mixing desk; you can bring in the different instruments as you're going along. And that was the joy of his life. I've kept it all these years. I've never got rid of it. That's where the name of the band came from. Stereophonic.'

Stuart was keen on the name for a number of reasons, not least because they were running out of time for the deadline for promotions ahead of the Aberdare gig.

'Wayne Coleman had asked us to let him know at least two weeks before the show so he could put the name on the flyers. I was sitting in my mother's house in the spare bedroom and just writing all these names down and I just looked up and saw my dad's old radiogram. He used to play 78s, Frank Sinatra and stuff like that. My father was a great fan of music. The radiogram had "Falcon Stereophonic" written on it and I don't know why I didn't suggest the Falcons. I haven't got a clue, but it just said "Stereophonic" and I thought that it sounded really good. I went straight down to Kelly's house.'

Kelly, though, wasn't immediately won over:

'I thought it sounded like Stereo MCs or something so I said Monophonic and it didn't really sound the same, so we ended up saying Stereophonics was cool. We told Wayne and we did a load of new flyers with it. We had a couple of gigs in London before the Aberdare show and so we informed Gil Goldberg of the name change. Little did we know we'd changed it at exactly the right time because one of those London gigs was our first big step, and then Aberdare.'

Tragic Love Company were officially consigned to history and Stereophonics emerged a little older and wiser than their earlier incarnation. They'd had a brief taste of the music industry and were learning by their mistakes. Richard admits they were making it up as they went along.

'We'd done a series of demos as Tragic Love Company with tracks like "Billy Davey's Daughter", "Raymond's Shop", "Looks Like Chaplin" and "She Takes Her Clothes Off". Every time we practised we'd do three or four songs and send them away to record companies. We also went to London to see a producer who had his own studio. There was one Yank and one cockney fella and they were into dance music. They told us we needed more choruses. At the time we took it as a bit of a downer but it did help us in a way because we worked on those songs to see what we could do.

'On another occasion, we went down to somewhere in Essex to see Dick Crippin, the bass player from Tenpole Tudor [early eighties cartoon punk outfit]. We stayed in his garage and recorded two or three songs. We gave him £300 to see what he could do, but we didn't hear from him again. It was just finding our feet. We thought that because people had big houses and the gear, they were in the know. We learned the hard way, but that's what you've got to do.'

'Stereophonics was certainly a better name, so we set about getting a better demo together. Kelly told me about this studio in Wales that would do a session for £100. I gave them £50 towards it and the following week they posted me the DAT. I got very excited when I heard "A Thousand Trees".'

With the Aberdare show looming, Stereophonics were booked at the Borderline, bang in the middle of London's West End. They were supporting a band called the Smalltown Heroes. As Stuart explains, it proved to be a very important evening indeed – their first meeting with Marshall Bird and Steve Bush.

'After the gig these two guys went over to Richard and handed him a card and said, "We're two independent producers and we've got a shit load of free time in Battery Studios." They used to work at Battery and the people there apparently gave them free studio time to do their own projects. Anyway, turns out that they'd just done an album with the band we were supporting, the Smalltown Heroes. They said, "If you want to come to London and record a couple of tracks with us, let us know – we want to do it because we like your band."

'So we were looking at his card on the way home and saying, "Oh yeah, they're full of shit. Just some idiots from London who probably want £2,000 or whatever."

'Then, the following week, I had a phone call saying, "Do you want to do it?" and we said, "How much is it going to cost?" and they said, "Nothing," and we said, "Fucking great!" '

With the prospect of entering proper recording studios on the horizon for the first time, Kelly, Richard and Stuart set about preparing for the Aberdare gig supporting Catatonia. The headliners had recently signed a deal with Warner Brothers offshoot Blanco Y Negro records. The world was beginning to wake up to the fact that there was a lot of untapped talent west of the Severn Bridge. A month or so later the *New York Times* would famously refer to nearby Newport as the new Seattle. However, that was of no consequence to the show openers at the Aberdare Coliseum on Saturday, 2 March 1996. Backstage, Kelly was once again indulging his lifelong passion for dressing up.

'The venue was an old theatre, so there were loads of old outfits hung up on rails. Just before we went on stage Stuart tried on this fur coat and we started laughing. He said, "Try it on 'cos it's too small for me."

'So I tried it on. I had a white shirt on, incidentally the same white shirt I wore three years later at Morfa. I tried this fur coat on and this voice comes on the tannoy, "Five minutes to stage time." Then this guy comes in and says, "You're on," and I still had this fucking fur coat on. I remember the guys from the Pocket Devils, who were also on the bill, taking the piss 'cos I still had the jacket on. So, I wore this fur coat and we did "A Thousand Trees", "In My Day", "Tramps Vest" "Eyelids" – quite a lot of stuff that was on the first record. Quite a lot of punky pop. There was an electric version of "Billy Davey". I think we also did "She Takes Her Clothes

Off" and "Local Boy" even. It was only a forty-minute set, if that.'

Unbeknown to the band, in the audience was a guy called John Brand. He was a friend of the promoter and had come down to check out the 'Phonics and the Pocket Devils. John was a producer and manager.

'We just went to watch the turn for the evening and the first act on was Stereophonics. I just remember sitting in the balcony with young A&R chap and just being hugely impressed by the band. Kelly had found an old fur coat backstage at the Coliseum and came on wearing it. He just looked like a total rock star. The songs were brilliant. They did "A Thousand Trees" and "Billy Davey's Daughter" – just really powerful stuff. After the set I went back and introduced myself and just said to them that, if they were looking for a manager, I'd be interested in talking to them.'

Stuart immediately clocked the unknown presence.

'He came up to Kelly afterwards and I can remember walking past the two of them in the corridor and thinking, who the fuck's that guy Kelly's talking to, 'cos usually you know everybody who's into the music scene in Aberdare and I'd never seen that guy before.'

Richard, though, was more interested in checking out the headliners.

'I can remember Cerys in her tracksuit bottoms and all her gold. I can remember seeing their gear all sprayed with their name and there was us with one amp each. Stuart borrowed their kit; it was just funny.'

In the weeks after the Aberdare gig, Stuart, Kelly and Richard were aware they had to make some major decisions. Gil Goldberg soon became aware that all was not well within the camp.

'The big mistake I made was not going to see them support Catatonia in Wales. I did promise to go and had arranged to borrow my parents' car. On the night, my parents said that under no circumstances could I take their car to Wales. I was upset and instead of getting the train, I stayed at home and argued with my parents.

'The following week I saw the boys doing a gig in the Dublin Castle in Camden. I knew that it was the end when Kelly asked me what was going on. I was waiting to get the new demos (from Bird and Bush) and then start playing them to A&R people. Looking back, Kelly's question was more of a statement and I should have been a bit more positive with my response.'

The reality of the situation was that someone who had years of experience and very good contacts within the industry had approached Stereophonics. As Kelly explains, John and Gil had very different approaches.

'Gil was only my age, so he didn't have any contacts industry-wise. People were telling us he went through different phases all the time. He was setting himself up as an entrepreneur, so one week he'd be selling sunglasses, the next week he'd be managing a band. We just thought that maybe this was another phase. John always talked a good talk and when he took the tapes round he got results. Gil probably wasn't capable of that, but he did get us those early important gigs. Unfortunately he didn't have the experience.'

6 Deliverance

Bird and Bush

ON 13 JULY 1985, BOB GELDOF achieved the seemingly impossible, putting together the biggest musical spectacle the world had ever seen. Live Aid featured sixty of the world's biggest rock stars performing for free in two venues, one on either side of the Atlantic. Wembley Stadium played host to the likes of U2, Queen, David Bowie and Paul McCartney, while the JFK Stadium in Philadelphia boasted a line-up including Madonna, Led Zeppelin, Bob Dylan and the Beach Boys. The two gigs attracted live audiences of 162,000 but the real impact of Live Aid was achieved through TV. Over sixteen hours that day it's estimated that one and a half billion viewers tuned in worldwide, and in turn millions of dollars were raised for famine relief in Ethiopia. The sheer magnitude of Live Aid earned it the nickname the 'global jukebox'.

Marshall Bird and Steve Bush had both grown up in towns on New Zealand's North Island, close to the Bay of Plenty. They migrated to the nearby city of Auckland in the mid eighties, where they became friends and started playing in bands together. Both shared an ambition to indulge their love of rock music and make a career out of it. As they adjusted to life in the big city it soon became apparent that Auckland wasn't quite what they had in mind. The local music scene was insular to the point of being claustrophobic, and New Zealand's contribution to thirty years of rock'n'roll had been so minor that it was invisible to most people. That July day in 1985 had quite an impact in more ways than one. The global jukebox was of course accessible via satellite to people living in the vale of One Tree Hill and indeed their neighbours in Hillsborough or nearby Waikowhai, but to Marshall and Steve watching Live Aid on TV only heightened the sense of dislocation. They watched Bob Dylan misguidedly bang on about the plight of the American farmers. They saw Simon Le Bon commit career suicide in front of the entire world by failing to reach 'that note' in 'A View to a Kill'. They understood the drama; they knew the music. The characters too were entirely familiar, but still it seemed like the whole thing was happening on a different planet. This sense of removal was perhaps heightened by the fact that New Zealand is several hundred miles from its nearest neighbour let alone the USA or the UK.

It was as clear as day. This global jukebox didn't really involve New Zealand, so Messrs Bird and Bush made a mental note to move on. Little did they know that a decade or so later they'd be producing one of the biggest bands in Europe.

On a wet February evening in 1996, Marshall and Steve jumped on the tube to Tottenham Court Road en route to the Borderline club in London. They'd been in England about seven or eight years now so the intricacies of the public transport system in the capital were no longer a problem. Steve had taken the plunge first after joining an aspiring Kiwi band, the Mockers. Marshall followed soon after and the pair settled into life in London. The Mockers, however, never caught on and soon admitted defeat, splitting up in the late eighties. Steve found himself on the other side of the world without a job. As luck would have it, it was the best thing that could have happened to him because within a matter of weeks he fell upon the opportunity of a lifetime.

Steve explains: 'I got a job at Battery Studios in North London, which at the time was basically an in-house studio for the Zomba Records group. They had acts like Billy Ocean, Samantha Fox and the Wee Papa Girl Rappers, plus a whole bunch of hip-hop stuff from America. Battery was there for the use of their own writers, bands and producers, so that meant there was no pressure to sell the studio time commercially. As a result, all of the downtime was freely available to the people who worked at the company. Not many people knew how to work a mixing desk and probably fewer were even interested in doing it, but we really loved the thrill of being there. Most people start with a little garden shed studio and try to work their way up. We kind of went straight in at the top and we taught ourselves the ropes really. We basically just both stuck to day jobs and worked in the studio in the evenings and at weekends. We took any free time there was going and invited all sorts of weird and wonderful characters down. The first band we actually recorded a proper album with was called the Smalltown Heroes.'

In 1996 the Borderline was well known, as it still is today, for showcasing emerging singer-songwriters. Over the years it's become synonymous with aspiring new country artists in particular. That said, its booking policy is nothing if not varied and in the mid nineties the Wednesday night indie disco, Midweeker, was a major success. The night featured a couple of fledgling bands followed by three hours of big tunes deep into the small hours. It was a good deal for all concerned. The bands got to play to more people than was the norm and the club boasted early gigs by many of the 'Britpop' hierarchy.

As Marshall and Steve walked briskly along Charing Cross Road, the bright lights of Soho lit up the winter night. Doubtless *Blood Brothers* was showing at the Phoenix Theatre and Foyle's bookshop could well have had window displays featuring James Ellroy's *American Tabloid* or maybe *Bridget Jones's Diary* by Helen Fielding. Kula Shaker had just released their debut single, Ocean Colour Scene were in the throes of resurrecting their career with the help of Chris Evans' Radio One breakfast show and the big talk in musical circles was of a recent show at the nearby 100 Club featuring two new Welsh bands, Catatonia and the 60 Ft. Dolls.

The Smalltown Heroes at the Borderline, therefore, wasn't a buzz gig. All the same, Marshall and Steve were keen to see how their new charges would fare. They settled into the pine benches at the rear of the Borderline and waited.

The assembled throng was informed that the second band on the bill had pulled out at late notice but the Midweeker crew had secured a replacement. Stereophonics took to the stage just after 8 p.m. and played to the handful of people present. Marshall was intrigued.

'It wasn't the best gig I've seen. Stu was originally one of the drawcards for us. We were looking for a band that kind of meant it and Stu sat there and belted the shit out of the kit. We were also impressed with Kelly's voice from the off, but it was one of those things that almost passed us by. There was definitely something. I thought to myself, no, this is good – this has really got something. I remember how big Richard was and how heavily tattooed he was and thinking, how the hell am I going to approach this guy and get him up to the studio?'

Steve, too, was impressed:

'We loved what Stuart was doing. Basically, he had a tiny kit, big drums but not many of them, but he just looked the part when he played.

'I don't remember thinking the songs were great but I do remember thinking the voice was good and the guitar sound kind of had something familiar about it. Of course, it transpires it's the whole AC/DC rock history of the band, which kind of comes through in most instances. So that was quite familiar to us, being from Australasia. But I remember quietly thinking there was something good there and I prompted Marsh to go up to Richard of all people and say, "I'm a producer!"'

Richard, of course, was sceptical:

'I'd been handing out flyers at the Borderline for the next gig we had, which might have been the Kings Head in Fulham or the Bull and Gate in Kentish Town. I'm not sure but I think it was Marshall who asked where we were from and if we would like to do some recording at Battery Studios. I thought he was pulling my leg. Then I went back to the van to Kelly and Stuart and said, "The Kiwi fella was asking do we want to do some recording in Battery studios." Anyway, we had the Aberdare gig the following week so we thought we'd leave it until then.'

John Brand

In September 1985, eight weeks or so after Live Aid, the British album charts were still awash with the artists who had dominated that historic day. *Brothers in Arms* by Dire Straits and Madonna's *Like A Virgin* jostled with *Now That's What I Call Music 5* for the top spot, while the new entries included *Hounds of Love* by Kate Bush, *Here's to Future Days* by the Thompson Twins and *This is the Sea* by the Waterboys. The latter boasted the Top 40 hit 'The Whole of the Moon' and featured a production credit for John Brand.

John had started work within the music industry over a decade earlier at London's Trident recording studios. By late 1975 he was 'elevated' to the role of tape operator on the Genesis album *A Trick of the Tail*, and engineering work soon followed with the likes of Kiss, Queen, Rush, Peter Gabriel and Bachman Turner Overdrive.

The turn of the eighties saw John take full control in the studio – production credits and hit records followed with the Ruts, the Members, the Cult and Magazine. His work on the latter's seminal record *Play* didn't go unappreciated. He made another album with Howard Devoto's highly influential outfit before moving on to the debut album from a 17-year-old Glaswegian singer-songwriter called Roddy Frame. Frame's band, Aztec Camera, released *High Land Hard Rain* to both public and critical acclaim. The album featured several hit singles, including 'Oblivious' and 'Walk Out to Winter', and charted on 23 April 1983 at No. 24 before moving up to No. 12 the following week. Orange Juice also made the Top 50 that week with their *Rip it Up* album, heralding the dawn of a new successful era for music from Scotland. Ireland too was slowly emerging as a creative hotbed with new albums from U2 and the Undertones. Wales also had a few stars of its own, but they weren't quite as credible as the Postcard Records-inspired renaissance happening north of the border or the post-punk guitar scene that was emerging across the Irish Sea. Still, there's no arguing with it – the highest album chart entry that week was *Faster Than the Speed of Night* by Bonnie Tyler, which debuted at No. 3. Doubtless Bonnie, or Gaynor as she was christened, was just a bit put out that Michael Jackson had made the most successful record of his career. *Thriller* may have been ruling the roost at the top of the album charts but it didn't stop the Welsh chanteuse pulling off a historic double in the singles charts. Jim Steinman's Midas touch, which made Meat Loaf's *Bat Out of Hell* one of the biggest selling albums of all time, worked again on Bonnie's 'Total Eclipse of the Heart', which went to No. 1 simultaneously in the UK and the USA. A year later, she would consolidate that success with a duet with her countryman Shakin' Stevens. America, though, didn't really take to 'A Rockin' Good Way', and the Welsh scene of the mid eighties slowly faded away.

John Brand, meanwhile, had got together with the Water-boys, who were touring with U2. Bono and Co. were in the throes of becoming one of the biggest bands on earth and John was fascinated. His ambitions now stretched beyond produc-tion and he started putting together plans for a management company. Production gigs with artists as diverse as The Beloved, Bros and the Go-Betweens paid the bills while he launched Marsupial management.

By the early nineties, Marsupial was looking after Sun-screem, who had a string of Top 20 hits including 'Perfect Motion', a cover of the Marianne Faithfull song 'Broken English' and 'Love You More', which was also a Top 30 single in the USA. The accompanying album, *03*, peaked at No. 36 in March 1993, but the band fell apart soon after.

John also had management contracts with To Hell With Burgundy, Sally Anne Marsh, Darren Morris (better known as Conor Reeves), JJ and Pooka, who by early 96 were signed to Island Records. Around this time, Cardiff-based promoter Wayne Coleman was putting together the Splash tour, which was to be headlined by Catatonia. The idea was that each night's gig would feature a couple of unsigned local bands and be preceded by a day of talks about aspects of the music industry. Wayne invited John to speak during the afternoon at the Aberdare leg of the tour and John promptly accepted, viewing the situation as a good profile-raising opportunity for Pooka.

'I was there with Pooka because part of the show day involved a lecture to an invited student audience on the Music Industry.

'Wayne had heard a tape of Stereophonics and had booked them to play that night. After the lecture was over the band started to perform. I went upstairs to watch the show from the balcony of the Coliseum, a theatre venue with a capacity of about six hundred. I was sitting upstairs and caught about five or six songs including "A Thousand Trees", which I thought that night was their most impressive tune. After they'd finished I went backstage to say hello and to introduce myself. I met Kelly on the stairs and told him who I was and that I really liked the show and that if he was ever interested in talking about management to get in touch with me.

'Not long after, the band got in touch with me through Wayne Coleman and we arranged a meeting at the Leigh Delamere services on the M4. I told them what I'd like to do and what I could do for them. They told me about how they'd been doing loads of gigs in London as the Tragic Love Company and sending out demos in cartons of Chinese food and trying all the gimmicks under the sun to try to get attention, which they hadn't achieved.

'My game plan was to try to develop them as a band within Wales using the Welsh media, which I thought was sufficiently strong to try to build a buzz for the band without having to go to London.

'Kelly gave me a set of lyrics because I couldn't really understand what he was singing on the demo they'd given me. As I was driving back to the office I had the lyrics on the steering wheel and had the tape in the cassette machine. By the time I got back to the office I was completely blown away by what he'd written. I rang Kelly straight away and asked him where he'd got the inspiration for them and all this sort of thing; we really had a long chat about the lyrics. There were about four songs on the tape, I really can't remember exactly what they were – probably "A Thousand Trees", "Tramps Vest", "Check for Holes" and "Local Boy". We talked about the songs and the band – we talked about everything really, and by the end of the conversation I was convinced I wanted to get involved, and he seemed pretty happy about the idea.'

Kelly was impressed.

'He phoned me up that night. I was living with my mother, and he said, "These words in this thing are brilliant!" I'd never heard anybody talk like that about our stuff before. I said, "What do you mean?" He said, "What are camping eyes?" I said, "It means when you go camping and you sit round a fire all night and your eyes are stinging 'cos you haven't had enough sleep. You come down in the morning and your eyes are hurting – it means you're tired." He asked me all these different lines to all these different things and I was explaining things to him and he was just blown away by it.

'I was getting excited that at least somebody understood what I was on about. We were on the phone for about forty minutes. My father said, "Who's that?" and I said, "I don't know." '

Throughout the summer of 1996, Stereophonics played a series of showcase gigs in South Wales. John Brand's tactic of building a media buzz in Wales in order to make the record industry come to them seemed to be working. At one show, at the Filling Station in Newport, the guest list pinpointed no less than 35 representatives from different companies. Kelly's father, Oscar, realised that they were on the brink of securing a deal.

'We were talking after the show in Newport and I said, "Make sure if you are going to sign, it's what you actually want out of the deal. It's a job: it isn't any more and it isn't any less. If you can keep it as a job and work at it and ignore the bullshit, you don't get carried away with it. If it's your job then you've got to be good at it and you've got to improve all the time. Don't get caught up in all the hype so that you become a crook." '

In between playing live they entered the studio with Marshall and Steve for the first time.

Kelly takes up the story: 'We did "A Thousand Trees" and "Eyelids". "Eyelids" was recorded in Straylight in Willesden Green. This is exactly the version that ended up on the album. That version of "A Thousand Trees" was also going to up until the very last moment, when we decided I sounded twelve years old – so we re-recorded it about a year later.

'I remember driving up to this house that Marshall and Steve were renting with a Geordie guy called Jimmy. Jimmy had gone away so we ended up sleeping in his room. Richard and Stuart were in the bed and I was on the floor. I remember we arrived in Stuart's yellow van. Steve and Marshall came out and they just started taking the piss out of our van looking like the one in *Only Fools and Horses*. We had a night on the beers and curry and then I remember waking up in the morning in someone else's house. I went into the living room and found an AC/DC album there. I put *Highway to Hell* on full blast and then we went to Straylight and did the demo.'

The demo certainly made an impact and before long the A&R community was working up a lather over 'A Thousand Trees'. This frenzy hit fever pitch when Steve Lamacq played the demo on the biggest alternative radio show in Europe – *The Evening Session* on Radio One.

Steve recalls: 'When I first heard about Stereophonics, it was still at the time when you'd have A&R men disappearing down to Wales looking for The Next Big Thing. I played "A Thousand Trees" from the demo on the Session Unsigned slot a while before they actually signed.

'It was the most solid demo we'd had on the show for ages. Bear in mind, I hadn't seen them live, but I thought the track justified the record company interest. The guitar sounded really full-on for a demo, and the voice sounded interesting. There was definitely something there.

'A lot of the demos we'd had in from Wales in the past year had been either pretty standard post-punk groups or rather quirky village hall-type bands. This just seemed like a good tune, well played with a bit of passion.

'Anyway, we played it, and I think that probably tipped off one or two late-comers from record companies or people who'd maybe not followed up the original demo when it had gone round.'

'Steve rang me in the office the night he was going to play the demo of 'A Thousand Trees' for the first time,' John Brand says. 'He told me that he thought it was a fantastic song and told me that he was really going to support this band. He also told me to add some zeros to the deal. True to form he did support us. He was the first person at Radio One to play anything by Stereophonics and he's supported them ever since.'

One of the many interested parties was Richard Branson's new venture in music, V2 records. V2 was so young that the offices were still being refurbished and the staff list comprised only three people – A&R man Ronnie Gurr, label boss David Steele and Jeremy Pearce, the CEO.

Jeremy says, 'The first time I became aware of them was when a friend of mine, Geoff Travis [MD of Blanco Y Negro Records], told me about Stereophonics. He thought they were very good and mentioned that they'd been played on Steve Lamacq's *Evening Session*. Our A&R guy, Ronnie Gurr, was also interested in them and so the next step for me was going down to see them play the Blackwood Miners' Institute in Wales. It was basically a room full of A&R people. I thought signing them was going to be very tough because V2 was just a small label at the time. All we had was a promise of our commitment and, obviously, we had the backing of Richard Branson.'

It wasn't just record companies who were sniffing around these gigs. There were representatives from publishing companies and the odd concert-booking agent too. Scott Thomas was working for International Talent Booking at the time and counted Cypress Hill, Fugees and the Manics among the artists he represented.

'I went to the Blackwood Miners' Institute on a Sunday night in July 96 having not even heard a demo, simply because of what people were telling me. The venue's an old, turn-of-the-century building that the miners used to use. You'd have brass bands playing there and there's a big bar, so it's like a social club.

'I remember everyone in the entire venue sitting down until the moment they came on and I'm thinking, this isn't going to work. Basically everyone knew the band, or knew of them, so there wasn't like a kind of clamour. I thought, this isn't going to have a gig atmosphere. Then they walked on and everyone stood up and suddenly it became a real gig. As an agent you always have to ask yourself, what are they going to be like in fifty gigs' time? That way you're not jumping to immediate conclusions. Most new bands need about thirty or so gigs to get into their stride before you put them anywhere near the public eye. They were already there! I remember "Looks Like Chaplin" and "A Thousand Trees" being the ones that stood out right away. John gave me the demo on the way out of the gig. It had the lyrics printed on the inside of the inlay. I remember thinking, what band gives you the lyrics?

'The following day I was on the phone to John going, "I have to represent them. Who do I kill to get involved?" I think we tied it up in the week afterwards.'

John Brand couldn't believe the situation. His plan was falling into place. He couldn't have written a better script.

'By 1996 I'd been shopping deals for bands for quite a while and because I had been in the music business even longer. I had just grown up with the people who were then the heads of A&R and are now the MDs of record companies. Wayne Coleman was involved with the local media in Wales and, between us, he was able to get the gigs and I was able to get the people to the gigs.

'I kind of fabricated a whole story in London about how big the band were in Wales. The reality was they'd never even played in Cardiff. They'd actually done more gigs in England than they'd done in Wales, but of course it was easy for me to bullshit people. The one legend compounded the other part of the legend so that people did actually start to believe that they were big in Wales and in turn the Welsh media started to believe that the English companies were really interested in them.

'Within about three shows we had HTV doing a feature at the big A&R fest at the Filling Station in Newport. They came down with a crew and filmed all the A&R men at the gig and ask them why they'd come all the way down to Wales to see a band called Stereophonics. At the end of the day, the band's demo tape was really good and all we needed was the right people to get to hear it.

'As far as shopping for the deal, I really wanted a set-up where the band could spend time developing and where they would be given the artistic freedom that I thought they needed. They're very creative people and a major label would have been the wrong move. Some bands don't have any ideas and you put them in the hands of a major and they can be moulded and made into decent bands. We didn't need that.

'Of course, I had to go to the majors in order to drum up the deal. I was looking for money obviously. I needed to get them some cash, some decent gear, good recording budgets, tour support commitment, opportunity to do good videos, you know, all the things that a band needs to really progress in its first year.

'So V2 came along – they were actually interested in another project I was working on and Jeremy Pearce came down one night and met Stereophonics at a gig for this other band. He *was* V2 at that time, he liked the boys and they liked him. It became clear in my conversations with him that V2 could well be the right company. Their worldwide expansion plans timed nicely with our own development plans. It gave the band the opportunity to tour extensively prior to releasing a record.'

Jeremy Pearce could see the prize slowly coming within his grasp.

'Personally, I thought "A Thousand Trees" was an outstanding song and I still do. It was very, very mature. It was one of the best new songs and you could hear it being a hit straight away. It made me feel very confident about the songwriting ability of the band. Still, it was going to be a challenge to get them against the opposition.'

By this stage David Steele had signed up as V2's label boss, almost doubling the staff count at the emerging company.

'It was a time when the Britpop guitar bands had started to fade. Oasis were still hugely popular and the Manic Street Preachers were still big. You knew that big bands were still there and it was all the middle ground minor bands that were starting to suffer.

'With the Stereophonics demo I just thought the quality of the songs and the voice meant that this was something that could really be developed and they could be a band for the future. They were never going to be one of the buzz bands that the *NME* love and who become very trendy and then disappear. They were much more a traditional band.

'There were some things going on in Wales, but that can work against you because everyone's saying, "Not another Welsh band!" I think that the thing that struck me about their nationality was that they were very true to their home and very down to earth. I think what happens is they just connect with people universally because there are small towns everywhere.'

Kelly, Richard and Stuart, meanwhile, were trying to make sense of the situation. Three months earlier they'd been Tragic Love Company doing 'pay to play' gigs to an invisible audience. Now the whole record industry was trying to woo them. However, Kelly knew to follow his instinct.

'We got a rumour about this company that Branson was trying to set up and you hear all these stories about how everything that Branson touches turns to gold. At the same time we were seeing Warner Brothers, Island, EMI, Parlophone, Virgin, Polydor, Chrysalis, Columbia – literally every company that there was in London. It was frightening because we didn't know which one to sign to. At the end of it we decided to opt for personalities because most of them were like car salesmen.'

John Brand soon sensed that Kelly was no fool when it came to working people out:

'We were sat in the boardroom at EMI and the A&R guy turned round to Kelly and said, "This 'Thousand Trees' track. Why did you write this song? Is it for Greenpeace? Is it about saving trees?" Kelly just looked at me and I knew that EMI was out of the window! There was really nothing to say after that. It happened on a few occasions where we met up with people that clearly didn't get what it was all about.'

Kelly, however, liked what he saw at V2:

'We had a meeting with Ronnie Gurr, the A&R guy at V2, in Branson's house in Holland Park. We had to drive up at the same time that the Notting Hill Carnival was going on. I was driving up in my Orion, which I'd bought off Rich for £200. It was more orange than silver 'cos it was full of fucking rust!

I had to fill it up with Radwell every fifty miles because the radiator was knackered. I had to stir it in with this pencil and the pencil got stuck in my water tank. So we were stuck at the Notting Hill Carnival and the car was overheating! We got to Holland Park and we had to stop the car and all this orange shit was running down the road.

'Branson's house was great. You got the little Virgin sweets in bowls and all that stuff. I remember this big huge table, which is now in Virgin's first-class lounge at Heathrow. So we're sat at this table and Ronnie says, "Look – fuck all these other companies. If you sign with us we'll be up and running in six months. By the time you make your album we'll be ready to go." He talked a good talk to be honest.

'There was also Ronnie and Jeremy's backgrounds. They'd both worked with some impressive stuff. Jeremy had signed Oasis and Suede during his time at Sony and Ronnie had found Kula Shaker.

'Also, a lot of the other A&R guys talking to us weren't much older than we were, and I didn't believe them. I didn't buy it. In one case the guy was the nephew of the MD and he was offering us bottles of Becks at 11 a.m. – just because he thought it was cool. I didn't want a bottle of Becks; I just wanted to know what was good for my career. I didn't give a fuck about people like that. We ended up taking the risk really – it could have really gone wrong.

'I don't know why we did it in the end, to be honest – it just felt right. They were nice people and they gave us the best contract.'

Stuart agrees:

'Everything they said made so much sense.

'They spoke about the rest of the world, which no other record company did. They spoke about America; they spoke about Australia, Japan, everywhere, and we just thought that this is a record company that really knows where they want to go. To be honest with you, after that first meeting not even a second thought came into my head. And the good thing about V2 was, it was all people who had been in that corporate situation but wanted to work for an independent. That's the thing with V2, it is an independent label but it's got the money of a major, so you get the best of both worlds.'

V2 had done their work on the ground. Now they decided to play their ace card to make completely sure that they'd secured the signing. As Kelly explains:

'I was in my house one day and Jeremy Pearce phoned and said, "Branson's going to phone you." I said, "What for?" He said, "To try to convince you that we're the right label to sign to."

'So you can imagine, I was living with my mother and father at the time and my mother was threatening to say, "Yeah, if you're Richard Branson then I'm Elizabeth Taylor." So the phone rings and he sounded more nervous than me. He said, "Hello, can I speak to Kelly, Richard or Stuart?" as if we all lived in the same house or something. Then he said, "I hear you're very popular at the moment but I just want to convince you that if you do sign to the label, it will be 200 per cent behind you." Richard Branson phoned my old girl's house? It was very strange!'

'The first thing I heard was a tape of them which sounded fantastic.' Richard Branson was determined. 'I think somebody had done a home video of them and based on that I was very keen that they should be the first band on our new record label. Switching the clock back many years the first record on Virgin Records had been Mike Oldfield's *Tubular Bells* which sold millions. We obviously wanted to have a band that was as important for this generation many years later.

'A number of people were interested in signing them and I think that perhaps what helped swing it our way was that phone call to Kelly at his mother's house in Wales. I wanted to make it clear how keen we were.'

John Brand at last was fully content that they were making the right decision.

'The V2 offer was no more lucrative than any of the others. We got to a point where we had serious offers from about four labels and a lot of other labels that were interested. I was looking for a label where we'd be a priority because I'd had bands on other labels and unless you have that big support behind you it's very difficult. The other thing I liked about V2 was the fact that they weren't really set up.

'Branson wanted to set up a new label; he'd hired Jeremy to put it all together and that was all it was. There was also the fact if we signed then we would be synonymous with the launch of the label all around the world and get all the extra press and attention as a result of that.

'We were also keen to avoid being thrown into that situation where major labels expect immediate results and don't give you any time to develop. The band didn't have a lot of experience; they hadn't done a lot of touring and so the V2 deal allowed us the space we needed. We made the first record in bits and pieces around the touring. So it was a good decision at the time, a risk but nevertheless a good decision.'

In fact, by the time the Stereophonics signed on the dotted line they had almost recorded their debut album as Steve Bush explains.

'Initially myself and Marshall produced the first demo which gave us two quality recordings. We had another four songs waiting to be recorded but we had no money. The first lot of demos I think we'd paid for somehow. I think I might have worked an extra two Sundays or something at Dreamhire!

The next time around we had these four songs and John Brand did a very smart thing by contacting not just one record company to ask for demo money but SIX! Of course, most record companies are happy to spend £500 on demoing a band. They think nothing of it, so he actually lined up six companies who paid £500 each! As a result of that we were able to record another four tunes to the same quality as the first lot. Consequently V2 had six tracks effectively, ready to potentially put towards an album. This was probably a key factor in how myself and Marshall ended up producing the whole album. If it had been Sony, or maybe another estab-lished label, the first thing they would have done is brush us off and move them on to a big producer and that would have been the end of it.

'V2 on the other hand only had two people and one telephone so they had no resources really to put a band in the studio and start building a promotional campaign. Instead they carried on funding essentially what had been these demos that we did and we just carried on until the end of the first album.'

So, job done. Branson had his prized first signings. V2 was about to start work proper and after years of beat-up yellow vans, working men's clubs and delivering school dinners, Kelly, Richard and Stuart were finally going to get paid to make music. V2 CEO Jeremy Pearce was intrigued by his new charges.

'Stuart was a big extrovert, a very Welsh sort of character with the booming voice and a sort of superficial resemblance to Tom Jones. Richard was always just the completely charming, reserved guy with no side at all, really a gentle giant, and Kelly was clearly very gifted and very intense, but in spite of that, very modest. So there was none of the feeling of the tormented genius who didn't want to speak to people. He was just a very nice, modest person in spite of his great talent. So they all had very individual characters.

'What was impressive was the tremendous feeling between them. I really had the feeling, which I always said to them, that this was the most precious thing they could have, this relationship between them. I told them that that would stand by them and they should look after that almost to the exclusion of all else.'

Pier Reid had joined the fledgling V2 staff as part of what would be the marketing department. She would become the band's product manager and so was keen to have a look at them to see whether they had pin-up potential.

'The very first time they came into the office I remember checking the three of them out. I can remember looking at Kelly and thinking, He's got the eyes, he's got the looks, the come to bed eyes. I remember looking at Richard and looking at his profile and thinking, he's a great-looking lad too and then looking at Stuart and thinking, he's a character! The three of them had this chemistry between them.

'I get involved with all the photography, sleeves and videos so I was sat there thinking art-work wise I could see beautiful photos of them. I was just listening to them. It was obvious that Richard was the quieter one. Kelly was also quiet that day.

It was Stuart who was doing all the chatting. Nothing's changed much there! I did think looking at them that they're not three lads you're ever going to change. I never thought they needed styling. Some people might need a bit of help, but the three of them were who they were and the main thing with the 'Phonics was the music.'

So everyone was happy. All that was left to do was actually sign and celebrate. The night of the signing was always going to be one of those nights. Kelly had a ball.

'That night, we were in a French restaurant in London and Ronnie Gurr mentioned that Kula Shaker were playing the Astoria and the after-show was at the Groucho club. Now we'd been invited to both events because we told Columbia we were interested in signing to them. As if that wasn't bad enough, Ronnie had signed Kula Shaker to Columbia and he'd left Columbia to go to V2, so he wanted to rub their faces in it by taking us to this party. So we went to see Kula Shaker at the Astoria and I can remember walking in and thinking, this gig is massive. It's not quite so big now we've played it a few times.

'Earlier, in the restaurant, they asked, "Do you want white or red?" and we said, "Both – and a lager!" That's how it went. We were having it all because it might not last long. They gave us £1,500 in fifties, so we were living it up. We were pissed by the time we got to the Groucho and we went downstairs and there was Bob Mortimer by the bar! We turned round and Jarvis Cocker was there as well. I was like, "What the fuck's this?" I said to Stuart, "I want to talk to him but I don't know what to talk to him about."

'So, we ended up sitting next to him and we were trying to buy drinks with cash and they were saying, "No, we can't accept that." We were like, "Isn't this money good enough?" It's all credit cards and that. We were probably getting really loud at this point. So, we sat down and talked to Jarvis for a while and I probably told him that I loved him from what I can remember. Then we went back upstairs to the party and I was leaning against the wall and there was this painting which fell off the wall and smashed! I kicked it under this buffet table.

Meanwhile the head of Columbia had got wind of us having signed to V2. He'd come in at this point and he was saying to Ronnie Gurr, "Get your fucking band out of here!" We were so pissed that we just wandered off to another room.

'Robbie [Williams] was there; he was talking to Bob Mortimer and I remember thinking, he's a lot bigger than I thought. He was quite chunky at the time. I said, "Can I have a word with you?" So we went out in the hallway and there was just me and him sitting on the stairs and I said, "We signed a record deal today and I know you just split up with a band and your single went in at number two." He was really nice, just talking about the business and what I was doing. That was the first time I met him and then he turned into this big star. It was about the time he did that George Michael song, "Freedom". I remember the bass player from Blur walking down the steps, so you can imagine us the next day! We'd met all these people, signed a record deal, and we had £1,500 in our back pocket that we were going to burn on Levi's because we didn't have any jeans. We were flying!'

2

Free Falling From a Stage

why don't you take a look in my mouth
why don't you take a look at yourself
so why don't you take a look around
so why don't we take a look inside

roll out the shock parade
free falling from a stage
performance and cocktails
roll up and shine

i hang the devil from a circus wire
face up seats four in love spittin' fire
so why don't you take a look around
so why don't we take a look inside

it's time to live it's time to love
it's time to do who's afraid of
it's time to breathe time to relieve
it's time to shine

7 Guess Who's Coming to Dinner

LESS THAN TWO YEARS after that memorable night at the Groucho the Stereophonics' world had changed beyond recognition.

It's 7 May 1998 and I'm strolling through St James's Park in Central London. The noise of the bustling capitol is humming in the background but here in the middle of the park there is temporary respite from the madness.

Ahead, Buckingham Palace is enduring the daily routine of clamouring tourists taking photos that will lie undisturbed in packets for future generations to throw away. To the left, Horse Guards Parade winds past the Foreign and Commonwealth Office to the Cabinet War Rooms, which never fail to inspire wild notions of espionage and guys with curly moustaches.

As I wander over towards Pall Mall, there are people scattered on the benches around the lake in the centre of the park. Some are grabbing a bite of lunch away from the glare of office politics. Others are grappling with broadsheet papers. Never a good idea turning the page on a breezy day.

At the water's edge there is a party of schoolchildren straining to see over to Duck Island as their teacher intermittently roars at one little fella at the back who is busy throwing stones at the duck aristocracy. Doubtless there are ducks in his local pond that don't swim around with their beaks quite this high.

I digress. I am en route to witness quite possibly the most surreal show that Stereophonics will ever play. Stuart, Kelly and Richard are due to play in front of about fifty celebs at a special function at St James's Palace in aid of the Prince's Trust. The fact that the venue used to be the official Royal household for three centuries until Queen Victoria decided to move up the road in 1837 is not lost on anybody. Neither is the potted history dished out in leaflet form upon arrival.

St James's Palace isn't open to the public, obviously, because it's Prince Charles's London residence. It was commissioned by Henry VIII between 1532 and 1540 and built by Sir Christopher Wren, who was also responsible for St Paul's Cathedral.

It's enjoyed its fair share of history. Charles I was confined here prior to his execution by Oliver Cromwell in 1649. Queen Victoria married Albert in the Queen's Chapel within the palace and, more recently, Queen Elizabeth II made her first speech here as Monarch in 1952. Today, though, we add another chapter.

Walking through the place is quite something. High ceilings and more art than you can shake a stick at. After all, it is still the Senior Palace of the Sovereign and the Court to which foreign Ambassadors and High Commissioners are accredited . . . and three-piece rock'n'roll bands from South Wales.

I meet up with 'the Cwmaman Three' in a small antechamber off the main function room. Nearby, the great and the good are sipping fine wine and tucking into canapés. Kelly, Richard and Stuart, on the other hand, have seen better days. They've spent the last two months touring the USA, Australia and New Zealand and, despite having had a couple of weeks to recover, they're feeling as rough as hell. Let's just say 'last night' wasn't particularly dark when it came to a boozy end. They may feel a little delicate but everyone is in good humour, especially Richard, who extends a warm handshake and welcomes me to 'Sid James's Palace' (What a *Carry On*, eh?).

'We've been told that Kevin Spacey's coming and Ben Kingsley's here. Who else?' Kelly asks. 'Ben Elton,' Stuart responds, 'and that guy who talks through his nose, you know, Braggy whatsisname.' There's much laughter before we find out that 'Braggy whatsisname' is in fact top broadcaster and cultural commentator Melvyn Bragg.

The plan is to do two songs, as Kelly explains. 'We are going to do "Chaplin" and "Traffic". "Chaplin" acoustic will sound

Left 'For Those About to Rock'. Kelly aged nine dressed as AC/DC's Angus Young, in his front room at Glanaman Road in 1983.

Below Richard and his brother Jason.

Right Richard and Kelly on holiday at Barry Island, South Wales, circa 1981.

Left 'Heavy Metal Chic': Richard and Kelly with Kelly's dad, Oscar.

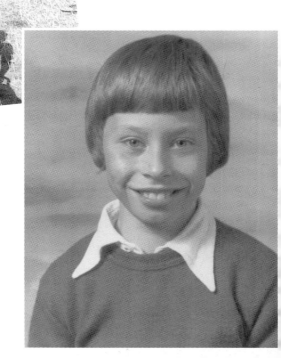

Right Stuart's school photograph.

Above An early gig at the Beaufort Ballroom, Ebbw Vale on July 20th 1996, just before signing to V2.

Left 'Nice To Be Out' (both Julian Castaldi)

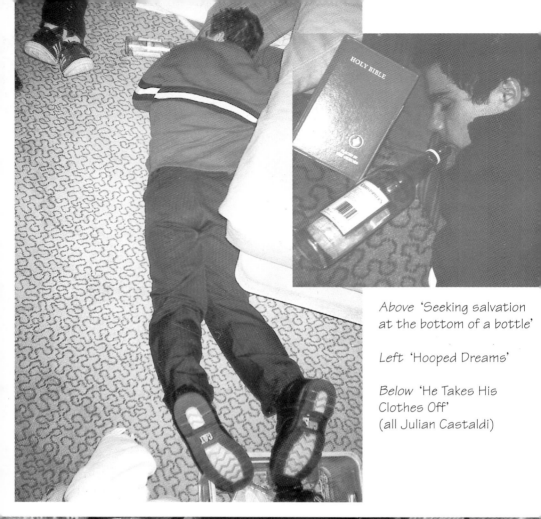

Above 'Seeking salvation at the bottom of a bottle'

Left 'Hooped Dreams'

Below 'He Takes His Clothes Off'
(all Julian Castaldi)

Right 'Magnum P.I.' Kelly with old friend, photographer and band archivist, Julian Castaldi on the tour bus en route from the V97 site in Leeds to Chelmsford, August 16th 1997. (Lucy Scott-Harris)

Below The Stereophonics perform the Beatles song 'I'm Only Sleeping' with Noel Gallagher at Air Studios, North London for the John Lennon tribute programme 'Shine On', September 9th 2000. (Julian Castaldi)

Left Kelly at the Lennon
tribute night.
(Julian Castaldi)

Right 'Who Are You?'
Backstage at the Royal
Albert Hall with Jimmy
Page and Roger Daltrey,
November 27th 2000.

Below With another hero,
Black Crowes' frontman
Chris Robinson, backstage
at the Toxic Twin Towers
Ball at Wembley Stadium,
June 26th 1999. (Julian
Castaldi)

Above And then there were four... Performance and Cocktails, 1999. (Julian Castaldi)

Right 'Pleased to meet you, hope you guessed my name!' Royal Albert Hall, November 27th 2000.

like some kind of cowboy campfire song, so here's hoping we knock 'em bandy!'

The performance is note perfect and the distinguished audience clap in accordance before the host, TV newsman Jon Snow, resumes the talk on the work of the Prince's Trust. Stereophonics are here basically because they got money out of the Prince's Trust in their youth. Today is payback time.

'About six years ago I sent them a letter explaining what we were up to,' Kelly says. 'They sent back a cheque for eight hundred quid. We bought some speakers and a mixing desk. It really helped us because we could then afford to start gigging regularly and we started getting a response from people.

'Today is hardly the most rock'n'roll event but every now and then you've got to forget about what is and isn't cool to do. Anyway, Kevin Spacey's here. That's pretty cool.'

Kevin Spacey certainly made an impression. He was invited to the Palace that day because he was in London appearing in a West End play called *The Ice Man Cometh*. Three years earlier he'd made the leap from respected actor to movie star with the release of three movies: *Swimming With Sharks*, *Seven* and *The Usual Suspects*. The 1997 release of *LA Confidential* further confirmed his A-list credentials and so, with all due respect to Stephen Fry and Ben Elton, he was undoubtedly *the* star presence in the room. He was also very impressed with the turn.

Kelly recalls: 'After the show, he came straight over to us and said, "I really love your band. It's great music." We asked him what he was doing in England and he spoke about the play. He said to get in touch if we wanted to come and see it, so we did a couple of weeks later.

'It was an amazing play. We met him after the show and went for dinner somewhere in the West End. There was this big round table and we arrived just before him and sat down.

'Afterwards we all went to the Met Bar, which is part of the hotel where he was staying. I didn't know what the Met Bar was then. I didn't know it was a celebrity hangout. I remember going in there with him and by that point I just didn't know what to say to him. I asked him what it was like working with people like Clint Eastwood. I knew quite a lot about Kevin Spacey but when someone's just finished work the last thing they want is to be interviewed, so you just try to play it cool.'

For John Brand, the whole episode signalled a departure point. 'It was their first exposure to that world. It was really good because Kelly is a massive film buff and Kevin is one of his favourite actors, so for Kelly to meet Kevin Spacey and for Kevin to be interested in what Kelly was doing was fantastic.'

Kelly interjects at this point: 'John phoned me up about three months later and said, "I've got Kevin's number. Can you phone him and listen to his answer message?" By this time my brother Kevin was with the army in Northern Ireland. So I phone this number thinking it was my brother and I put on this Irish accent: "Kevin, there's a bomb under your bed, a bomb under your bed." And then I hung up.

'The answerphone message was an excerpt from a film and I thought Kevin had carved it off a video and put it on his phone and I was laughing at it. Then, much later, I thought, bollocks, this isn't Kevin's number. So I phoned John and said, "The number you gave me a couple of weeks ago, it was my brother's, wasn't it?" He said, "No. It was Kevin Spacey's number. I wanted you to listen to the answer message." I said, "Where is he now then?" and John says, "He's in Ireland doing a film." I thought, I bet he's had security going mad everywhere! It was a coincidence, but we haven't seen him since. He was a nice guy. I don't pretend to be best mates with him, but it was cool having dinner with him.'

A month after 'Spaceygate', Stereophonics continued to live like royalty. This time around, though, they decided to play a castle in the principality. Palaces in London may be all the rage but you just can't get ten thousand people into them.

Three hundred and forty-three years before Stereophonics played Cardiff Castle, Charles I sought refuge there while on the run from Oliver Cromwell's Parliamentarian forces during the Civil War. He was eventually seized and imprisoned at St James's Palace. Another tale of the same two venues, albeit with rather more historical repercussions!

To say that Cardiff Castle has had a colourful history is an understatement. It's a miracle the place is still standing in any shape or form, and that's nothing to do with the skirmishes outside the last gig there in the late 1970s.

The Romans first settled on the site during the first century AD. Ten centuries later the Normans developed it into a fortress, but in 1183 the native Welsh populace revolted and almost reduced the structure to rubble.

Things weren't great for the next 180 years but they took a real turn for the worse when the notorious English DeSpenser family moved in. Within a decade they had executed the Welsh leader who had instigated the revolts against the English overlords. The now legendary Llwelyn Bren was killed and his body was dragged through the streets for all to see. Bad idea! Predictably there were further rebellions in the early fifteenth century when the Welsh avenged Bren's death by setting the castle and most of the town on fire.

You get the picture. The castle rocked long before the invention of the electric guitar. By the twentieth century it had been rebuilt and improved several times, most recently by the 3rd Marquess of Bute in the mid 1800s. He was noted for his flamboyance and gaudy taste, which would explain why today the place is bedecked in astrological symbols and biblical characters in gilt robes. There are flowing fountains, rich greenery and incredible marble fireplaces all over the place. There aren't many cities with a building like this located right in its centre.

In 1947 the castle was finally turned over to the people. Cardiff City Council became responsible for maintaining what is in essence still a Norman fortress and duly opened its doors to the public. During the seventies they also began to stage rock shows in the grounds as a way of raising cash for the upkeep of the building. The gigs, however, became more of a headache than they were worth and so the last guitar solo drifted off over Cardiff City Centre in 1978.

That was until 12 June 1998.

When the show was announced, Stereophonics were unsure as to whether they could attract ten thousand people on the strength of their own name. It soon became apparent that they had nothing to worry about.

'I don't ever think a Welsh act had ever headlined there before.' Scott Thomas from International Talent Booking takes up the story. 'The Queen was in town that weekend for the beginning of the EU summit, so there was an awful lot of behind-the-scenes stuff. The local authorities were quite keen on the idea of the band playing for the Queen. We weren't really into that idea.

'The show only went on sale about ten weeks in advance so, with ten thousand tickets to shift, it was a bit of a challenge to say the least. I don't know if an English band would feel the same about Windsor Castle but the great thing about Cardiff Castle is it's got no royalty. It's just basically this bizarre symbol in the middle of Cardiff.'

A few weeks before the show Kelly was characteristically modest about the fact that ten thousand tickets went in ten days.

'We would have liked Catatonia or the Super Furry Animals playing with us but obviously they're bigger than us. It would be nice if they came down for a drink anyway.

'We said years ago, as a joke, that one day we would play the Arms Park in Cardiff, but they're knocking that down so the closest we're going to get right now is the castle. It makes sense that this is happening in Wales because we've made a real effort to play here. In the same way that the Scots have really supported us, the Welsh have been unbelievable. It's only six months since we were playing Cardiff University.'

'I think Welsh people are proud of what's going on at the moment,' Stuart adds. 'I hope it carries on. I hope there's another million and one bands to come out of Wales.'

Kelly picks it up now: 'Everybody was saying a year ago that it'll be interesting to see who is left after the so-called Welsh scene dies away. At the end of the day, it's all about writing songs. That's why Catatonia are getting so big. It's about the songs. It's not because we're Welsh: it's because we have real songs. It's good for us to know where we come from but it's no big deal really. It's other people who make a big deal of it.'

On the day itself there's no mistaking that this is a Welsh event. The gates open at five o'clock but people have been gathering since early morning. By lunchtime the grass verges outside the castle wall are home to one giant party. There's a carnival atmosphere amidst the sea of Welsh flags and T-shirts bearing the name of the event – 'Cwmaman Feel the Noize'. One organised bunch have brought a barbecue and are busy turning sausages. The majority, though, have opted for nourishment of the liquid variety. The pre-show knees-up is further enhanced by baking-hot sunshine. It can't have been anything like this twenty years ago when the likes of Queen, 10CC and Status Quo graced the same venue.

The band arrive for a soundcheck around one o'clock but it's limited to an hour because the court across the road reconvenes at two. Kelly, meanwhile, is trying to take it all in. Their dressing room is the castle's resplendent Peacock suite, which is effectively the Queen's private apartment when she's in town. The fact that she's due to arrive tomorrow means they've been warned to be on their best behaviour. This is one dressing room that no one trashes!

'Two years ago we couldn't sell out the pub across the road. When we were playing in Sam's Bar we had to take the money on the door and then go and do the gig, so it's changed days. This is definitely a different kind of venue. I live twenty-three miles from here and, to be honest, I hadn't ever set foot inside the castle grounds until recently.

'I've got to say the waiting around is the worst part. Once you get onstage it's a relief. It's been handy that we've been in the studio for the last six weeks, so we haven't had a lot of time to think about this. Now though, I really want to try to forget about all the cameras and stuff and just enjoy the gig.'

Outside the walls, expectation is reaching fever pitch as the Friday evening rush hour kicks in. Tickets are changing hands for anything up to seventy quid. The pubs nearby are packed to the rafters with buoyant punters who are paying absolutely no attention at all to the Denmark v. Saudi Arabia World Cup match on the TV.

At five the gates open and two hours later Subcircus get the show on the road. They're followed by the Warm Jets but, while the crowd give both bands a polite reception, they're here for one reason only.

Meanwhile Kelly, Stuart and Richard wander out to a platform towards the rear of the venue to check out the atmosphere but once they're spotted there's pandemonium and they run for cover. The days of mingling with the crowd prior to a show are officially over.

At 9.25 p.m. a deafening roar goes up as a cheesy organ backing tape dies down and Stereophonics take to the stage. They look tiny set against a giant shell-like construction, which itself is flanked by the stone ramparts of the castle.

Clad in trademark jeans, T-shirt and a brown leather jacket, Kelly says, 'Hello, Cardiff,' and the band launch into their debut single, 'Looks Like Chaplin'. It's followed by a foot-stomping 'Check My Eyelids for Holes' and then comes the first sign of what to expect from the next album.

The new song is called 'Bartender and the Thief' and the first impression is of AC/DC colliding with Supergrass. In fact there are four apparently new tunes tonight. The other three, 'T-Shirt Suntan', 'Wouldn't Believe Your Radio' and 'She Takes Her Clothes Off', hint at a more mature collection of songs. What's also clear is that, lyrically, Kelly has moved away from the drama of small-town life.

We get all of *Word Gets Around* with 'Local Boy' and 'Big Time Drinkers' as the two stand-out moments. The former is complemented by 10,000 voices singing every syllable. That's one of the amazing things about tonight – the crowd not only know the choruses, but they also know every word. Not bad for a debut album! 'Drinkers' is dedicated to anyone who likes a tipple, before Kelly mentions his hero, the late AC/DC vocalist Bon Scott who ironically choked on his own vomit after a particularly heavy session. 'Drinkers' also features a particularly manic performance from Stuart, reminiscent of Keith Moon or indeed Animal from the Muppets, while Richard works the stage with an air of cool not usually associated with bass players (Mark King he ain't).

The stools are brought on towards the end of the set as everything chills out. Dusk has settled and the castle is bathed in red and green light. It's quite a picture as Kelly's voice grows to fill the entire castle grounds with two of the more mellow new tunes: 'She Take Her Clothes Off' is a lament and tells a tale of a woman trying to regain her youthful beauty; 'Wouldn't Believe Your Radio' sounds like a country song and is rumoured to be the first single from the forthcoming album.

The band then disappear, only to re-appear soon after. Kelly tells the assembled throng that a guy called Paul Jones has asked him to ask Nicola if she'll marry him. The show winds up with a dedication to the Manics, the Super Furries, Catatonia and the cast of *Twin Town*, most of whom are watching from the guest enclosure. 'More Life in a Tramps Vest' prompts an ecstatic response from the audience who, unknowingly, are part of a coming of age party for a new Welsh generation. The lights go up and the band are gone, but things have changed forever.

The after-show at the nearby Angel Hotel is packed full of family and friends draped everywhere from the reception area to the bar.

James Dean Bradfield is having drinks with friends whilst various Super Furries wander about. Owen from Catatonia sums up the mood.

'I bumped into a mate of mine from Cardiff who lives in Denmark. He travelled home yesterday for this event so that gives you an idea of what it means to him. I'm really pleased for Stereophonics because, like us, they've had to work really hard for their success. The first singles didn't really do very well and they've won people over the hard way – by playing live.'

The 'Phonics' agent, Scott Thomas, has the look of a proud dad at a school sports day.

'James from the Manics is here because he wants to be here and he wanted to see it. The great thing is that there's no rancour; there's no cynicism or reviewing of the gig or chin stroking. It's just, "Wow it happened!" and that is the nice thing about it.

'I come from not too far away and I've got about twenty mates and about seven members of my family here tonight. It just feels like something is really happening. Something is happening in a place where nothing's been happening for so long. It was a joke to be a Welsh act like Shakin' Stevens or the Alarm and now suddenly something is happening like Manchester or Seattle and we're in the middle of it.'

Across the room, Richard's mother, Mairwen is laughing heartily.

'There we were in the Peacock Suite in the castle before the show and someone happened to mention that the Queen had visited that room. They told us that the toilets we used were the ones the Queen had used! So, of course, Kelly's mother, myself and Stuart's mother had a bit of a joke about that: "We're using the same toilet as the Queen used!" That was quite something.'

Stuart's mother Mabel also has a grin from ear to ear:

'I was so proud seeing them there. A little bit worried in case anything a bit awkward occurred, but it didn't. It went off well, and the fans, they were fabulous, absolutely fabulous. I'm proud of the fans as well because they're so dedicated to them.'

Once again Graham Davies, the former landlord of the Ivy Bush in Cwmaman and one of Kelly's early mentors, is struggling to get his head around what has just happened.

'During "A Thousand Trees" Kelly barely sang a note. The audience just sang it. They knew all the words and it was a real lump in your throat job. All these kids know Kelly's words, this boy from Cwmaman who was playing in the Bush two years ago. Now all these kids know the words of his songs.

'I can only speak for myself, but everybody in the village is proud of the boys. As proud as they are of being from Cwmaman. That comes across to me as well: they haven't forgotten their roots. No matter how big these boys are going to get, they are still Cwmaman boys.

'They're still "the boys". That's what we call them. We watch TV in the house and my sons will shout to me, "Dad, quick, the boys are on TV." It's not Stereophonics, it's the boys are on the radio. They'll always be the boys; that's who they are: they're our boys.'

Kelly is a little shell shocked by the whole experience, especially their foray into the crowd to check out the support bands.

'I didn't know that people were going to, react to us in that way. They literally did go mental and we got dragged away by security people and people were diving on us. At that point I thought, What is going on? The security guy also handles Oasis and he says, "You can't do it any more! Liam always does that, goes out and tries to watch bands." I said, "Yeah but I'm Kelly Jones, he's Liam Gallagher!" He said, "You just can't do that any more. Not in Wales!" I think that was the part when we all looked at each other and thought, Something is happening.'

Kelly's father Oscar is also musing over his son's graduation into the big league:

'I don't think success will change him in a bad way. The thing is, he'll be meeting more and more people now and so you become more confident and a little wiser, but I think they've all got their feet on the ground. He's still the same cheeky sod I've always known. It's early days yet. It's not even two years since they were signed, since they were playing to twenty or thirty people in some pub in the north of England.'

8 Blow Up

Back to 1996, and to the Duchess of York in Leeds, a typically down-at-heel pub venue that used to reek of the sweat and dreams of a thousand fledgling bands. Over the last quarter of the twentieth century it indelibly imprinted its smoke-filled, drink-fuelled stamp on what has fondly become known as the 'toilet circuit'. Unfortunately the late nineties saw Leeds city centre undergo an overhaul that saw the arrival of Harvey Nichols, Café Rouge and a bunch of Pitcher-and-Piano-type bars. Something had to give and the Duchess closed its doors just before the millennium, bringing the curtain down on two decades of shabby brilliance.

In late 1996, however, it was very much alive and on 21 October it played host to Scottish band AC Acoustics and their support, Stereophonics.

Within six weeks of signing on the dotted line with V2, Kelly, Stuart and Richard had hit the road with a vengeance. The tour had started at the Lomax in Liverpool and would eventually drive into the heart of the rock'n'roll wasteland, pitching up at the Angler's Retreat in West Drayton.

Leeds, though, held some significance. First, Kelly had been a die-hard fan of the football team since his early youth and, second, anyone involved in music couldn't help but be impressed by the myths that surrounded the Duchess. After all, everyone had played there. Three years earlier, a Manchester band called Oasis had crossed the Pennines to blast their

Yorkshire neighbours into submission. Four years before that, Nirvana had travelled slightly further, crossing the USA and the Atlantic to support Tad in the dingy confines of the Duchess.

Richard's memories of that October night are somewhat coloured by the logistics of the situation.

'We'd bought a splitter bus with some of our advance, which meant we were mobile and didn't have to spend a fortune hiring vans and coaches. We also saved V2 a fortune in hotel bills because we had to drive everywhere, like from Leeds back to Aberdare. Six hours in a Mercedes splitter van after playing this famous venue! It's not quite the glamour you imagine.

'We weren't complaining though. We thought we were kings because there was a TV and a video and a six-track CD changer in the back.

'AC Acoustics were nice. The crew were a nice bunch as well and I think we all learned a little bit from them. We got on with everybody just doing all the pubs and clubs up and down the UK.'

Scott Thomas from ITB was the man responsible for setting up their tours.

'You do have to get out there and play every city that you can. If you have the option it's a case of do the thirty-five shows and get them under your belt. With AC Acoustics it was like, "Right, that's a tour. We'll have it." Some of the venues on that tour I've still never heard of since – the Angler's Retreat in West Drayton being a particular case in point. I had to guess where it was on the map so the attitude was very much, "You've got your songs, you've got your live set, now let's get you going."'

John Brand was also getting to know the band.

'I was standing in one of those early gigs and Kelly said to me, "How are my clothes and everything?" and I said, "Fine, you look great." I then suggested to Richard what to wear and he just looked at me and said, "You can tell me what to play and you can tell me this and that. But never tell me what to wear!" It was really funny; it was like, "OK!" He gradually emerged as a kind of fashion pundit for the band.'

Two days into the AC Acoustics tour Stereophonics played their first ever headline gig as a signed band. It was at Cardiff University and, encouragingly, it attracted four hundred people. Six days later they would play to just thirty people at the Boat Race in Cambridge, so it was becoming obvious from the start that Wales was going to be their key market.

After twelve dates in twenty days with AC Acoustics, Stereophonics returned to Mid Glamorgan for a celebratory homecoming gig. It took place, fittingly, at the Aberdare Coliseum, the place where the madness had begun six months before.

However, behind the scenes, Kelly was having a bit of a confidence crisis over his vocal abilities or lack of them. His father, Oscar tried to allay his fears.

'He was having trouble with his throat and I said, "The more you do it the stronger your voice will become. It won't reach its peak until you're about in your mid to late thirties." But he was having problems with his throat, he just couldn't sing, couldn't get it out.

'He went to his local doctor who told him he'd have to have his tonsils out. When I went to the recording studio in London I said, "It's all in your head, Kelly, it's all in here and you're afraid to let it out." He wouldn't believe me and I knew from experience. Every now and again when you're really getting uptight and you're really thinking about things, your throat sort of closes and it doesn't perform like it should perform. Eventually he went to a Harley Street specialist. God knows how much he spent but the specialist said exactly what I'd told him.

'Since then his voice has gone from strength to strength. The longer he's been on the road the better his voice has become. As long as he looks after himself he shouldn't have too many problems. The more singing he does the more control he'll have over it and the more he'll be able to do different things with it.'

The first single was released a week or so later. 'More Life in a Tramps Vest C/W Looks Like Chaplin' came out as a limited edition on Monday, 11 November 1996. The songs had been recorded at Battery Studios with Marshall and Steve during the summer, soon after that first session at Straylight.

The single release meant, of course, that the team working around the band had to be expanded and promotions people were appointed. Hall or Nothing at the time handled press and promotions for bands like the Bluetones, the Stone Roses and Feeder. They also managed the Manic Street Preachers. Julian Carrera at Hall or Nothing was given the task of steering Stereophonics' profile within both the mainstream and the music press.

Scott Piering ran his own TV and radio promotions company and at the time was responsible for artists including Pulp, the Verve, the Smashing Pumpkins, the Prodigy, Metallica and the Charlatans.

'I remember meeting Scott,' Kelly says. 'He's very eccentric and he did this thing with his glasses. I thought, Cool guy but to be honest I had no idea what you had to do to get a song played on the radio. Meeting all these people in less than six months was mental. I can remember we set up a dream team. Everybody we met we got on with really well, Nicky, Sam and Vicky at Appearing and our agent, Scott Thomas, a big six-foot bald-headed guy. All these people, they were all new characters to us.'

Scott Piering's task was basically to get the band exposure on radio and television by securing airplay for the single. This task was delegated to his radio and TV teams. Nicky Sussex headed up the radio team.

'We were keen to take advantage of the launch of V2 as a means of getting the band exposure and so set up their first radio interview as a signed band. It took place at a studio in Willesden in North London. That's when I first met them. They struck me as being very sweet, really keen and eager and rather naive with it.'

So, as I explained earlier, this is where I came in to the picture. I was that interviewer on that miserable Sunday morning in November. The interview started with a question about the single.

DANNY: So tell me about 'Looks Like Chaplin'.

KELLY: Most of our songs are about where we come from. They're all about one area, phrases you hear, people we know in that area. I try to make them like mini-plays. Basically the band live are quite a high-energy band and then hopefully there's a bit of depth behind it when you take it back and listen to the lyrics and stuff. It's not throwaway stuff.

DANNY: You've just signed a record deal, so do you dream of playing massive gigs and selling obscene amounts of records?

RICHARD: Over the next twelve months, by the end of '97, we're going to get as many people to see us as possible and as many people to hear us as possible. It would be good to get them to know us, get to like us and hopefully everybody will enjoy what we do as well.

KELLY: I think January is the first proper release and then continuing on from January there are three singles and then hopefully an album in the summer.

STUART: We're trying to build it really slowly basically because we're finding it really hectic and if things did really take off we'd find it even more hectic.

KELLY: There's 14 songs recorded already, six of them were done before we even got signed. There's no shortage of songs, it's just you've got to do the groundwork before you release them to get people to know who you are. It's pointless just putting something out there just for the sake of it. So we want to do all the hard work next year, do the touring.

DANNY: Are you looking forward to supporting the Manics this Christmas?

STUART: Yeah, definitely. It's the biggest show we ever played. We are obviously chuffed with them picking us to actually play with them and I think there's going to be a lot of nerves on the nights that we do play.

KELLY: We're getting more confident with playing live. We played Cardiff University a couple of weeks ago and we were surprised with how we played. We've only played Cardiff three times under the band's name and there were about 450 people there. Apparently we sold more tickets than the Super Furry Animals which was really nice because we haven't even got anything out.

DANNY: So it would seem to be a good time to be Welsh?

STUART: Well we can't play football, we proved that last night didn't we, 7–1! I think we better stick to music myself, you know what I mean, not sport.

RICHARD: In the '70's we had the sports.

KELLY: And now we haven't got the sports at all, it's music now. It's all down to Max Boyce. Actually I've never bought a record by any Welsh band, as much as I respect what they do. We've never been influenced by any of the Welsh bands.

STUART: The good thing about the Welsh scene is that all the bands sound totally different. It's like Catatonia don't sound like the Super Furries and the Super Furries don't sound like the Manics.

KELLY: It's a bit harder for them to pigeonhole you. They're automatically going to say to us that we sound like the Manics because we're a three piece, I've got short black hair and we're from Wales. Just because you're Welsh they've got to compare you with someone else and it's a bit annoying sometimes, but there could be worse bands to be compared to, they're a class band.

The reaction to the single was encouraging. *Music Week* gushed: 'In "Looks like Chaplin", Stereophonics have come up with one of the strongest debut singles of the year.' *NME* commented, ' "Looks Like Chaplin" is a mosh-pit stormer, stout and sterling grunge without the "grrrr" . . . Leekrock is with us. Rejoice!'

Predictably, the self-same publication took a more vitriolic stance some weeks later. The band had played the infamous Monarch pub/club in the Britpop heartland of Camden, North London, and *NME* were there to review it: 'Hardly the most rapaciously unique aural cocktail known to rock-kind, obviously, and you get the sneaking suspicion that the threesome's current guise is hardly crafty enough to sustain a career of the long-term variety.'

However, *Kerrang!* disagreed on the subject of the trio's prospects: 'In two years, Stereophonics will be writing about the world. Who knows, they may even own shares.'

December 1996 was quite possibly the most bizarre month in the history of Stereophonics. Scott Thomas at International Talent Booking had pitched his sights a little higher than the AC Acoustics tour and had secured prestigious support slots with Skunk Anansie, the Manic Street Preachers and, incredibly, the Who. The month would finish with a Hogmanay knees-up in front of tens of thousands in Edinburgh, and there was the comparatively small matter of three Kenickie supports as well.

'The first of those gigs, the one-off Skunk Anansie support show at Leicester's DeMontfort Hall, came about because two of Skunk Anansie came to one of the early shows,' Scott explains. 'One of my roles is to invite other music business people down to the gigs so the word gets around. That of course includes people in bands – especially if they're bands I already represent. You hope that they'll like it and then you never know what might happen.'

The gig with Skunk Anansie was a roaring success and the two bands immediately struck up a lasting rapport. Stuart was delighted.

'Ace and Mark came to watch us at the Monarch pub in London. Mark has told me since that he started off at the back of the room but, as the gig got better, he got closer and closer. So, after we finished the show they came over to us and they said, "Do you fancy doing some dates with us?" We didn't have to think about it for too long. When it came to actually doing the show that December, and the tour the following March, we were treated superbly. They are very much the same as us, an honest band. The success of a band is fifty per cent based on musicianship and then fifty per cent to do with the spark between those involved. Individually we're not great musicians, but at the end of the day we're honest in what we do. We go onstage and try to do the best we can and play from the heart. It's the same thing with Skunk Anansie, that's what they do. We got on with them great and we still get on great with them now.'

'We were on our way up to Edinburgh to play with Kenickie after the Leicester date with Skunk Anansie,' Richard says. 'Usually everything is planned way in advance but that day John was in the van and he took a call from Scott Thomas. John stopped halfway through the call and turned around to us and said, "Do you fancy doing two nights at Earls Court with the Who?" We were like, "Are you fucking joking?" So we did Edinburgh with Kenickie but then we had to pull the following two dates to get back to London for the Who.'

So how exactly did Scott pull this one off? Surely Pete Townsend wasn't at that Monarch gig as well? Scott explains: 'With next to no notice I got a call saying the Who wanted a British rock band to support them at Earls Court. I'd sent four songs off to them and the choice was made. They or their people were hearing stirrings about the band anyway. Obviously we presented them to the right people, but I think in the end it was a case of the Who hearing the stuff.

'Their dressing room at Earls Court was bigger than the gigs they'd been doing earlier the same week. When they went on, obviously lots of the audience weren't in the arena but there was still about six to seven thousand people, which was by far the biggest crowd they'd ever played to.'

The two Earls Court shows had sold out well in advance and the prospect of supporting the Who was intimidating enough without having to think about it for too long. As ever though, nothing is simple. There's no gain without some pain at least, as Richard explains.

'Kelly was really ill on the first night because he had the flu. He had the shakes and the sweats and spent most of the day trying to get some shuteye. His mother and father came to the show. My sister was there as well, so it was a bit hairy. Afterwards John introduced Kelly and Stuart to Roger Daltry. He said, "Be lucky," and jumped into his car and shot off straight away with his bag of money.'

As discussed in that first interview, the Manic Street Preachers were doing an arena tour that Christmas and they'd asked several Welsh bands to support them, including the Super Furry Animals, Catatonia and Stereophonics. Scott

Thomas also represented the Manics but denies any hint of insider dealing.

'The Manics loved them and wanted to give them whatever gigs they could. They definitely knew the material and wanted to get them on the gigs. It seemed like a totally right thing to do for both sides. I don't think we ever discussed, "Do you want to go and play with the Manics?" They just wanted them on and they were keen to do it.'

'The first time we met them,' Richard explains, 'they were really quiet. I remember the show at the Apollo in Manchester. The power cut out midway through "Traffic". It was really weird. We didn't know what to do or where to look. The place was pitch black, so that was a new experience.'

A Hogmanay special on Princes Street in Edinburgh, where the band propped up a bill featuring Ocean Colour Scene and Babybird, wound up 1996. It was quite a day with temperatures close to freezing and, as the evening approached, the sleet and snow seemed to get worse, which is obviously not ideal for an outdoor show. To add insult to injury the Stereophonics convoy driving north from Wales was plagued by a series of mechanical problems. The icing on the cake came just after the show when chart favourite Babybird was not at all 'gorgeous' by all accounts.

Stuart certainly wasn't impressed: 'He was a bit of a fucking prick to be honest. He had a couple of hits in the charts and he thought he was Laurence Olivier. He turned up and him and Kelly were arguing over something and he said to Kelly, "I'm just as Welsh as you, my name is Jones!" He went on stage and he said something about us being "dad-rock". We didn't go on stage slagging him off, so afterwards we were just going, "What's your problem like?" He wouldn't come out of his dressing room. Fucking prick. He knew he'd had it if he left there because we were all standing round and things were a bit heated. We didn't see him for the rest of the night; I think he just stayed in his dressing room. It all got a bit silly in the end but it just goes to show, at the end of the day, the bigger you are, the harder you fall.

'I think they headlined that show which was a big thing. There was an estimated 250,000 people there and it also went out to millions of people on TV. They were the headliners but where are they now? It's simple really: don't fuck with people on the way up because you always meet them on the way down! That's why we always keep our mouths shut unless someone else starts it.'

Whereas 'Looks Like Chaplin' had been a limited edition single, Stereophonics' first real assault on the UK singles chart came in the form of 'Local Boy in the Photograph', which was released in March 1997. The band were back out on the road, but this time they were headlining venues like the Stage in Stoke on Trent, the Room in Hull and, memorably, the Coal Exchange in Cardiff, where the tour kicked off on 1 March, St David's Day. They also went back to the Duchess of York in Leeds, which is another date that sticks in Richard's mind.

'We were driving from Hull to Leeds and Steve Lamacq played "Local Boy" on the *Evening Session*. We heard it and it was really exciting hearing your song on the radio and then someone speaking about it and bragging it up. It was excellent.'

The Stereophonics' sound wasn't archetypal *Evening Session* fodder. Britpop was at its height. Oasis were playing Knebworth and Blur, Pulp and Elastica continued to sell hundreds of thousands of records. The show's presenter, Steve Lamacq, however, liked what he heard.

'Kelly was writing songs, I thought, a little like Mike Leigh would write plays. You could imagine him wandering down the street, people-watching, and coming home full of these images of characters who would play roles in his songs. Either starring, or cameo parts.

'It was like he was writing a piece of fiction. The songs were based on real people, but the rest was the product of his imagination, which was sometimes quite stark, and occasionally a bit romanticised.'

Back on the bus though the band were unaware that they were gathering some influential admirers in the media. Richard was understandably more interested in sorting out some rather more important matters.

'We didn't want to blow the record advance straight away. John told us to set up a company and a wage structure was introduced. To this very day we're on the same wage, which is cool. We started paying ourselves wages, which we could enjoy by spending it all on booze! It was just an excellent laugh. You couldn't ask for a better job, just travelling around with your mates, free booze, free food, hotels now and again and playing music. It's everybody's rock'n'roll dream.

'Of course, whenever you get tired and there's a lot of noise around you, you snap every now and then and tell them to shut the fuck up. I think we learned a lot in that time as well by giving each other space and knowing what each of us could cope with. You've got to learn the good points and the bad points; you've got to know what to say and what not to say. It's like any good friends. You know what to bring up and what not to. If it's a sore subject, you leave it, and if it's a funny one, you play on it for months.'

The 'Phonics' own headlining dates were mixed in with two short support stints. Midway through the month the band opened for Skunk Anansie in halls and arenas ten times the size of their own shows. They then joined Subcircus for a brief Scottish jaunt.

'We became quite popular up in Scotland before anywhere else,' Richard explains. 'We just put in the hard work. Not a lot of bands were up there doing gigs and we were up there every other week getting pissed and being in the Uni papers.'

It was on the day of the London show with Skunk Anansie that the all-important debut chart position was announced.

'I remember taking a phone call in the Columbia Hotel in West London. I was told that we'd charted at number fifty-one. I thought it was absolutely brilliant. Funny really – that probably meant more than a lot of what came after.'

Kelly, for one, was pleased, as was John Brand:

'I remember when we first started doing shows I used to wonder how people would react to the music, how they would move to it. Are they going to sing the chorus? Will they even remember the chorus? I watched people gradually get into it and they became familiar with it and eventually they didn't just remember the chorus, they sang the whole bloody song, which I thought was extraordinary. That doesn't happen with too many bands.

'As the gigs picked up pace, we went back to the same venues over and over again. That way we found that we grew an audience more quickly.'

David Steele from V2 records was pleasantly surprised: 'There was obviously a plan from day one. We were aiming for certain chart placings with each single and so on. The thing that surprised us was that we expected that to be achieved through conventional routes, i.e. press coverage and radio play. That didn't really happen and so really getting to number fifty-one with "Local Boy" was because of the fans who had seen them play live.'

The touring was obviously paying off, but not without a few character-defining shows where next to no one turned up.

'Twenty-three people at the Southend Esplanade on March 24th that year was a particular low,' Scott Thomas whispers ruefully. 'The venue doesn't have the best location and that part of town smells of fish and seawater quite heavily. The rider was nicked by the support act and everyone was left wondering why they bothered. The band are working hard and spending what in effect is their own money to be there. They went on and did a great gig and talked to the 23 people present.

'It was a case of saying this will happen but I don't think it'll ever happen to you again. I'm glad I was there to have a chat to them about it and get their feelings as to where they think they're going, and if they feel they're achieving things. I think in the end we went back to the tiny B&B and played Playstation for most of the night. But there were a few, not a massive amount of stiff gigs. Their attitude to that was "We've had a bad gig, let's move on."'

The second single, 'More Life in a Tramps Vest', signalled Stereophonics' arrival in the Top 40. It was released two months after 'Local Boy', charting at No. 33 and, in keeping with the band's image, the boys hit the road *again*! It was their fourth UK tour in seven months and it began at the Barfly in North London on 1 May: Election Night. Times were changing in more ways than one. Among the crowd that night were Supergrass, another successful outfit who would soon employ the services of Britain's leading support band.

The now road-weary Mercedes splitter bus hit the motorways of the UK – from London to Glasgow, Glasgow to Wolverhampton and so on. It was a classic 'dartboard' tour, with long distances in between gigs. Sometimes it's impossible to make a tour make geographical sense but the increasingly cynical Cwmaman contingent was running out of patience with their itinerary. However, there were a couple of stand-out gigs en route to take their minds off the milometer.

The first was the Hillsborough Justice concert, which took place at the home of Liverpool FC. The aim of the day was simple: to raise awareness of the plight of the bereaved families who lost loved ones in that horrendous crush on the terraces during Liverpool's cup semi-final against Nottingham Forest a decade earlier.

The bill at Anfield featured local heroes Space and the Lightning Seeds, as well as the Manics and the Beautiful South. The day was full of mixed emotions for Stereophonics. It was the first time they had played in front of such a large crowd but Kelly, Richard and especially Stuart (who's a Liverpool fan) were more than aware that there were thousands of other people in the ground who were dealing with something far tougher.

One thing that did have a major impact on Kelly was the uncomfortable relationship between the electrics onstage and the rainy conditions. Pier Reid from V2 records travelled to Liverpool that day to see the gig:

'It was pouring down with rain and he touched the microphone and literally flew back and got electrocuted! I thought, we're going to kill the artist, but he just looked a little bit confused and then carried on. You could see on the big screens he'd obviously had a shock. In fact it happened a couple of times while he was up there.'

The following day they made their way south to Cardiff for the Big Noise event. It was a one-day festival held on the building site that was Cardiff Bay at the time. Intriguingly, the stage was separated by a moat from the car park, where the punters were gathered to watch the show. The idea was to re-invest the profits from the gig into the wider development of the area, but question marks hung over the timing of the event.

Rumour had it that the Manics turned it down in order to do the Hillsborough benefit the day before.

However, the day passed without real incident. There were performances from 60 Ft. Dolls, Catatonia, Space, Gene and Paul Weller. The 'Phonics again rattled through their well-rehearsed set but made a mental note that there would be better Cardiff gigs to come.

The year's diary was rapidly filling up. This current tour was due to wind up in Brighton in a fortnight with an opening slot at the Essential festival. The Essential was the curtain-raiser to a summer of British and European festival appearances for the band, culminating with Reading in late August. The album would be released at the same time and then there was another UK tour pencilled in for late September/early October. Hot on the heels of that was their first European tour, followed soon after by their first US stint. They would return home on 14 December.

Only a year earlier they'd signed their deal, but now it felt like they'd been on the road forever. As the 'Phonics bus pulled on to the site at Stanmer Park in Brighton after an overnight drive from Sheffield it was clear the haphazard routing of the gigs was far from appreciated. Kelly had virtually lost his voice and everyone was exhausted. Still, they made it onstage at 1 p.m. to open proceedings, but minutes later they were gone. Kelly's voice was shot, the set was cut to just three songs and the band were left asking serious questions about their schedule. Time for a break.

' "The most unessential start to the Essential festival" – that's how it read in one of the magazines.' Stuart is warming to his theme. 'We were seriously big-time frazzled. We played up at the Sheffield Leadmill the night before. We got to the gig and we went in and we looked at the schedule and we weren't on stage until midnight. This was two o'clock in the afternoon and we'd just driven up from Wales. We were the headline act and we had to do an hour and a half. Kelly's voice wasn't feeling too good so we decided we'd have to do an acoustic set because his voice wasn't going to be any good to do the Essential festival next day.

'We don't like to put gigs in order of importance but we thought the Essential festival was going to be more important because there would be more people there. So we had a couple of hundred people in the Leadmill and we played this acoustic set and it went down OK. It wasn't great. We must have come off stage about half past one. We had to drive then and try to get to Brighton by fucking nine or ten for the boys to set the gear up. We were going on stage about twelve. We drove down, stopped about fifteen miles outside of Brighton at this B&B and then we were onstage. We got through the first two songs but as soon as we started "Same Size Feet" Kelly went to the microphone and nothing came out!

'Me and Richard were going, "What's the matter with him then?" The next thing he takes his guitar off, chucks it in the air and walks off. Me and Richard were still playing and I'm thinking, he's just gone off for a fucking laugh. Next thing, you see him walking and he's gone! I'm looking and he's down by the backstage area and me and Richard were like, "I think we'd better fuck off – he's not coming back on!" So we waved to the crowd and walked off.

'It was getting ridiculous in the end. Everybody sits back and has a joke about doing dartboard tours. The first three tours we did were the three biggest dartboard tours I've ever done in my life. Going from one end of the country to another, with no stops in between. You can't go on stage at twelve o'clock at night and then expect to drive three hundred miles and get into a gig at twelve o'clock the next day. It just doesn't work. So that was that: the most unessential start to the Essential festival! We just told John, "We've got to get more sleep. See yer. Bye!" '

9 To Have and Have Not

KELLY IS STANDING IN THE AISLE of the tour bus dressed in jeans, a pink, green and turquoise-blue Hawaiian shirt, plastic shades and a black woollen hat. Julian Castaldi (band PA, hairdresser) is stood next to him dressed equally appallingly. The band have just played the first leg of V97 in Leeds and the bus is charging down the M1 en route for the second leg in Chelmsford. Outside, the early afternoon sun is cracking the ditches but inside the lights are off and the cabaret is in full swing. It's one of the more surreal aspects of being one of the opening turns on the bill that the after-show kicks off at silly o'clock. Anyway, Kelly is leading the assembled throng in a campfire-style singsong. There's a comedy version of 'Tramps Vest'. There's the old folk staple 'Dirty Old Town' and, as the beers flow, I could swear that Kelly is belting out a version of 'Chain Reaction' by Diana Ross. Everyone is in great form, primarily because the gig was a real success. The debut album *Word Gets Around* is only a week away from release and the accompanying single, 'A Thousand Trees', is nestling neatly on the Radio One B-list. Everyone is enjoying the larger and the more luxurious confines of a proper tour bus. There are two lounge areas with all mod cons, at least ten bunks and a large fridge! The tried and tested ten-seater splitter bus seems a lifetime ago. Everyone's had plenty of sleep and Brighton is a distant memory.

Hours earlier, midday temperatures in Leeds had been in the 80s as the bus pulled on to the site. The Driven had the dubious pleasure of going on first and then it was 'Phonics' turn. The crowd went mad from the opening chords of 'Local Boy'. A football was kicked up on stage and the band joined in the party atmosphere. 'A Thousand Trees' was sung almost word for word and you could sense that there was, for the first time, an audible fan base. The twelve months touring have obviously paid off. Kelly's rapport with the audience was intimate, despite the outdoor setting, and he seems to have finally developed a neat blend of confidence and vulnerability, which makes him a really engaging frontman. 'Traffic' is also emerging as a major crowd-pleaser and 'Tramps Vest' and 'Looks Like Chaplin' are now treated like long-lost friends.

The response wasn't lost on the band either. Sitting backstage immediately afterwards, Kelly was in buoyant mood.

'Things are really good right now because the venues we go to are starting to sell out. As good as it is playing Brixton Academy with people like Skunk Anansie and the Manics in front of four thousand people, it's much better now that we sell out venues of five-hundred capacity for ourselves. That way it's our crowd, which is people singing the songs . . . like today everybody was singing the songs.'

So, back on the bus, the gig has been well and truly dissected. The conversation then turns to tonight's headliners in Chelmsford, Blur. Kelly is really keen to check them out and goes off to consult with the outside world (i.e. the driver), to see how far away we are. Given that we've been on the road for over three hours we must be near. Wrong! The bus is knee-deep in a major hold up on the M1 and we're somewhere near Sheffield. Three hours and we're not even out of Yorkshire! It gets worse. Apparently there's been a terrible accident in Leicestershire and tailbacks are conservatively put at thirty miles. Least favourite Blur tune of all time? 'There's No Other Way'!

The party has lost its swing and one by one everyone slopes off to read or watch TV, so Kelly and myself decide it's the perfect opportunity for an in-depth chat about his imminent album.

DANNY: You started playing in bands at the age of twelve. When did the first songs come along?

KELLY: I remember making songs up as a kid in the bathtub and then you get out and you forget them. To be honest, the first proper songs are on this record: 'Goldfish Bowl', 'Billy Davey's Daughter' and 'Local Boy'. All those ones with the same four chords really. Before that it was like anyone in any band – you write loads of songs and they're rubbish and you throw them away and they don't even have a name really. We started making demos in 91. Each demo had about ten lame songs on them and we did about three of them before we started writing this sort of stuff, so there were quite a lot of songs before. Probably about fifty songs before we got to the level of the album. There was a song called 'Better Than a Cure', which was about a town in Cyprus that was deserted after a Turkish invasion. Basically, the place is just as it was when everyone fled – washing on the line, knives and forks on the tables. I was listening to Pearl Jam and Neil Young at the time and I liked melodrama. When you're eighteen you think it's all great; you start writing songs that you think are deep and meaningful, stuff about the IRA. Bottom line is you know fuck all about the IRA, but it's topical at the time. I was trying hard not to write songs about love because you don't want to do that when you're eighteen. You want to write angry songs, but if you're not that angry then it's a bit difficult, so you find other people's situations and you try to write about those.

DANNY: When, then, were the seeds of this record planted?

KELLY: From day one really. I can remember making up tunes when I was an eight-year-old kid. Every Sunday night was bath night before you go to school, and I'd be there just thinking of tunes and stuff. I remember singing tunes and not knowing what they were, but I didn't remember them because I didn't play guitar at that point. When I had a guitar, when I was about eleven, I just used to sit in a room and I wouldn't try and learn how to be Jimi Hendrix. I couldn't be bothered to try to learn other people's songs; I just wanted to try to learn my own.

That was unless you had to learn covers for a gig and they were the only ones I would learn. For years, until I was about eighteen, I just used to go on stage and make up words a lot of the time. Some song titles ended up coming about that way because I didn't think people were interested in the words. I just thought they were into seeing the band. I was just trying to be in people's faces and then, all of a sudden, I started listening to people's dialogue. It was around the time that *Pulp Fiction* was in the cinema and *Our Friends in the North* came on TV. I really got into the dialogue in those certain scripts and films and dramas. I can remember writing conversations on a laptop in college because I was bored. I'd started writing because I found the conversation about the hamburger in *Pulp Fiction* interesting. I started writing stuff like that. Stuff that hasn't made it on to the album, early songs like 'She Takes Her Clothes Off' and 'Raymond's Shop' – that's where those types of stories came from. It was then that I really started listening to words, people like Bob Dylan and Neil Young. I'd write stuff and give tapes to Graham, the landlord in the Ivy Bush. He used to read the words for quite a while and then you'd give him a song that was something about nothing and he'd say, 'It's shit.' I knew then – it was the words.

DANNY: So the album is a collection of dramas based in or around Cwmaman, which I presume for the purposes of fiction could be called 'Goldfish Bowl'?

KELLY: Put it this way. I'm working at the market and going to college, so the only experience I have is what anybody has at that age – your friends, your family and whoever you're going out with. I hadn't travelled anywhere, so the main thing around me at that point was the pubs and the culture of the pubs. Obviously, my old man being a singer meant I was used to pub life from an early age. So all these characters that I saw around me in the pubs started to become the focal point of the writing really.

The song 'Goldfish Bowl' came about because I was listening to the Kinks and the Jam and getting into that kitchen-sink style – songs about going to a football match, that sort of thing. Everybody always says living in Cwmaman is like living in a goldfish bowl because everybody's always looking at you. It is physically like living in a bowl because there are the four mountains surrounding the village. So that song is about the characters I knew. Cliff Chips used to own the Bush and he used to play dominoes. He was this character with the white hair. My old man – his band was called Oscar and the Kingfishers. There was a bloke called Mel Crisp. He lived next door to Stuart and he kept pigeons. He became Caramel Crisp in the lyric. At the time, we were doing all types of cover material, including 'Friday I'm in Love' by the Cure, so there were influences coming from all over the place. That was the first time I tried doing all the quick-fire rhyming stuff ('I'm drinking sinking swimming drowning working smirking . . .'). The line that sums that song up is 'I'm deep in a goldfish bowl, it's sink or swim'. You either play along with things or you get out. Everybody's lives are like that, especially if you live in the valleys.

DANNY: Is there a danger with these songs that people back home will think you're patronising them?

KELLY: I don't think so. The lyrics are observational rather than judgemental. 'Last of the Big Time Drinkers', for instance, is a celebration of where we come from. It's not a put down. People work all year and they're happy having two weeks' holiday. If you don't want that then you can get out. People always thought we wanted to get out of Cwmaman. We didn't really; we just didn't want to work in a factory.

In fact, the phrase 'Last of the Big Time Drinkers' is part of the language in our area. I always remember my cousin Leighton saying it when we were kids and out on the piss. I thought it was a great title for a song so I built the song around it. 'Drinkers' is basically about people working in factories all year round. They get a bit pissed off with it but they just look forward to those two weeks in the sun.

Same with 'Tramps Vest'. It was just a great phrase from Malcolm, one of the boys I worked with on the market. He was known as Mac the Knife and when it got quiet he'd always say 'There's more life in a tramp's vest'. The song is a story of all those characters coming into the market at a time when the market was dying because of all the big superstores. Even though the subject matter was sad, the song is quite quirky and, if I'm honest, that's because I wrote that and 'Drinkers' to try and get a record deal. Blur and Pulp were all over the radio at the time and I thought that quirky style was what everything was about, but when we sent all that stuff away no one was interested anyway.

In the end, 'A Thousand Trees' proved to be the song that did it – which was the last thing I expected because I thought it was too wordy. I couldn't imagine anybody dancing to it or singing along to it because it had too many lyrics. Moral of the story: you can't write to a format because it's not going to work.

DANNY: So 'A Thousand Trees' is one of the oldest songs on the record?

KELLY: Definitely. I had the line from a box of matches when I was a kid. England's Glory boxes of matches used to have slogans on the back and I remember reading it when I was about ten. It just said, 'It only takes one tree to make a thousand matches; it only takes one match to burn a thousand trees.' It just stuck with me and when I went to college we were doing this short animation flick-book thing. The one I made was of a tree burning into a match and a match burning into a tree.

So the song began at about the same time, except it was a punk song with totally different words for ages. It was called 'Murray Walker' for a while because he'd just got sacked. It was all sorts of shit. Eventually I think I wrote the words and I had to rewrite the music because there were too many words.

The story is about a football coach who coached us when we were kids. He was well respected within the community. I was in his under-twelves team. We were called 'Billy's babes'. In fact we had that written on the back of the shirts. Anyway, one day a couple of girls complained that he'd been messing with them in the changing rooms. They told their parents and then it all got blown up into a court case and he went down. I don't think he served the full sentence because he's now in his seventies.

I just remember being in the club, I think it was Christmas morning, and he came in and everybody shook his hand, welcoming him home. I thought it was weird because if it'd been anyone our age, the guy wouldn't have been given the time of day. He'd have been given a slap. The village was completely split in half: half the people believed it; the other half didn't.

The song is more about how rumours in a small town can change people's perspectives about somebody else. It's not about saying if he was guilty or not. It's about people living in a small town and either buying the story or not buying the story and the metaphor sums it up I suppose.

DANNY: Is 'Local Boy' also based on a true story?

KELLY: Yeah, I was working on the market with a guy called Justin. His best mate was called Paul Bogus. Anyway, one afternoon I was doing weights with this mate of mine, Beanie, who lived a couple of doors away from Stuart, when this other lad came in and he said, 'Have you heard about Bogus? He jumped in front of a train.' We couldn't believe it. We didn't know what to think because he's a kid your age and, even though I didn't know him well and hadn't seen him in ages, it was a shock.

Working on the market you hear a million stories, but the one that stuck in my mind was something he said to Justin. Justin told me that Paul had asked him one day if he knew anything about the local train times and, of course, after the event you wonder whether he was just asking innocently or whether he was planning something. The song, though, doesn't go into the detail of what happened and how it was treated in the press. Ironically, the photo of him in the paper showed him sitting on a bench, smoking a joint and smiling, but the song's not about that. It's more about the reaction of the kids. I remember experiencing that because I was in the square in Aberdare all the time 'cos I was working there on the market. Everybody was just talking about it and stuff, so that's that.

DANNY: 'Billy Davey's Daughter' would seem to complete the small-town real-life tragedy element to the record.

KELLY: I remember us being in Stuart's yellow van going up to Colchester or somewhere for someone to take money off us, saying they were going to make us famous. We were going across the Severn Bridge and Stuart mentioned that it was there that Billy Davey's daughter had jumped. Someone had told me the story, vaguely, before, so I only ever heard half the story – which is the whole point of the song really. I don't know which half's true and which part of it's rumour, and I thought that was the good thing about it. I don't know why she did it, if she got pushed or if she jumped, or if she had an argument with her boyfriend. Some people say she jumped, some people say she was pushed off. That's why at the end there's the line 'Word gets around' because, again, it's like Chinese whispers. Every time someone tells you something, something changes or something gets added.

I thought using the real name was the cool part about it 'cos you never think you're going to get a record deal. Then when we did get a deal, and we were finishing off this record, I didn't want to put it on. We tried a version where we changed the name. We changed it to 'Millie Navy', 'Millie Davey' and all these different things – and we were actually contemplating this when we thought, this isn't right. We went to see Billy Davey and said, 'Look, we've got this song' – I think Graham from the Ivy Bush asked him for me and he said it was all right.

117

DANNY: The album was recorded in stages, wasn't it? It wasn't a case of being holed up in a studio for a couple of months, was it?

KELLY: We did 'A Thousand Trees' and 'Eyelids' in Straylight Studios with Bird and Bush early last year. We hadn't even got a record deal then but those songs got lots of A&R men interested. So, there were all these record companies who were interested in signing us and they were giving us money to do demos. We took it all and we did 'Tramps Vest', 'Chaplin', 'She Takes Her Clothes Off' and 'In My Day' in one session. Two of them made the record. Basically, over the last year we've been touring and recording in bursts. I think the next session was at Parr Street in Liverpool, where we did 'Last of the Big Time Drinkers', 'Traffic' and 'Carrot Cake and Wine'. Then we moved on to Real World to finish things off. It was there we did 'Same Size Feet' and 'Not Up To You'. We also tidied 'Traffic' and re-recorded the vocal on 'Thousand Trees', because I sounded about twelve on the original.

DANNY: 'Traffic' sounds almost like it belongs to a different record. The subject matter is different, and the sound.

KELLY: We were coming back from London in a hired car. It was a Mondeo Estate, or something like that, and there was a bass drum in the back seat, so I couldn't see out the back window. We were stuck in this traffic jam and I remember that's where I got the idea but I didn't write it then. I wrote it in my parents' house, in the bedroom. It literally came as a list, that song, and the music came after.

It's pretty self-explanatory lyrically. It was seeing someone next to me and just trying to make up as many different scenarios or pictures about her that I could possibly think of. Was she a mother of three kids? Was she a prostitute? Had she just killed someone? The idea is that each line contrasts completely with the previous one. I suppose it's influenced by stuff like 'That's Entertainment' by the Jam. I used to love all that sort of stuff.

DANNY: 'Not Up To You' has a similar detached feel to it. Was that also one of the more recent songs on the album?

KELLY: That's a song about destiny and fate. I heard a story about this guy waiting for a lift to work one morning and a bus came past. The wheel came off the bus, rolled down the street and knocked him into a ditch, killing him. I think it's hysterical really, but it's not, is it?!

I just remember waiting for a lift when I used to go to college and I used to love the orange streets. They always seemed that way because of the lighting. I put that into a line, 'The street orange glow', 'cos everybody who works early and comes home late in the winter never really sees the daylight. You come home with orange lights and you go to work with orange lights, so it's just a good description line I suppose. It goes through all different lines like that: if he'd kissed his missus just for a bit longer, or if he'd lost his shoe, or cut himself shaving, then he wouldn't have been at that particular point at that particular time.

DANNY: What exactly does 'check my eyelids for holes' mean?

KELLY: It's kind of a watered-down version of 'Traffic'. The phrase, again, comes from pissed-up talk in a pub. If someone falls asleep in the pub and they're being encouraged to go home, it's a classic reply: 'I'm not sleeping; I'm just checking my eyelids for holes.' The song is about someone trying to get to sleep, like a comedian wondering if he's still funny or a model worrying if she's getting fat. It's all those things that go through your head when you go to sleep. I just picked different characters for each line. A girl worrying if she's pregnant – 'I got to lose weight' is the first line. 'Is my stand-up show still a laugh?' It's just people from different walks of life worrying before they go to sleep. We all think about something just before nodding off. It's pretty simple – it's not that deep.

DANNY: Who 'Looks Like Chaplin'?

KELLY: My street got flooded when I was about eleven years old. The river burst its banks and everybody was fucked really. The house was full of water and the whole street was shagged. On the night of the flood, our street looked like a river. There were boats going up and down – it was all a bit surreal.

There was this old bloke who looked like Charlie Chaplin because he always had his eyes squinted and he used to walk with his hands behind his back and his feet faced outwards in that 9:15 shape. At the time, the street used to dip, so the water would gather and get deeper as you walked on. There were fire engines and police and people screaming, but he just walked on as if there was no water there; he just kept walking straight through the water. In the end, Beanie's brother dived in and pulled him out and he put him in Eileen's house at the top of the street. I used to love all that stuff when it used to happen because it was like everybody just pulls together and it was like one house was the community. Everybody's in there drinking tea and stuff, almost like World War Two. I just used to love that situation because I thought it was funny. I remember this other bloke sitting there without anything on, just a pair of Union Jack pants, shivering and drinking a cup of tea. It just stuck with me for a long time – people pulling together and poor old Chaplin in the middle of it.

DANNY: 'Same Size Feet' has that same kind of poetic rant that crops up in 'Goldfish Bowl'. This time, too, it seems to be about someone drowning.

KELLY: It's a story about a man and a woman. I heard the story from somebody else. This married guy was having an affair with a widow. She couldn't contact him for fear of the wife finding out, so she relied on him calling her. So a week goes by and he hasn't called. Then she started to worry about him, especially when a body was found in the bay close to where he lived. The description sounded like him and yet she found herself not being able to go forward and find out. She couldn't get information on the most important person in her life. That was it for the story really, but then I tried to imagine what had led to this. Did they meet in a club? Maybe he lied about who he was? Maybe if she did enquire she'd find out that she'd been duped as well? Maybe he was pretending to be someone else? It was always the idea for a script. I'd still like to make it into a film.

During the course of the conversation day has turned to night and the coach has crawled down the M1 and eventually on to the V97 site in Chelmsford. The place is emptying because Blur finished over an hour ago. Campfires are burning but it's lights out on the Stereophonics bus. Another big day tomorrow. Rumour has it that Richard Branson's coming down to hang out.

The morning starts disastrously. The bus has completely packed up, so the equipment is being ferried over to the second stage by a motley combination of cars and vans. It's another beautiful day and already you can hear Feeder getting things going on the main stage.

Behind the scenes at the second stage there's already an air of celebration in the Stereophonics camp. John Brand has arrived with good news: 'A Thousand Trees' has charted at No. 22, making it their biggest record to date.

Their 'hit' single gets a special introduction and, despite the fact that it's barely lunchtime, there's about two thousand or so people watching. The mosh pit has expanded beyond four or five rows, so the ferocious drumming on 'Too Many Sandwiches' and 'Last of the Big Time Drinkers' is matched beat for beat by sweat-drenched punters pogoing in unison. The gig, if anything, has even more energy than Leeds, and the boys leave the stage in jubilant mood.

The sidestage contingent has also grown and no one can ignore the presence of V2 supremo Richard Branson with his assured demeanour and gleaming teethy smile. Of course, he has a vested interest in the event in general, but he's adamant he's here to see Stereophonics.

'We wanted to see if we could start V2 off with a really credible band and they've got everything we could possibly want. We've got three stages here and Stereophonics are on one of the smaller ones, but they've got a tremendous reaction considering the band are in their early days. I'm absolutely certain that within a year or two they'll be topping the big stage.'

John Brand, too, has a grin from ear to ear:

'Over the last few months we've sold out all the club shows we've done, and just by going through all the festivals we've managed to increase the amount of people who are watching. There was probably two or three thousand people there today, so it's certainly improving all the time. The fact that the record is being played on the radio really helps – also the power they have on stage. I think the bonding between the three of them is really important. They come across very much as a single unit. They've been together for so long that they know each other instinctively, and that really comes through in their music. It's very strong, very united.'

10 The Only Game in Town

'DAVID STEELE FROM V2 RECORDS phoned the hotel in Hamburg. I think it was Hamburg. We were out there doing some press and radio interviews. I can remember it – we were eating chilli and David says, "You're number six!" and I was like, "Fucking hell!" The top five was like Oasis, the Prodigy, a lot of the big boys at that time in 97. I think Elvis was number seven. It was a weird ten. It was a lot of big names. We were really happy with it.'

Word Gets Around was released on Monday, 25 August 1997, two days after the band played the Reading festival. It charted at No. 6 in the UK Top 50 album chart and, as Kelly remembers, it was no ordinary Top 10 that week. Oasis were No. 1 with *Be Here Now*; Texas were at No. 2 with *White on Blonde* closely followed by the Prodigy and Radiohead respectively. The highest new entry was the Levellers at No. 5. Stereophonics came in two places ahead of their contemporaries and countrymen the Super Furry Animals, who had just released *Radiator*.

However, while the fan base was expanding at an encouraging rate, the press were still undecided. *Melody Maker* drew bizarre parallels with Sleeper: 'It's the outsider-in-Nowheresville stance that Sleeper try too hard to evoke, only Stereophonics do it for real. Y'see, Louise, you can't simply move out and mock; you have to acknowledge that you were there in the first place.'

Confused? You will be. *NME* picked up on a similar theme: 'The Welsh valley town of Cwmaman is their birthplace, and it seeps through the 'Phonics' debut album like apricot jam oozing between a nymphet's naked toes ... Stereophonics, then: orthodox and amiable; occasionally get a bit uptight when they should go fucking loopy. Oh yes, sing if you're glad to be grey ... 7/10.'

Kerrang! though, had no qualms: 'From a tiny town somewhere between Cardiff and Swansea comes one of the most exciting new bands in Britain ... 4/5.'

Vox, too, were impressed, giving them 8/10. 'Kelly Jones sings like the devil himself, and the world ought to know it. Something in that Welsh water has imbued his voice with a quality both raucous and immaculate ... If there's to be any criticism, it's that he seems a bit too keen to give 110 per cent all the time and we'll have to wait for album number two to feel the real range of a startling talent.'

Q magazine concluded that it was a 'smouldering' debut, adding, 'The result recalls the bastard son of Creedence Clearwater Revival and Buffalo Tom but also a bluesier Manic Street Preachers.'

The broadsheets were also split. The *Daily Telegraph* declared that 'It rocks, it's about something, and, if you're significantly over 25, you've heard it before.'

The Times, though, took a different tack: 'It's easy to imagine these first signings to Richard Branson's new V2 label being huge by the millennium.'

The *Independent on Sunday* was equally impressed: 'When is stadium rock not stadium rock? When the sound is as gritty as it is passionate, and when the superior lyrics, by Kelly Jones, peer into the secrets and lies of small-town existence.'

None of this, of course, mattered over chilli in Hamburg. Kelly was elated. The album's chart placing justified the grind of the last twelve months and the beauty of it all was that no part of the media could claim any credit. Stereophonics had achieved success, albeit comparatively minor success to what lay ahead, simply by touring. They had taken a leaf out of the old school rock'n'roll manual and done it the way Sabbath, Zeppelin, U2 and REM had done it. So, with a Top 10 album under their belts, the band started to prepare for their first trip to the States. Stuart, though, was far from well.

'On the Monday the album was released, my temperature was through the fucking ceiling. Initially I thought I had a kidney infection but John Brand put me in touch with this specialist who, after taking my temperature, ordered me straight into hospital. So off I went straight into this infectious diseases ward! Kelly and Richard went off to do some promo in Germany and, on the day we found out that the album had gone in at number six, I had that many needles in my arm that I looked like a heroin addict. Anyway, soon after, the nurse came back and she says, "We know what it is: you're anaemic." She came back the next day and said there was some problem and they had to take more blood. That day they decided I was diabetic. On the fourth day the actual doctor came in and he said, "We've done all these tests and we've found out what it is." I had glandular fever combined with pneumonia! The pneumonia was the bad chest and the glandular fever was everything else.

'At this stage we were about to go to America for the first time and so John called the hospital, wanting to know if I could go. I told the doctor. I said, "There's my manager on the phone, can I go to America?" The doctor went through the roof. He said, "You're going nowhere for at least a fortnight. You can't risk it." So he got on the phone and I could hear him shouting at John.'

Kelly and Richard, meanwhile, had finished their promotional tour of Germany and were preparing for their assault on the Big Apple. You don't spend your life drinking in pop culture without getting wildly excited at the prospect of New York City. The images were already tattooed on their brains. There was Bob Dylan in Greenwich Village, Big Yellow Taxis, the Empire State, Wall Street, the Dakota Building, Simon and Garfunkel in Central Park, Woody Allen, the Beatles at JFK, Dylan Thomas(!), salami sandwiches and coffee to go, Broadway, David Letterman, Times Square, CBGBs, 'Throw the body in the east river' . . . Kelly, for one, couldn't wait.

'I remember being on the plane with John and Richard. I was pretty wound up, sitting in first class with the TV and the big chair and thinking it was great! I just kept thinking, this is going to be fucking mad when it lands now! And it was. You get there and we had to go through all that immigration nonsense and then they pick you up in a limo because they're cheaper than taxis. We thought we were clever and special! I got in the limo and you just got a stiff neck from looking. Oasis came on the radio, 'Don't Go Away' off *Be Here Now*. That's my favourite song off that album – I think it's a great track. I can remember seeing lots of Oasis stuff in the shop windows – and the Prodigy.

'So we got there and it was a weird trip. Matt Pollack was the radio plugger in the States for V2. He looks like Bruce Springsteen and he's got a really dry sense of humour. If you don't like Americans then you'll never get him, but if you do then he's a funny guy. He's so in your face. I love him. He took me and Richard round to show us Howard Stern's room in the KROQ radio building and then set us up in the lobby. Then he'd say, "Get your guitar out and sing to these people!" There's nothing more intimidating. He'd come and sit in your hotel room on a morning and say, "What can you do acoustically?" And I'd say, "Quite a lot of them," and he'd say, "Play me a couple." So I'd sit there on my bed and play these songs acoustically to Matt. Then he'd take me to all these different radio stations all over New York where he'd stick me in a kind of broom cupboard and then invite these people in. I'm thinking, I'm going on the radio, but I'm not – I'm just playing for them. I'd be in restaurants playing for people who were having dinner.

'There's no two ways about it. It is sucking the devil's cock really – all in an attempt to get your songs played on the radio. I didn't know any other way and I did it with Richard.'

Richard too was a bit overwhelmed by the assault on his senses.

'Everything was just too fast there. You walk out of the hotel and everything is just going in all directions and you're straight into a car, straight to here, straight to there. Then it's back to the hotel for a meal and time to do it all again. I got freaked out playing for all these college students who were working for some record distributors. They were eating pizza and we were playing "Traffic". Light entertainment with lunch!

'Having said that, because it was just me, Kelly and John out there, we got to see quite a bit of New York. We went to Central Park, saw Strawberry Fields, went up the Empire State, went down to Lady Liberty to have a look. It's a really good atmosphere in New York, really quick, and if you can take it all in it's a really good buzz.'

So with Lady Liberty, pizza and broom cupboards behind them, the next stop was Los Angeles where they were joined by V2's in-house video director, Pinko. He would go on to direct all of the videos for *Performance and Cocktails*, but for now the task in hand was the video for 'Traffic'.

Pinko had a clear idea: 'We thought, let's go to the heart of what people know as America – and that's Hollywood, basically. The whole idea was really this one-take thing where you start with the crowds crossing Hollywood Boulevard. We'd pick up Kelly sort of singing into a telephone and then follow him in and out of buildings because, basically, the video just tracks him. That would then be intercut with a performance in a car park. Obviously Stuart wasn't well, so we had a stand-in drummer. He got mysteriously blurred in the edit so you couldn't tell it wasn't Stuart. In fact we shot some footage of Stuart later on, back in London, so, even more miraculously, he appears in the video playing in a car park in Los Angeles when he was in fact in a South Wales hospital.'

The video aside, that first American trip proved to be fruitful in another way. It inspired two of the songs that would appear on the next record, 'Pick a Part That's New' and 'Plastic California'.

'The music and the main chorus for "Pick a Part" came about in the Gramercy Park Hotel in New York,' Kelly explains. 'I was just jet lagged and generally knackered. I can remember waking up in the hotel and actually coming up with the line "You can do all the things that you wanna do." I was thinking about how, when you arrive in America, you think you've seen everything before.

'It was also on that trip that I started "Plastic California". There's lines from there like the "gin/amnesia problems". That's when I just fell asleep in this bowl of gin in Pinko's hotel in LA. They were bringing us gin, but it wasn't in a glass, it was in these big bowls, and I was just wanging them down. I was just jet lagged, drunk and completely fucked.'

Kelly was blown away by the whole situation.

'We were staying in the Roosevelt Hotel and I've got to admit it was an amazing trip. For the first time, we couldn't take it in until we'd left.'

Meanwhile, on the other side of the Atlantic, Stuart was dealing with his own problems.

'Kelly and Richard were phoning me and a week later I was still in bed and they were in LA. First time they'd been to America and I didn't get to go. I got discharged and I went back to see the doctor and he told me the reason I had what I had was because I was so run down. Apparently, my defences had packed up through too much drinking and too many late nights. I said to him, "What can I do like?" and he said, "You can't drink for six months." Fucking great! So there we were starting our British tour three weeks later, and there's me – couldn't drink.'

The UK tour of autumn 97 took in thirteen of the nation's grassroots venues including the Princess Charlotte in Leicester, the Northampton Roadmenders, the Venue in Edinburgh and the University of London Union. The music press turned out in force at the latter, which was the first date of the tour. Again opinion was split.

The *NME* remained cynical: 'They're excellent, in fact, and somehow it's not enough 'cos they don't really matter, possibly because they're not saying anything much . . . and their clothes are rubbish.'

Ian Gittins at *Melody Maker* had actually listened to the tunes: 'Take "A Thousand Trees", the blistering tale of a respected village sports coach whose life is ruined by Chinese whispers of sexual abuse. Is he guilty? Innocent? Who knows? Or "Same Size Feet", a real-life mystery of adultery and vengeance. "This is a song about sex and murder – the kind of things which happen in Wales," singer Kelly Jones mumbles . . .

'Naturally these lyrics can't all penetrate tonight, so some of the primal impact is lost, yet live Stereophonics are still a visceral and vibrant concern.'

Kerrang! pinpointed the age-old problem with playing to the London media pack: 'There are too many trendy, too-cool-to-lose-it types packed into ULU on the strength of the Welsh trio's recent hit single, "A Thousand Trees", rather than people with a true understanding of what the band are about.'

The UK tour wound up at Nottingham's Rock City, but far from taking their foot off the gas, Stereophonics prepared to join Supergrass for a brief European stint. Things were looking good for 'Traffic', the fourth single from the album, which was due out at the end of the month. The reviews, for the first time, were universally gushing. 'Wales' finest band of the moment are to be congratulated for weaving a ballad full of pathos about the dull agony of the everyday,' the *NME* commented.

Comedian David Baddiel was the guest singles reviewer for *Melody Maker*. He voted 'Traffic' single of the week, adding that it was 'really beautiful'.

Kerrang! also voted it single of the week and urged their readership to jump on board: 'It should be their first major hit single – it's the best song on the album. Bored of waiting for the next Manics album? Get into the Stereophonics now. They rock; they've got tons of good songs; they're a bit like the Manics without the pretentious bits, and you'll love 'em.'

Closer to home, Kelly's father Oscar saw 'Traffic' as his son's great leap forward: 'I thought some of the stuff that he wrote first was a bit obscure. I was impressed with some of the stuff he wrote but I wasn't blown away until he came down from London one day. He came back home and he said, "I wrote this today." He played the new tune, which was called "Traffic", and I thought, this is really good. This is unbelievable! I actually realised for the first time that he is *really* good at writing real songs.'

'Traffic' entered the UK Top 40 singles chart at No. 20, their highest chart positioning to date, but the band were hundreds of miles away on the Supergrass tour, which was winding through Germany, Austria, Italy and France. However, before they left they filmed a mimed version of the song for *Top of the Pops*. It was shot outside the front door of Oscar and Beryl's home on Glanaman Road and featured virtually the entire young population of the village gathered around the band, who were trying to keep it together despite pouring rain. That didn't matter though: *Top of the Pops* had finally come to Cwmaman, and the fields across the road from where Kelly and Stuart grew up eight doors apart were now on national TV. However, once again things were moving so quickly that Richard, Stuart and Kelly could only really focus on what was actually going on at the time – and that was the Supergrass tour.

'The Supergrass tour in Germany was good. At first it was strange to be doing a tour with a band we loved but who probably didn't really know who we were.' Kelly continues: 'John knew their management and we got the tour through that. I can't imagine Danny and the boys sitting there and asking for us but then, halfway through the tour, you could see them coming to soundchecks and standing at the side of the stage while we were on. They're really quiet and when I first met them I was like a kid because they're like cartoons of themselves. Danny, Gaz and Mickey – they're three real characters. I was really into it. I had a brilliant time on that tour and to watch them every night was class. My brother Kevin was tour managing us at that time as well, so we took Kevin to Europe.'

It was around this time that Stereophonics on tour developed organically into the 'Highway to Hell, Cwmaman Away-day Permanent Stag Party'. Kevin, Kelly's brother, was at the helm. Cwmaman trio Julian Castaldi, Simon Collier and Chris Stone (aka Swampy) were also on board. Julian had started out as their driver but had since carved out a niche as the band's all-round personal assistant, video diaryman, acupuncturist(!) and photographer. Simon was Kelly's guitar tech and Swampy joined on that tour as Stuart's drum tech. He would later bemuse both the audience and the headliners by standing sidestage butt naked during Supergrass' set on the final date of the tour in the Magazzini Generalli in Milan. While everyone else wondered what this madman was doing, the Stereophonics party was in tears.

'As you can imagine, we were green, but not as green as he was,' Stuart explains. 'The whole tour was a real laugh. We got asked to do this thing for this TV company in Germany. They'd had a competition and the prize was tickets to the gig and a chance to hang out with both bands in this bar where they'd set up all sorts of board games like Connect 4 and nonsense like that. In the process they were hoping that the fans would ask us all questions and that would be broadcast as the interview. Thing was, after about an hour of this, Danny form Supergrass got bored and started playing the piano. He made up this song with obscene lyrics and of course no one, apart from us, knew what he was on about. I couldn't believe it – they filmed this and broadcast it at about four in the afternoon on primetime kids TV.'

Stereophonics' first full year of trading, 1997, wound up in celebratory style with two homecoming gigs at Cardiff University on 16 and 17 December. The latter was their 100th show of the year and, as you would imagine, it was quite a night. In typically modest style the band had billed the show 'Happy With That – Stereophonics live in Cardiff' and from the beginning it was always going to be one of the those nights. 'Looks Like Chaplin' led the battle charge and the crowd went ballistic. Outside, the temperatures were below freezing. Inside, they were rapidly approaching boiling as the band ploughed through 'Thousand Trees', 'Local Boy' and 'Not Up To You'.

The highlight came, however, when Kelly, Stuart and Richard walked back on for the encores. The support band, 'Head', followed them out armed with silver discs, which they duly handed over. *Word Gets Around* had clocked up sixty thousand sales and the Cheshire cat grins said it all. Kelly accepted his with the quip, 'Happy With That,' before launching into a heart-wrenching soulful version of 'Billy Davey's Daughter'.

Not a bad end to a year that started in the freezing sleet and snow of that Hogmanay show in Edinburgh. Since then, Stereophonics had covered virtually every bit of the UK. They'd made their first major forays into the heart of Europe, not to mention dipping their toe in across the pond. There had been four singles, three of them Top 40 hits and a Top 10 album that had established Kelly as a writer to be reckoned with. More importantly though, work had started on the follow-up to *Word Gets Around*. So, while the Christmas of 97 provided time for reflection, by New Year all energies were firmly fixed on the road ahead.

Kelly is staring at a list of nominees for the Brit awards. 'You've got to go for the craic. We know we're just in the Best Newcomers but I'm fascinated. I remember watching Oasis win, and then Supergrass and Kula Shaker. Years ago we used to say, "One day that'll be us," and now we've been invited, so it would be rude not to go. I don't think we've got a hope in hell of winning. It'll be All Saints or someone like that but, anyway, it's nice to be nominated.'

Stereophonics are sitting in the backstage area of the Red Box in Dublin. At first glance they look unfamiliar and then suddenly it dawns on me that Richard's long locks have gone and he's sporting a cropped blond number. By way of contrast, Stuart looks like a walk-on from the film *Boogie Nights*. His hair is big. In fact his hair is the closest a white man has come to an Afro for quite some time. Kelly reassuringly looks like the Kelly of 97 – and 96 for that matter.

It's the opening night of the *NME* Bratbus tour and, given that it is 13 January, it'll come as no surprise that it's pissing it down outside. Inside, various members of Theaudience, the Warm Jets and Asian Dub Foundation are milling about waiting for showtime. The headliners, however, are relaxed. They've just got news that they've been nominated in the Best Newcomers category at next month's Brit Awards. The opposition looks tough. All Saints, Shola Ama, Embrace, Travis and Finley Quaye are also in the running so, while All Saints are the odds-on favourites, it's not an open-and-shut case. That's because the result is down to Radio One listeners who are being urged to phone in with their vote.

For the time being though, Stereophonics are focused on the task in hand. They've only ever played in Dublin once before, at a music industry conference shortly after they were signed. Throw in the fact that we're only a fortnight into the New

Year, the weather is far from clement and the tour is the brainchild of a paper that has done them few favours in the past, and Kelly could be forgiven for at least a minor anxiety attack. Instead, though, he knows exactly what he's got to do and why he's doing it.

'It's not the best time of year to go to gigs. Everybody's skint after Christmas. It's a strange one all round. There are so many writers at the *NME*, so one minute you're great and the next minute you ain't. We've had a lot of good reviews and a lot of average reviews but we never ever thought that we would be asked to do the *NME* tour. It's good for us to come to Dublin though. It's good to be in Ireland because we've barely played here at all. Basically the tour is just a good opportunity to go back around Britain because we've been away in Europe and I don't want to let it slack off at home.

'We've been recording new stuff and we want to release a new single by August, and then it would be good to have an album out this year. Whether that fits in with the record company's way of doing things is another matter. The songs are ready. We have nine written and I'm really happy with the way the writing's going. We just want to keep people interested and that's why we're doing this tour and that's why we always play live a lot. We don't want people to forget about us, because this business can be so fickle.'

The news about the Brit nomination is met with a mixture of amusement and downright bemusement. They're also in the running for Best Newcomer at the *NME* Brat awards. *Melody Maker* readers have voted them Best New Band in the end-of-year polls ahead of Embrace, Travis, the Seahorses and Symposium, but it doesn't end there. *Q* magazine have listed them among the five nominees for Best New Act in their own polls, and *Kerrang*'s readership have declared that Stereophonics are the seventh-best new band in the world, just behind the likes of Feeder, Limp Bizkit and the winners, Coal Chamber.

'It would be nice to win anything really. A fucking wooden spoon would be all right.' Stuart is on characteristically blunt form. 'I like the trophy with the fist and the finger sticking up. There's one of them in Supergrass's management office.'

Talk turns to the recent reworking of 'Local Boy in the Photograph', which is about to be re-released in three weeks' time.

'We were trying to figure out which would be the best song to release,' Kelly explains. 'It all depended on how "Traffic" did. I was really happy with the fact that "Traffic" sold eighteen thousand records, which was twice as many as "A Thousand Trees". "Local Boy" has turned into one of the most popular live songs and when we released it early last year no one knew who we were. Initially we wanted to put out "Same Size Feet" or "Not Up To You" but the single coincides with the tour and "Local Boy" is one of *the* songs of any tour.

'Why has it been remixed? You've got as much idea on that one as me. They want to remix everything we do and I don't know what's the matter with the originals. It's got to be a little punchier for radio is what I'm told. It's madness. The "Traffic" single was remixed for three grand and we turned it down because it was a pile of shit. So then they go and do the same thing with "Local Boy", except this time it costs six grand! Anyway, this time around it's a good mix.'

Since 'Local Boy' was released the first time around, Kelly has met the father of the lad who threw himself in front of a train. 'He approached me in a club and I thought I was going to get a glass on my head, but he actually took it as a tribute, so that was good. It's hard to know how people relate to it in a way. God knows why they relate to anything that we do because you write it for yourself. It's only after the event that you think about other people listening to it.'

Stereophonics will return to Germany and France throughout February before de-camping to the USA for March, and then in April they do their first dates in Australia. On paper it looks quite gruelling but, then again, what band gets into this business without having dreams of driving through the deserts of Arizona or lazing around on the Gold Coast?

KELLY: We've got to spend four days off on the Gold Coast. People just don't understand what that actually takes out of your body.

STUART: I don't understand why anyone would go into this business, to be honest with you.

KELLY: I think it's a complete waste of time.

DANNY: It does make me mad when I speak to certain bands who imply that going around the world is a great hardship when the majority of the population has to grin and bear the everyday grind. You obviously don't subscribe to that.

KELLY: I haven't been able to take anything in. I haven't been able to take in that we supported the Who. There was the gig at Anfield, the record charting at number six, then the night we got the silver disc in Cardiff. You can't take it in because it happened so quickly. In about five years, when we look back, then it will probably sink in, what we've actually done.

RICHARD: You look at the silver disc in the morning . . . Is it real? You tap it and it's like clunk, clunk, clunk. Yeah, it is.

KELLY: A good way of explaining it would be like, when you're a kid and you go on holiday once a year, and you look forward to that airport but you're nervous about the flight. We go on so many planes now that it's like getting on a bus and you totally don't think about it. It doesn't even enter your mind that you're going to step on to a plane. You don't even tense up when you're taking off. And that wouldn't have happened a year ago. It's the same kind of thing when you achieve something. You think, all right, thanks, and you move on to the next thing so quick. It's a really strange thing.

The first couple of months of 1998 saw Stereophonics become a regular fixture on the pages of the UK music press. The initial scepticism of some publications seemed to have disappeared perhaps because they finally realised they could no longer afford to ignore the band. It was at this time that the Stereophonics met Scarlet Page, a photographer who would become a good friend. A year or so later she would shoot the front cover of *Performance and Cocktails* but at the beginning of 1998 she was in Cwmanan to take some hometown shots for *Kerrang!*

'I'd seen all their pictures and they all looked so serious and just very straight. There seemed to be no character there at all.

The photos were very stiff and I wanted to try and get some fly-on-the-wall kind of shots. We went down to this really grubby wall close to where they live. There were these kids running around going wild. Two little boys and two little girls. One of the little girls called one of the boys a prick and Stuart's booming laugh erupted and I think it frightened them. It was just that split second. That's the photo that's wound up on the front of this book.'

Julian Carrera at Hall or Nothing recalls his first impressions of being the Stereophonics press officer:

'The first set of overseas trips we did with Stereophonics were in Germany in early 1998. Berlin and Halle (*Melody Maker*) and Hamburg (*Q*). Berlin was freezing cold. We met up with the band outside this lush art-deco venue called The Loft that seemed to be on the third floor of a renovated Nazi meeting hall. The gig was great – slow burning, powerful. I remember that everyone smoked, and queued for the bar. The capacity crowd was quiet through the set but were rapturous in their applause at the end of the show.

'After the gig the German record company took us to the grimmest "rock" bar, and the band and crew played pool. It was on this trip that the snapper Tom Sheehan took a "team shot" – the band and crew all together. It was a point that the band made time and again: how tightly knit the band and touring crew was, although both parties always knew where the line was drawn.

'Halle is in East Germany and was pretty depressing to be honest. The town seemed to be completely dilapidated. The venue, The Wortesaal, was huge but decorated with hideous eighties Whitesnake rock murals. It was also quite under-attended as a show, but we did get to hear three or four new songs in soundcheck, including "T-Shirt Suntan". In Hamburg, the band rocked and *Q* liked it.

'This was just after the band had headlined the *NME* tour. We did the band's first *NME* cover in Dublin on the first date. The photos didn't go so well so we had to shoot them again. *NME*'s then editor reviewed the show in Sheffield and described "Tramps Vest" as sounding like The Wonder Stuff, not unfair but not pleasant all the same. Still, they were beginning to sit up and take notice.

'Up to this point we'd had reasonable but not spectacular press. During the band's first year of activity, broadly October 1996 to the end of 1997, we traipsed up and down the country following them with various magazines. We seemed to do an inordinate amount of on-the-road stories (*Kerrang!*, *Melody Maker*), quite a few bits in London (*Vox, Dazed And Confused*) and a couple of stories in Cwmaman.

'By the beginning of 1998 the tide was turning. I was getting more calls and those calls certainly got more frequent after one night at the Docklands Arena.'

Less than a month after Dublin the setting is the London Docklands Arena. The occasion? The Brit Awards 1998 and the glitterati are out in force. The venue itself is perhaps better suited to hosting the Ideal Home Exhibition but for one night only someone's attempted to transform it into an ornate dining room. 'Table for 157, please!'

The place is a cliché. It's packed, in the main, with ageing wealthy guys in dinner suits and their attractive, younger, female staff all out for the annual office knees-up.

This year there's an air of expectancy. After all, last year Jarvis got arrested for that most heinous of crimes – wiggling his arse during a Michael Jackson performance! It's only twelve months, too, since Oasis indelibly stamped their presence on the proceedings by winning everything, drinking more than anyone else (which is no mean feat) and generally looking like they strolled in from a nearby fairground.

What a difference twelve months makes. The British music industry is still enjoying unprecedented sales. Over the past twelve months the Spice Girls have been hanging with Nelson Mandela and confirming their status as a worldwide phenomenon. Pop is on the way back but Noel Gallagher has sounded the death knell for Britpop. The minute he set foot inside Number Ten, New Labour officially embraced 'Cool Britannia'. A government-endorsed music scene? No thanks! Thankfully, Chumbawumba share the sentiment of real rock'n'roll fans everywhere and decide that the sycophantic shenanigans going on around them are too much. There's the big record company moguls pressing the flesh with their political counterparts. Contemporary music has been hijacked by the baby kissers! This rabid, dribbling marriage of corporate cash and political power needs a wake-up call. Quite whether some bloke called Danbert Nobacon from Chumbawumba throwing a bucket of water over Deputy Prime Minister John Prescott is the solution is debatable, but it provides a welcome diversion from the nonsense.

It goes without saying that this year the line-up is not very rock'n'roll at all. The Verve have refused to show up, preferring instead to do a benefit gig for the homeless across town at the Brixton Academy. There will, however, be a video link, which is handy because they proceed to dominate the evening, picking up Best Band, Album and Production Team. Elsewhere the role of honour includes Shola Ama (Best Female Artist), Finley Quaye (Best Male) and All Saints (Best Single/ Best Video).

It will come as no surprise then that Stereophonics cut an uncomfortable dash in among the hoi polloi. Kelly is dressed in a V-necked T-shirt and jeans. Richard is sporting his blond crop and a biker's jacket. Stuart has opted for a jazzy shirt with multi-coloured zigzags. They look and feel like they don't belong. Oasis handled a similar situation with a combination of innate style and swagger. Kelly, Stuart and Richard are, by their own admission, confused by the whole thing. That confusion, though, is thrown to the wind when the winner of the Best Newcomers Award is announced.

Now, with the benefit of hindsight, the whole episode brings a smile to Kelly's face.

'Jeremy Pearce, the CEO of V2, came up to me just before the show started and said, "Have you written a speech?" I said, "Yeah, have you? What are you talking about?" He said, "Just remember to thank your mam and dad." I was looking around going, "What the fuck's going on then?" Stuart was going to go for a piss and then it all went mental. I thought, there's no way we've won this award, but they called the name and my chair just went. I was up there like a chicken with no head! I said before, "If we do win it, nobody swear or say something fucking daft," so we said thanks to everybody. But I couldn't resist it and so I said, "It's about fucking time we got some recognition," because we got booed as we walked up that night. They cut out Richard and Stuart's speech from the TV show and just put that bit in, so my mother gave me a slap and said, "You're like those Oasis boys!" '

It's a night that Stuart won't forget in a hurry. 'When we heard the announcement the table went up and me and Richard got up and we were looking round thinking, savour this moment. We were looking round at all the faces, and the next thing Kelly's on the podium! It was a very good night. We went back to the Columbia Hotel and got drunk really. Branson was around. We had a few drinks with him and then we went back to the hotel, and I had the old statue with me! I drove home the next morning and everybody was raving about it back home, which was nice.'

Cwmaman, too, was waking up with a hangover. Graham Davies recalls, 'As soon as it got around that the boys were nominated for the Brit Awards, there was a buzz. Everybody was sitting by their radios. I can remember us sitting by the radio, everybody listening, thinking, are the boys going to do well? When they won, it was like, "Let's all go and have a party."

Back in London, John Brand knew a little more than he was letting on: 'When it was first announced that we were nominated I knew we had 17,000 people on our database and I knew we'd only need to get about 6,000 of them to vote to give us a really good chance, so we did a mailshot saying, 'If you ring up Radio One and vote for us, we're going to win this thing; support the band." Fortunately they did in droves, it was brilliant.

'I had no idea what the scores were but I had a phone call from this guy at All Saints' record company, London Records, on the Friday before saying, "What the fuck are you doing? You're cheating!" He then told me that we were miles ahead and I had no idea at this point! I said, "How do you know we're miles ahead? It's not me who's cheating, sounds like it could be you! All I've done is my best to motivate the fan base to vote for us. You're telling me that we have been successful, and that's great, isn't it?"

'So, I sat down with the boys and said, "I don't know if you've won this or not but be prepared, maybe write a little speech just in case you win."

'On the night, I couldn't stop laughing. First of all, to be in this situation was completely ridiculous. Our original plan was a record deal within four months, an album within a year and maybe some hit records. It wasn't Top 10 album within a year and then of course we're going to win a Brit award! And there we were, eighteen months later, sitting in this place with all these people, surrounded by all these other pop stars. When they went up to accept the award I just cracked up. The speech was just Kelly being Kelly.'

The Brit award certainly changed the perception of the band, which was sweet music to their record company. David Steele from V2 takes up the story: 'It was then that everyone started getting interested. The press could see what they were achieving and that they were doing well despite the lack of media support. In retrospect, that original fan base were thinking, this is ours. No one else had discovered them yet. I think that was more rewarding really than the Brit award for me, that we were achieving and selling records and doing well despite not getting the support where we would have liked it.'

It was handy really that 'Local Boy' had been re-released that week. It subsequently charted at No. 14, providing Stereophonics with their biggest hit to date. Nicky Sussex, the band's radio plugger, was delighted.

'At first it was difficult to get radio to pay much attention to the band. We were far more excited about them than they were and, although we had good support from the *Evening Session*, we didn't really get any daytime play until "A Thousand Trees". The first real turning point came with the re-release of "Local Boy", and that was when it really felt that they had firmly become a Radio One band.'

Kelly, though, was aware of the irony of the situation.

' "Local Boy" had been "A" listed by Radio One and we'd just won a Brit award. It was like, "This is it. Here we go." Thing was, it all stopped because we had to make a new record. It was like, "We're on a roll and now we've got to make a new album." '

3
Long Digging, Gone Fishing, Love Drinking

when you think about it he's watching every word you say
hey dazed and when he's sussed you out he calls her up
and out she comes and hustles us

long digging gone fishing love drinking

the bartender and the thief are lovers
steal what they need like sisters and brothers
met in a church a night to remember
robbing the graves of bodies dismembered

he watched the lesbian talk she kissed and groped
but mostly talked in lust crushed he couldn't make the call
his eyes were gripped on licking tongues
enough's enough failed for once

long digging gone fishing love drinking

the bartender and the thief are lovers
steal what they need like sisters and brothers
met in a church a night to remember
robbing the graves of bodies dismembered
saved what they stole to meet at the altar
place where they first set eyes on each other
flew to the sun to start life all over
set up a bar and robbed all the locals

11 High Society

NEW YORK CITY IN THE RAIN. Broadway is glistening in the early evening rush hour. The traffic is slow and heavy as yellow cabs snake through the gridlock. On the sidewalks people rush for cover as the downpour starts to literally bounce off the shiny roads.

Despite the conditions, Times Square still gives off an air of admittedly squalid glamour. The neon signs light up the twilight with larger-than-life images of Calvin Klein models, Coca-Cola cans and MGM's latest movie release. Down below this multi-coloured attack on the senses, a crowd has gathered outside the MTV building where some guy who looks like Tom Cruise's cousin is broadcasting to the nation.

Tonight, you see, is the annual MTV Music Video Awards show and some of the stars are stopping off here en route to the main event uptown at the Metropolitan Opera House. While the beautiful people are whisked from the comfort of their limos into the studios, the threat of a monsoon is not deterring the hapless souls outside who have claimed their places by the barriers.

About ten or so blocks north of Times Square there's a similar crowd gathered outside the studios where *The David Letterman Show* is filmed. This lot are a little older and seem to be better prepared for the elements.

Just around the corner from the Letterman studio, Stereophonics are waiting patiently at the Ameritania Hotel. It's 18 months since they won the Brit award and Richard Branson is due to pick them up but he's stuck in traffic. Eventually he shows up and the car heads north from the theatre district to Columbus Circle. It's a short crawl up Central Park West and then a swift left on to West 62nd street and suddenly they're at the 1999 MTV Music Video Awards show. On the bill tonight: live performances from Aerosmith, Lauryn Hill and Ricky Martin. Thing is, though, Stereophonics are at the wrong end of the Lincoln Center and therein the entrance to the Metropolitan Opera House. That all-important red carpet is around the corner.

Lesser mortals would have walked away but, as you would imagine, this small hiccup is not a problem for a captain of industry like Richard Branson, as Kelly explains.

'The main point was to walk up the red carpet through the media like the celebs, name-dropping Stereophonics as many times as possible. We walked down towards the start of the red carpet with Branson being called at by media and fans alike. We got turned away so Branson said, "Fuck it", and jumped the fence. We followed and we walked the carpet talking to as many TV shows as possible. It got to the point where Branson was answering every question with the word Stereophonics.'

Richard continues: 'We followed Branson, jumped the fence, sneaked past all the security guards, jumped another fence and then got on to the red carpet and did the walk with him. It was hilarious because those events are all about egos and there we were like some comedy SAS team.

'It didn't get any more straightforward either. We got in there and we had three tickets. Two of them were third row from the back and one was in the box with Branson. We didn't care though, it was an adventure.'

The actual show lasted an interminable three hours and was hosted by the comic actor Chris Rock. The big success stories of the night were Lauryn Hill, who picked up four awards for 'Doo Wop (That Thing)' (Best Video, Best Female Video, Best R&B Video and Best Art Direction), and Fatboy Slim, who wasn't far behind with three for his 'Praise You' video (Best Direction, Best Breakthrough Video and Best Choreography).

Richard, Stuart and Kelly watched on indifferently until they were summoned by V2's promotions people.

'During one of the intermissions of the actual show we did the circus-like press-cum-media circle downstairs,' Kelly says. 'Aerosmith were in front of us and Tommy Lee and Pamela Anderson behind us. It was exposure, but it was a strange way of doing it. Tommy Lee had a brown raincoat on and very little underneath it and was running around flashing at photographers. It was all a bit odd.

'After the show we went to a Chinese restaurant for dinner with Richard Branson. He was telling us that he'd had dinner with Paul McCartney the night before. McCartney told him that he'd heard of us and the town we came from. We couldn't believe it.

'When we finished the meal, Stuart had gone to the toilet so Branson convinced us all to hide at the back of the restaurant, leaving Stuart to pick up the tab for the dinner. Stuart was confused with the guy asking him to pay but then we all showed our faces, pissing ourselves laughing. Stuart laughed, calling Branson names. I think he was quite relieved.

'We then squashed into the back of the car and went to the Virgin party at the Four Seasons Hotel. It was just one of the after-shows for the MTV awards. We walked in with Branson.

'Anyway, we made our way through the hordes to a side room. Me and Stuart stood in one of the corners. There were a few people in the room drinking. We glanced around and spotted David Bowie talking to someone. Then we clocked it was Paul McCartney. We kept staring. I think I sloped off to whisper to Richard but Stuart kept staring. McCartney noticed him staring and he stuck his two fingers up at him. Stuart returned the compliment. Macca laughed. Stuart then told me what had happened so we thought we've got to meet him. We walked over and by now it was just Richard Branson and Paul McCartney talking. Branson introduced us and McCartney then told us stories about hitching to Wales as a kid with George Harrison. He thought we were from Carmarthen, but we didn't correct him. That was close enough for me. It's Paul McCartney!

'I called Richard over. He doesn't really do the celeb thing but McCartney is one of his favourite bassists. I introduced him to McCartney as Richard – the bass player. McCartney lit up to a fellow bass player and gave Richard a big hug. The drummer from Bush came over for a chat and McCartney asked him, "Are you from Carmarthen as well?" '

While Kelly then wandered off to find the restroom Paul McCartney carried on talking to Richard, Stuart and John Brand. As John explains, the former Beatle was on top form:

'McCartney that afternoon had bitten into a baguette and had broken his tooth. He was telling us that he'd seen someone being attacked and gone to help and got punched. So Stuart's never met McCartney before and he's giving him this ridiculous story in this silly Liverpool accent. It was just totally surreal.

'The supermodel Caprice was there too. When we started to become successful Caprice was asked who her favourite popstar was and she said, "Richard Jones from the Stereophonics." I was urging him to go and say hello but he declined.'

Kelly meanwhile spotted Steven Tyler.

'We'd just played Wembley with Aerosmith a couple of months before. Tyler raised his glass to Stuart. I walked over. Tyler looked at me, grinned, raised his eyebrow and clinked his glass against mine. My picture was in *Kerrang!* with him a week or so before. Maybe he recognised me from that. Maybe he was being polite.

'While I was talking to Tyler, Pamela Anderson and Tommy Lee were behind me. Tyler is standing there chatting to me, holding his wife's hand, and he leans over and starts whispering this X-rated stuff about Pamela Anderson in my ear. I nearly spat my vodka and tonic all over him.

'Stuart came back and we noticed David Bowie about to leave. Stuart and I were talking about him when Steven Tyler overheard us. Tyler asked us, "You know David?" We said, "No." Tyler then calls him over and introduced us as the Stereophonics. Bowie said hello and began to apologise for not speaking to us at the NetAid press conference.

'Tyler commented on his hair being long, called him a bit of a rocker. Tyler asked, "Why the long hair?" Bowie said he'd just been on tour and had let it go. Then he looked at me and Stuart and asked, "Do I look like the David Beckham of rock'n'roll?" Me and Stuart laughed but Tyler didn't get it. He said in a mock English accent, "Who's David Beckham?" Bowie laughed and pointed at us. "They'll tell you," he said, and on that note he walked away and left myself and Stuart to try to explain to Steven Tyler who David Beckham is. It's not that often that happens really is it? That was one of the weirdest nights of my life.'

Richard Branson looked on as the band revelled in their surroundings.

'The MTV awards was a fun night. We tried to get their profile up in America and I suppose at this stage I was better known than they were there. Amusingly as we walked into the MTV awards the idea was to use my profile to help their profile. The press kept saying, "I didn't know you had three sons!" I was the proud dad of Britain's best band but in America they weren't even heard of at the time.

'I remember Paul McCartney telling me he was a fan which can't be bad and David Bowie. It was a tremendous boost for them to have fans of the calibre of Bowie and McCartney.'

The MTV Music Video Awards took place on 9 September 1999. The day before, Stereophonics had attended a press conference for the newly formed charity NetAid. The music-friendly organisation had put together a major concert to launch itself upon the world.

In an attempt to emulate the success of Live Aid, NetAid was to take place simultaneously in different locations. This time, though, there were three, rather than two, venues – Wembley Stadium in London, Giants Stadium in New Jersey and the Palais des Nations in Geneva. The concerts would take place a month later, on 9 October, and be broadcast globally and streamed live on the NetAid website. The line-up was full of big hitters. Puff Daddy, Sting, Bono and Jon Bon Jovi were among those scheduled to perform at the US show. The bill in Geneva had the likes of Bryan Ferry and Texas, while Wembley boasted David Bowie, Bush, Catatonia and Stereophonics. The aim was simple and honourable enough. All of the monies raised through NetAid's website would be dished out to anti-poverty projects worldwide. The proceeds from the concerts would go to specific crisis-hit areas including Kosovo and parts of Africa.

This was the rallying call that brought Quincy Jones, Bono, David Bowie, Puff Daddy and Wyclef Jean together for the press conference in the Big Apple. Stereophonics were also in town and so added their support, but again it was to be another surreal collision with what they considered *real* celebrity.

Kelly grimaces as he describes the situation. 'There were three chairs at the side of the big table for us to sit on and we were like, "John, do we have to do this? Nobody knows who we are."

'We all turned up with sleeveless T-shirts, flares, sandals, and yellow sunglasses like David Soul trying to look cool, and still no one knew who we were. We sat there and everybody did their speeches really impressively.

'Afterwards they organised the speakers for a photo. So they were doing this photocall and someone shouted out, "Can we do one with the Stereophonics as well?"

'We walked over and Bono was with Wyclef and Puff Daddy but he left them and came over and started shaking our hands. He told us that Edge had been at the Slane Castle gig where we appeared on a bill headlined by Robbie Williams about ten days before. He said, "Really nice to meet you. The Edge was really moved by your gig in Slane the other day." We'd seen Edge at the side of the stage at Slane Castle. Bono said, "Apparently it was a good gig." I said, "Yeah, really good." I was thinking, Bono and the Edge have had a conversation about us, how weird is that? He said, "You've got to take America on! Oasis tried to take it on but then they decided they hated Americans, but you've got to take it on!" '

'Then Puff Daddy walked past and Bono goes, "Have you met these guys?" and he said, "No." Bono then said, "Do you know them?" and he goes, "Yeah I know them, man," and I'm like, "Yeah? Right on, Puffy!" '

The rest of September and the beginning of October were spent touring Australia and New Zealand supporting the

Living End. There was a brief return to London for the actual NetAid show before the Stereophonics roadshow flew back across the Atlantic for a handful of dates in the USA.

By 3 November they had joined the likes of Travis, Keith Richards, Blur, the Chemical Brothers and Ian Dury at the tenth annual Q magazine awards back in London. The bash took place in a ballroom at the exclusive Park Lane Hotel.

Keith Richards was honoured with the Special Merit Award. Ian Dury and Chas Jankel picked up the Songwriter Award while Travis got best single for 'Why Does it Always Rain on Me?' Best album went to the Chemical Brothers for *Surrender* and Blur got the Best Band in the World Today trophy. Stereophonics, meanwhile, beat off stiff opposition from REM, the Rolling Stones, Suede, Gomez and Nick Cave and the Bad Seeds to pick up Best Live Act.

'That was a mad day,' Kelly says. 'We had a Lear jet to get us to London for the awards and we had to be back in Sweden and on stage by 7.30 p.m.

'So we got there, walked in, walked up to the stage to collect the award and then had some pictures taken with Madness and Fran from Travis. Keith Richards and Ronnie Wood were lolling about. In fact it was Ronnie Wood who dished out our award, which was odd because the Stones were nominated in the same category. We weren't confident because when you hear names like REM you think you haven't got a hope in hell. Anyway, Ronnie Wood went up to the microphone and said, "About fucking time – Stereophonics!" I thought, did he say that by coincidence or did he know that's what I said at the Brits. It was probably written on the prompt for him.

'There's a good picture of us walking off with the award and Travis are on the table there and they're all clapping for us, which was cool.

'Straight away we were rushed off to do interviews and then we had to get back in the plane and go to Sweden.

'I remember when the relevant Q issue came out they said to Keith Richards, "Who did you meet?" and the only word he could say was "Stereo dot dot dot phonics". I thought, wow, he remembered us! We were delighted with that.'

12 Apocalypse Now

NEW YORK MAY HAVE TOASTED Bowie, McCartney, Bono and the like but the previous summer still took some beating.

At first glance, it appears that Lemmy has got his arm around a young teenage boy. Upon closer inspection though, the diminutive character being dwarfed by the infamous Motorhead frontman turns out to be none other than AC/DC guitar hero Angus Young. At six foot plus, 'the Lemster' looks like a Wild West outlaw dressed in a shirt unbuttoned to his waist, a leather waistcoat, white cowboy boots, jeans and a bullet belt. His Antipodean friend has opted for something a little more casual – jeans and a T-shirt. The pair are standing in one of the opulent hallways of the Intercontinental Hotel on Park Lane in Central London, doubtless discussing the pressures of being a living legend. Half an hour before, Lemmy was presented with the Classic Songwriter award. Angus and his colleague Brian Johnson were honoured with a Lifetime Achievement award, acknowledging the quarter of a century that AC/DC have been making music.

It's the *Kerrang!* awards 1998 – Heavy Metal Heaven to some, Rock 'n' Roll Babylon to others, but there's no denying this is *the* awards ceremony for partying. The pleasantries get under way at four in the afternoon; the awards are dished out an hour later and by 6.30 p.m. the whole place is wasted. Green Day are in attendance, as are Sepultura, the Deftones,

Queens of the Stone Age, Pitchshifter, Cradle of Filth, Ash and five hundred other hedonists including Stereophonics.

The band were nominated in the category for perhaps the most coveted award of the night – Best Newcomers. In previous years it has gone to the likes of Placebo and Skunk Anansie but this time around there were ten nominees. They included Idlewild, One Minute Silence, Pulkas and Groop Dogdrill, among others. The award was dished out by Terrorvision's Tony Wright, who announced to the assembled throng that the Best New Band in the UK was Stereophonics. Cue much clapping, backslapping and just a little flapping because 'Kelly's Heroes' were in town. He mentioned in his speech that himself and Richard had once gone to a fancy dress party when they were about eight years old dressed as Malcolm and Angus Young and to see Angus sitting on the next table was an experience that would take some getting over.

Now, though, the awards have been given out and everyone is milling about the place doing interviews. Kelly is elated. Angus has drawn a special little devil creature on a beer mat for him.

'I remember when I was a paper boy delivering *Kerrang!* to all the cool kids in the street and it was classed as one of *the* papers. I'd never heard of *Melody Maker* or the *NME* in those days. Anyway, Stuart is going to be kicking himself. He's not here on the day we got to talk to Angus and Brian Johnson. It's unbelievable.

'I only found out yesterday that we were actually coming, so there was no build-up to it. We decided we were coming and then we won the award. It's maybe not as big as winning the award at the Brits because it's not televised. The Brits is a real big deal, but that was the best *craic* of an awards ceremony ever. There's no bullshit; the awards are over and everyone's getting pissed and Angus Young and Brian Johnson are over there on a table. I didn't have a clue they were coming. When we got here, Scarlet, who does a lot of photography for *Kerrang!* showed me the table list. I couldn't believe it.

'Stuart's in Dublin – he'll be gutted. We wish he was here because this is the ceremony to be at. I mean, *Back In Black* is the background music!'

'I went up to Angus earlier on with a table mat. I said, "Can you sign this for me?" and he wrote, "To Kelly from Angus". He drew a little devil on it from the "Let It Rock" video. We had to have a photo with them then for *Kerrang!* I didn't know what to say to them. I had to stand next to him; there was me and Richard and Angus Young and Brian Johnson. I said, "All right?" and he said, "Yeah." That's all I could say. Nothing else.'

As the night wore on it provided a perfect opportunity to reflect on the summer that had been. It had started with that great day out at Cardiff Castle and then progressed to yet another Glastonbury mudbath. Last year, Stereophonics got things under way on the Sunday morning of the festival on the second stage in a scene reminiscent of Woodstock at its muddy, sodden worst. I remember the 'Phonics agent, Scott Thomas mentioning that the scene resembled the Somme. He was worried that no one would show up so he was pleasantly surprised when about five thousand punters braved the atrocious conditions. In the face of such dedication he declared at the time that it was going to go 'all the way'.

A year later the conditions were the same but *word had got around* and the event had more of a *Platoon* vibe as swamp veterans battled against the elements armed with the lessons learned twelve months before. As Kelly recalls, their billing blissfully came during a let-up in the monsoon.

'I remember seeing Neneh Cherry on the back of a tractor in a pair of wellies. She had this stunning blue eyeliner on and looked amazing! We did the main stage and Robbie Williams was watching us in the pit. That was good. Stuart had broken his foot before that, so he had all these security people carrying him around because there was mud everywhere, which isn't good when you're on crutches.

'We bumped into Robbie again at T in the Park about a month ago. It was a few weeks after Glastonbury and, while it was hardly sunny, it wasn't too bad. We were watching Catatonia at the side of the stage and Robbie came up and said, "I've really been listening to your album," and I said, "That's funny – the crew have been listening to yours a lot on our bus." We had a good *craic*. Shortly after, we had a request asking us if we would like to collaborate with him on a version of "Ant Music" for the film *A Bug's Life*. Ironically, that was the first single that Richard ever bought. Kevin Spacey is involved in the film, so we thought it might be good to get involved. We recorded the song but when we listened back to it, it just didn't sound like us, so we axed it.

'Robbie sent me a fax saying he was sorry that we didn't like it but there were no hard feelings. He's a nice guy. He'll sit down and have a heart to heart with you when he's had a few, which is cool. He probably does it with a lot of people but what the hell, he's a nice guy.'

The summer of 98 also saw the Stereophonics start work on the follow up to *Word Gets Around*. Producers Bird and Bush were once again summoned and the 'Phonics family moved into the Fruit Farm studios in Oxford for a fortnight. Marshall remembers it well.

'There was suddenly a whole new stylistic approach. It was one of the first times where Kelly had a bunch of material, some of which the boys hadn't heard until we got to pre-production. Certainly Stu and Richard had not played all the tracks for *Performance* before we got to pre-production. So we had this two-week session in Oxford and worked through all the tracks together. Kelly basically taught the songs to the boys and then we kind of thrashed the songs around and made demos at the same time.

STEVE: Some of the demo recordings, again like the first album, actually survived for this album. For instance on 'Roll Up and Shine', the drums had been recorded in Courtyard Studios in Oxford and they just sounded right. Sometimes the first time you do something, you capture a performance that you can't re-create 'cos you think too hard about it. We moved on to Peter Gabriel's Real World studios near Bath and re-recorded the tracks properly, and as is usually the way, being in the right environment inspire the band to come up with new ideas.

Subsequently three or four of the songs were written in or around the studio or were inspired by ideas that were in the studio.

I think it's difficult when you try to move an album on, to perhaps leave behind the songs that have made you what you are in the past, but you have to do that. And that's what we are always doing. It starts from day one – Kelly brings a song in; we all listen to it or we live with it for a week and sometimes they go and sometimes they stay. But that is a typical production process for most bands, really. Self-editing all the time, non-stop.

MARSHALL: The memorable tune from that time is 'My Day', which was resurrected from *Word Gets Around*. It still didn't make it second time around. Prior to meeting in Oxford Kelly sent a tape for pre-production which hadn't exactly blown us away. However by the time he started he had written 'Pick a Part', 'Just Looking' and 'Hurry Up and Wait'. We took one listen and thought, we're in business now!

STEVE: Another song which was potentially for *Performance and Cocktails* was 'Mirror Falling'. Kelly had sent us a tape which although we were unsure of we had a go at recording fairly late in the session. It didn't really come up to scratch so we had another idea. Marco our studio assistant is actually the star of that, believe it or not. Marsh downloaded a load of quotes from various famous movie stars and basically did the David Bowie trick of chopping them all up and just reading them out willy nilly. Basically we got Marco, who's Italian, to read the quotes out and it became a song called 'Postman Do Not Great Movie Heroes Make'. So that was the key casualty from the record. I think, in its original form as 'Mirror Falling', it was a strong contender but it wasn't to be.

After the *Kerrang!* awards, Stereophonics embarked on a short promotional tour of the Far East, stopping off in Thailand to shoot the video for 'Bartender and the Thief'. It had been confirmed as the first release from the second album, which was almost finished by the autumn of 1998. The videos on the first album had failed to capture the eye of the powers that be at MTV and so the pressure was on to come up with something special. The man in charge was Pinko, V2's own video specialist.

Pinko recalls, 'The track had this really American rock feel and for some reason I just thought of that scene in *Apocalypse*

Now where the Playboy bunnies arrive on floating pontoons in the jungle to play to the troops. There's a quick performance, then the crowd goes mental and they have to make their escape on a helicopter and disappear. I wrote down the idea and, as fate would have it, the band were in Thailand on a promotional tour. I just thought – the River Kwai, cheap soldiers, a barge and a helicopter and we're in business.'

Once Pinko had aired the idea for the video everyone set about trying to make it an economical proposition, which isn't easy when you're trying to ape a Francis Ford Coppola movie, never mind one that involves soldiers and helicopters and the like. However, Stereophonics' manager John Brand had a plan:

'The guy who runs the Thai V2 office is like the Richard Branson of the Far East. They were gagging for us to go over there and I said, "Why don't we ring this guy and put it to him that this is what we want to do and give him a budget and see if he can actually put it together for us." So we rang him up and I said, "You want us to come to Thailand to promote the record. We want to come to Thailand to shoot a video. Let's get something organised." The guy was amazing. He didn't say no to anything. Admittedly in the end Pinko had to push and push to get what we wanted. Mr Richard Branson from Thailand was dishing out money left, right and centre!

'In my wildest dreams I never imagined I'd ever stand on the bridge over the River Kwai to make a bloody pop video. It was a logistical nightmare to set it all up, but it all happened and it paid off – it was a great video.'

'I arrived out there with the crew about a week before we were due to shoot,' Pinko continues. 'Within three days we'd found our location right in the middle of the jungle on the edge of the River Kwai. The authorities quite happily hacked down trees for us, created a whole landing area for us and we managed to get two hundred soldiers from the Thai army. I think they were on about eight dollars a day.

'Of course, the day before the shoot, the biggest monsoon rains came down and flooded the entire area, so the band had to get into the location by speedboat and we basically shot it in one 24-hour period.

'We had one helicopter at our disposal, so myself and Cameron, the cameraman, went to the local army base to get on board. We set off to go to the location and after a while we got the impression that the pilot had no idea where we were going. The pilot and the co-pilot didn't speak a word of English and myself and Cameron didn't speak a word of Thai, so I was tapping on the back of his helmet saying, "I think we're in the wrong place." The pilot then landed in a school playing field in the middle of nowhere and got out and asked the kids if they'd seen a film unit anywhere. We got back in the helicopter, took off, flew for another twenty minutes and actually found the location at last.

'The next hiccup came as soon as we got there. The plan from the start was that it would be a night shoot. There are two types of pilots' licences – one that allows you to fly by your eyesight only and another where you can fly by reading your instruments. We found out that the pilot didn't have the latter, but we insisted that he flew at night.

'So we go up to do our grand helicopter shots of the band below. We're flying around and suddenly the helicopter goes out of control; the engine splutters; it's total darkness and all we can see is the fire and the location below and nothing else but darkness. Cameron was leaning out of one side in a harness at this stage. The helicopter flips so violently that he actually fell out and was relying totally on his harness until I pulled him back in. Then the helicopter flips the other way, but I wasn't on a harness. I was on some crappy little seat belt. I was literally thinking of jumping and hoping I landed in the river but something in the back of my head told me that helicopter blades kind of go round quite fast. We finally landed in this bit of wasteland in total darkness. It was a swamp and the helicopter sank down about a foot into the gunge. If you see the video, there are some aerial shots but that was all we could get.

'That aside, we just filmed throughout the night and it was great fun. You actually did feel that you were in a *Boy's Own* adventure. It was dark; there were flames; there were helicopters and there were soldiers – and the band did a great playback performance.

'The band weren't quite risking life and limb but, from the moment they arrived in Thailand, the culture shock was enough to be getting on with. The influence of Western pop culture was so dominant that the place looked like the Saigon we've come to recognise from the Vietnam War movies.'

Kelly gives his version of events: 'We had Scarlet and Paul from *Kerrang!* with us, doing a feature, so when we arrived everyone naturally fancied a night on the piss basically. We sent this little Thai boy out on a moped on a mission to find vodka and crisps. So he heads off into the wilderness on this moped and half an hour later he reappears with two bottles of Smirnoff and loads of bags of crisps. It was a big night so the following day we were all half-cut doing that video.'

The opening shot of the video sees the band aboard a boat making its way up the dusk-cloaked River Kwai en route for the landing pontoon. Upon arrival they're due to jump off, break into a performance of 'Bartender' for the assembled troops and then leg it once the army boys get a little overexcited.

So as the boat gently meanders up the river with all the sounds of a tropical jungle piercing the evening hush, Pinko has got a few surprises in store just to liven things up. Kelly continues:

'Pinko told us that we would come down the river in the boat and the helicopter would be overhead. Next thing we know we're sitting there playing cards hoping that the aerial shots are working out, when suddenly it sounds like Armageddon. Boom! Boom! Boom! These three explosions go off and first of all it was like, "Fucking hell," and the back of your head and your ears kind of singe and all your hair gets singed. Then we did it again, knowing what was going to happen, but the actual take that's used in the video is the first one because I think you see the three of us just turning around in a state of shock. We thought it was fucking Vietnam!'

'We hired 200 personnel from the Thai army for the day, up until about 4 a.m.' Richard adds. 'They were paid something like £4 each. The boss of the record company in Thailand had contacts with the government so he managed to get a helicopter, a boat and the army for something like £50! When

157

the music started you could tell by the way they were dancing that they'd never heard music like that before. They didn't know how to go with the beat; they were just bizarre.'

So, with freshly acquired suntans courtesy of the explosions, Kelly, Richard and Stuart took a break before filming the performance section. They were hungry, but the on-site catering wasn't exactly appetising.

'We were all starving and this woman was cooking fish,' Kelly explains. 'We'd smell the garlic and it smelled good – but she was washing the dishes in the River Kwai, which was black. There was sewage in it and flies all around it, and she was trying to serve us food in these dishes. It was grim. We were happy to go hungry.'

Pinko, meanwhile, thought his brush with the other side wasn't quite in the same league as the poor sod who fell into the river:

'At the end the band were meant to jump back on the boat and escape. On about the third take, the guy who was responsible for holding the boat close to the river just slipped and fell. The River Kwai is renowned for two things – filth and really dangerous currents – so this security fella jumped in and helped him out. So there were about three or four near-deaths on that shoot!

'We laughed it all off of course. I get back on shore and the band go, "Can we send out for a pizza?" I was like, "We're fucking sixty miles from the nearest hut, never mind a fucking Pizza Hut!"

'Anyway, we wrapped the thing about five in the morning, got our boats back up the river, got into our jeeps and went back to our hotel and got pissed, as we always do before and after video shoots. It was then that Kelly and I decided, "Let's just do all the videos on this album based on our favourite movies."'

13 Pulp Fiction

Kelly is miming 'a thousand trees' while pretending to play his guitar. It's not quite his bedroom in Glanaman Road. His family aren't downstairs eavesdropping and cracking up laughing while he attempts to sing along with Rainbow (the band, not the TV show!). In fact it's a far cry from his bedroom-mirror days. This time there's 75,000 onlookers and most of them are Welsh and male. Stereophonics have been invited to 'play' on the pitch at Wembley Stadium ahead of the international rugby match between Wales and the world champions South Africa.

It's only four days since they played their biggest headlining London show to date in front of two and half thousand people at the Forum in Kentish Town. It rounded off a hectic UK tour that started in Aberdeen almost three weeks previous.

'The Bartender and the Thief', the first single from the forthcoming album *Performance and Cocktails*, hit the shops on Monday and the latest signs indicate that it could debut in the Top 10 come Sunday. The video went down a storm at MTV, and Radio One has been giving the single maximum rotation since the tour began, so the signs are good.

Prior to the London gig, Stuart was trying to get his head around the speed at which things are happening. The last single from *Word Gets Around*, the re-release of 'Local Boy', got to No. 14 and the last UK tour, the *NME* tour in January, saw them playing venues like the Garage in Glasgow and the Junction in Cambridge. This time around they're playing places with an average capacity of 2,000, rather than 500, and of course there's the small matter of a couple of tunes at Wembley.

As Stuart says, 'There's only a few people who've done it. Somebody told me the other day that Bonnie Tyler played before a game at Cardiff Arms Park and now it's us at Wembley. I think it's brilliant. It's going to be a brilliant day for Wales – everybody's going to be travelling up and maybe it'll give the fans a bit more voice to sing along and get behind the team and, hopefully, spur them on to victory.

'It's going to be quite funny. It's one of those things: they'll either love it or they'll hate it. I think it's going to be a shock to a few of them. You can imagine some of the older fellas: "What the bloody hell are they doing here? It's a rugby match!" '

On the day itself everything seems to go to plan (that is, to the unknowing eye). The boys walk out on to the podium, mime their way through 'Bartender' and 'A Thousand Trees' and then retire to the VIP suite to watch the game. Talking to the 'Phonics manager John Brand later on, you soon get the impression it wasn't quite as easy as it looked.

'We had to fit in between the choir and the marching band. Basically we had to get the band, their instruments and the podiums on and off the pitch in no time at all. When the small podiums arrived, no one could lift them. They were ridiculously heavy.

'I was in the tunnel beforehand and the guy from Wembley came down and said, "So those are your stages, are they? How many people have you got to put them on?" I said, "Oh we've got three – there's three stages and we've got three crew." He said, "OK, you've got thirty-five seconds to get them on and thirty-five seconds to get them off. How are you gonna do that?" I said, "I haven't got a clue, but give me half an hour and I'll work it out!" So, I went and found the head of security and managed to blag a whole load of security guys to come and do it, which was fortunate.

'The guy who was running the place didn't want us there at all. He wasn't into the music and he couldn't understand why we'd been invited. We were here making all kinds of demands because we used "in-ear monitoring" and I had to run a DAT with the songs on. It was all a big hassle for him. Plus we had half the bloody security people walking on and off the pitch on camera in the middle of the pre-match build-up.

'To top it all, when he cued the band to come on to the pitch it took them about a minute to get out to the podium, so they had to cut back to the studio. Meanwhile, the band had come on and started playing. Eventually they went back live. We did lose some airtime because the idiot cued us wrong but it was well worth doing.

'That was also the beginning of our relationship with the Welsh rugby team – it was the day we found out that not only did the Welsh people like us, but the Welsh rugby players liked us as well. They actually sang "A Thousand Trees" in their dressing room before they came on!'

The one downer of the day was the result. With three minutes to go it looked like Wales were going to sneak a shock victory but the South Africans had other ideas. A late surge saw them win the game by 28 points to 20. Still, it had been quite a day out and the weekend was about to get even better.

The following day, the UK Top 40 was unveiled. Cher stayed at No. 1 with 'Believe'. The highest new entry was Steps with 'Tragedy' but hot on the heels of Pete Waterman's puppets were Stereophonics. 'The Bartender and the Thief' was No. 3. Steve Lamacq, who had been the first person to play the single on Radio One, was pleasantly surprised.

"Bartender" was a strange one, because while many of their peers had started slowing down, writing songs at what was the New Meaningful Midtempo pace, "Bartender" was the fastest thing they'd done. Obviously it wasn't representative of the album as a whole, but it was a real barnstorming single. I almost got the impression that it was there to grab people's attention. Like a quick slap round the face was better than trying to be subtle and chat people up or flirt with them. It was more like, sod that, let's rush at them.'

It was a great end to a breakthrough tour. Not only had they notched up a Top 5 single, but also the band had begun to witness the euphoria that would later become the norm at their gigs.

During the summer they'd employed a professional tour manager, Neil McDonald, who had previously worked with Supergrass and the Wannadies. Neil assumed responsibility for the ever-expanding touring crew as the band embarked on their first major production tour. Up to this point the crew had been made up of a guitar tech (Simon Collier), a bass tech (Rooster), a drum tech (Swampy), a sound engineer (Dave Roden) and a documentary-maker, biographer, designer and all-round useful person (Julian Castaldi). Now the more elaborate shows demanded a monitor engineer/stage manager (Mick Brown) and a lighting team (Abbiss and Arturro). There were, of course, bus drivers, catering people and PA riggers but the basic difference was simple: the shows were bigger and the band could no longer just turn up, tune in their instruments and play.

Neil's first major UK stint at the helm was eventful to say the least. It's not every tour manager that takes the wheel just as his charges are scoring Top 5 hits and playing at Wembley ahead of rugby internationals. That said, the autumn 98 tour also threw up quite a few headaches, which, as tour manager, is your area of expertise. Cue the Edinburgh Assembly Rooms on 25 October.

'The Assembly Rooms is within an ornate council building. It looks like an old ballroom with moulded art-deco features dotted here and there. Anyway, about halfway through the gig I got a call to come downstairs.

'I went down into a room below this ballroom and there was a lot of council workmen and officials saying that we had to stop the show. Myself and John, the manager, could see that the floor above was bouncing so much that the ceiling seemed to be about to come through. Thing was, though, the floor above was sprung and so it was expected to make the ceiling look wobbly.

'Anyway, they got this structural guy in and he was up a ladder in the corner. There was a crack along the panelling and he just happened to get up there during a quiet song. It wasn't really moving much upstairs and he was very calmly explaining that the wooden beams were designed to accommodate the sprung floor.

'Then the band started another song and this crack was opening up by about three inches. He just took one look at it and got very flustered and said, "We've got to stop that!" I think it was at that point that John went on stage and tried to tell everybody not to jump up and down, which is no easy task. The crowd took it on board for about half a song and then went mad again. I don't think we'll be playing there again!'

Crumbling ceilings in Edinburgh are one thing. The snowy winding roads of Norway in the depths of winter are another. Neil's initiation was challenging in many ways.

'We were doing some promo dates in Northern Europe ahead of *Performance and Cocktails* but the band and crew were travelling separately. We were travelling from Oslo to Bergen and the band were flying because they had to stay behind and do some interviews the next day, fortunately.

'Snow was everywhere so we were aware that it was going to be a dodgy route. The bus drivers had been to the bus station and asked all the local guys who had said, "No problem, you'll be OK." So after the show we loaded up the trailer and had a few pints before we left and everyone else proceeded to get pissed on the bus. I remember about three hours into the journey there we were, twelve people in a bus, asleep, careering across dark roads in Scandinavia.

'There was one point where we came out of a tunnel. It was about a mile long, the tunnel in the mountains, between Oslo and Bergen. Suddenly you could feel the bus stopping and then starting to slowly move in a backward direction and it was obvious it wasn't controlled. We were sliding backwards down an icy mountain road. It was terrifying when all of a sudden we hit something.

'I jumped out of the side door and it was immediately obvious that we'd come through this tunnel and hit some black ice and the wheels hadn't gripped. It had started sliding backwards and the only thing that had stopped us sliding down the mountain was a motorway crash barrier.

Although anaesthetised to the danger of it I thought it was probably a pretty good idea to get everybody off the bus since we were balanced somewhat precariously. I went round the bus saying, "Everybody get up." My shouts were met by the usual, "Fuck off, I'm staying where I am," but eventually I managed to get everybody off. By then I started thinking about how to deal with the situation, nobody else was bothered. They were all pissed and throwing snowballs at each other!

'So, it's the middle of the night and I'm trying to wake up someone from the Norwegian equivalent of the RAC. Around me a couple of the team were skipping around in the snow naked.

'Anyway, hours later this guy turned up and proceeded to put the bus up on some planks of wood and put snow chains on it and we decided we'd try to find somewhere to turn around and go back. Fuck the gig, we're not going any further! Moral of the story. Don't play mountainous parts of Scandinavia in the winter!'

By Christmas everyone was thankfully in one piece and back in the UK for the now traditional festive gigs in South Wales. Preparations were also under way for the second album. Scarlet Page was approached to take some photos for its front cover.

'I got a phone call from V2 saying that Kelly had an idea for the album cover. He really liked this Annie Leibovitz photo she'd taken in the sixties of prisoners kissing their girlfriends outside the prison gates. The central figures were a couple kissing and the woman was looking elsewhere. She was miles away.

'Basically that was the idea. There wasn't a huge budget for it so we couldn't have hundreds of extras. We ended up using a lot of the V2 staff and two models. We had literally an hour to do it because we hired this football pitch in West London as the location.

'It was literally, right, "Lucy and George, can you snog now please! I know you've never met before but can you just look quite passionate about it and, Lucy, can you just look a bit disinterested!" and, "Can you just not quite put your tongue out so much!"'

* * *

Stereophonics hadn't played in Newport since the summer of 96, when half the A&R world travelled down from London to check them out. In fact, many would argue that it was that show at the Filling Station that changed everything. That was the show that kick-started the feeding frenzy which six weeks later resulted in a record deal. It goes without saying, then, that the prospect of returning to Newport was an exciting one, especially when they were booked to play the Newport Centre.

It's 2 December 1998 and Stereophonics' dressing-room area is a hive of activity. Stuart is entertaining friends; Kelly's girlfriend Emma is putting her hairdressing skills to use on John Brand and Richard is chilling in the corner.

Outside the venue it's cold and dark but the touts are doing a roaring trade. As hordes of fans flock through the nearby bus station it's obvious that Cardiff Castle hit home hard. Virtually everybody has either a Welsh flag or a Stereophonics T-shirt on, suggesting that the band have come to embody the dreams and ambitions of a young population who have been largely ignored until recently.

Inside the warmer confines of a small room off the main dressing-room area, Kelly has settled down for a chat about the new record, which is due to be mastered at the end of the week. It will be released in a couple of months on St David's Day, 1 March.

DANNY: 'She Takes Her Clothes Off' features on this record. Am I right in thinking that was on one of your early demos?

KELLY: It should have been on the first record but at that point it was a punk song and it only became an acoustic song when I did an acoustic session. Then all of a sudden the lyrics made more sense.

I was in two minds about putting it on the album actually because it was the B-side to 'Bartender'. It was only after 'Bartender' was released that people started saying 'She Takes Her Clothes Off' was a really good song. Then I had second thoughts and put it on.

Lyrically, the bridging point from the first album to this one was probably something like 'Not Up To You' or 'Traffic'. 'Not Up To You' led on to stuff like 'Hurry Up and Wait' and 'Just Looking'.

'T-Shirt Suntan' was about for the first record as well, so it should have gone on *Word Gets Around*.

DANNY: 'Bartender' would seem to be a real departure because you're no longer basing the narrative of the song on real-life events. This is pure fiction, I hope.

KELLY: It was the last song I wrote and yes, it is a completely fictional story about a situation I saw in a bar in New Zealand. The place is called Tabac and is owned by Neil Finn's wife. [Neil Finn was the singer/songwriter in Crowded House.] So his missus owns a really small cigar bar. We'd finished a gig and we'd gone on the piss, but there was nowhere left open, so me and Richard and a few other boys went round there.

I'm sitting at this bar and these people start coming in dressed in sailor suits and I'm like, 'Is this the drink or is this really happening?' Then there were these two girls at the bar who started kissing and we were like, 'This is a really good bar!' Obviously we were really pissed but you don't see stuff like that in Aberdare, so it was a definite influence.

Anyway, I had the riff and the melody and I thought, what the fuck am I going to write about? I always think it's harder to write the lyrics for rock songs because you've got less time to tell the story – and less room because there's loads of guitar.

The title kind of got inspired by *The Cook, The Thief, His Wife and Her Lover*. I was trying to make up a story like *Frankie and Johnny* but it turned into 'the bartender and the thief were lovers' rather than 'the waitress and the short-order cook were lovers'. Why they are stealing bodies from graves I'm not quite sure, but it all sounded good at the time.

I made up this story that this lesbian was going out with a bartender and she would hassle all the customers who would come into the bar. They would think that they were on to a promise but she would pickpocket them and give the wallets to the geezer behind the bar. When it gets to the end of song and they start feeling really guilty about doing this so they decide to knock it on the head. They take the loot and leave and start up a new life but then, when they get there, they can't resist it and they set up a bar and they do it all again. It's like a Quentin Tarantino script really.

DANNY: You've said in interviews earlier this year that the title *Performance and Cocktails* was taken from a flyer in a New York club called Shine. Isn't that the Fun Lovin' Criminals hangout?

Above 'I'd like to teach the world to sing!' – backstage at Brixton Academy prior to a Manics support slot, December 14th 1996. (All photos: Julian Castaldi)

Right Back to the toilet circuit! The Stage, Stoke-on-Trent, March 20th 1997.

Left In between electric shocks on stage at the Hillsborough Benefit gig at Anfield, Liverpool, May 10th 1997.

Right Stoke-on-Trent, 1997.

Below Cwmaman Feel the Noize. Backstage at Cardiff Castle, June 12th 1998.

Above Performance and Cocktails – Kelly in lounge lizard chic.

Left The Prince and Princess of Wales.

Below Kelly bonds with Liam Gallagher.
(James Avery/All Action)

Above 'Last of the Big Time Drinkers' - on tour, 1997.

Below Paris, November 1997, prior to a gig at the Cigale.

Above Teaching Ray Davies the tune to 'Sunny Afternoon' at The Forum, London prior to the Kosovo benefit gig on May 30th 1999.

Below The Stereo family at Gothenburg airport, June 18th 1999.
(L-R) Stuart, Richard, Julian Castaldi, Kelly, Dave Roden (sound man), Simon Collier (guitar tech) and John Brand (manager).

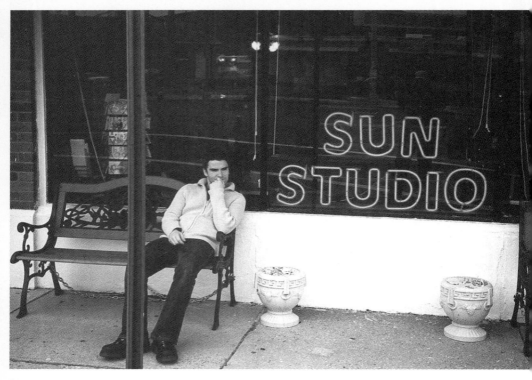

Above Kelly outside Sun Studios, Memphis, where Elvis cut his first records.

Below Tour fatigue takes hold. USA, April 2000.

KELLY: It is, but the story of that coming about has nothing to do with Huey or Fast. We were actually playing in the place at the beginning of an American tour. We didn't think anything of it. It was a really small stage and it was packed. It was a really good gig. So, we all got a bit tanked up before we went on, which is rare. I can remember us going on and it was all a bit frantic and we were giving it more than the audience were expecting really. We were playing as if we were in Wembley.

The owner of the place, Nicholas, came up to us after and said, 'We'll get you a little booth and you can stay the rest of the night.' He said, 'Leonardo Di Caprio was sitting there last week.' So, they put us in this booth and the record company were buying us drinks. It was a really good night.

Then the security guy came over and said, 'This club's going to turn into something a bit more weird at 2.30 a.m.' At the appointed time, this guy called Dominique goes on stage and starts talking about sexual fantasies. It reminded me a bit of what Madonna was doing with 'Justify My Love'. Behind him there were like all these men and women on trapezes blowing fire with hardly anything on. There was all this weird shit going on. People were coming on with masks on and he just carried on talking as if they weren't there. When he announced that the finale would feature a woman in a pig's mask pissing on herself a few people complained and so he pulled it.

You can imagine it – we were steaming in a New York bar at four in the morning and all this is going on. As we're leaving he hands a card to Stuart which says, 'Shine: Performance and Cocktails'. We were like, 'Too right, that was definitely a performance with cocktails!'

I don't like using album titles as song titles so we used the line in the song 'Roll Up and Shine'. The idea is like, 'roll up for the magical mystery tour', I suppose, and the club was called Shine, so that's where that came from.

DANNY: The next single has been used on the soundtrack to the Kathy Burke/Ian Hart film, *This Year's Love*. The film is about the idea that everyone has seven key relationships before they find Mr or Mrs Right. 'Just Looking' seems to focus on a similar theme – that whole issue of not knowing what you've got when you've got it.

KELLY: I wrote 'Just Looking' in Amsterdam. It started off as a list. I was thinking of new ideas for songs and I wrote down,

'Things I want, things I think I want, things I've had, things I want to have.' I wrote it and I read it back. I sang it back and it actually worked as it was, which was almost like a memo really.

I've found, being in a band, you get quite a lot of attention. You get people coming on to you and you've got to try to work out in your head why these people are talking to you. You've got to try to work out whether you're going to buy all this shit or just enjoy it.

I suppose you can analyse it: 'What do I want? The perfect wife?' People are led to believe in this day and age that the perfect woman is like a supermodel, size eight. The song goes on, 'Maybe the word perfect ain't quite right'. Maybe size eight isn't perfect at all.

Then there's the bit, 'They say the more you fly the more you risk your life'. That could be taken in a lot of ways . . . It's just an analysis of men and women I suppose. Some men have always got one foot out of the door waiting for a supermodel to come around the corner, whereas some kind of accept that that's never going to happen and they live with it.

DANNY: In the track 'Is Yesterday Tomorrow Today?' it sounds like the main character is seriously disillusioned.

KELLY: We were coming back from this V2 launch in Sweden and our bus driver (whose real name, incidentally, is Mel Gibson) drove via Hamburg. So we were wandering along the Reeperbahn with all these images of the Beatles in their day. Of course, it's pretty sleazy and we wandered down this street where all the prostitutes are in windows. I suppose I wrote a song from the point of view of one of these women. I realised her job is as much a routine as our job, in the same way that working on a building site or a factory is routine as well. She does the same thing every day.

I was wondering what she was thinking about. When it says, 'Write down all the things that you want to do, All the places you'd like to see', it's because she's probably dreaming of escape but, financially, that is impossible.

The title comes from a conversation I had with a friend back at home. He was telling me this two-year-old said to him, 'Is yesterday tomorrow today?' It's a bit profound for a two-year-old. I wrote it down because I thought it was an interesting phrase really. It was just one of those titles that had to be used.

DANNY: 'Hurry Up and Wait' again goes for that wordplay in the title but the sentiment doesn't seem a million miles away from 'Just Looking'.

KELLY: I stole the title from my brother Kevin, again. He'd been in the army and there are all these phrases. He was on tour years before us with different types of people in the army, so we always had words of wisdom from him when he tour managed us in the early days.

When you see everyone around you having kids, buying houses and settling down, you wonder how long you have to wait for your dog and your two kids or whatever. It's that idea of what life should be that seems to be drummed into everybody. They think they've got to follow that pattern. It's about expectations, about women, about life.

Again I did a list and 'Hurry Up and Wait' ties it all together really. How long do you have to wait to be happy? How long do you wait to achieve what you want to achieve? Maybe you just accept that it's never going to happen.

DANNY: You've said in the past that 'Pick A Part' is based on that first trip to New York – is that right?

KELLY: I had that riff for quite a while, the chorus riff, and I couldn't think of anything to write about, and then one morning it just came out of my mouth. I couldn't sleep because of jetlag and there I was in this hotel room trying to get my head around the whole New York experience, when I suddenly came up with 'You can do all the things that you wanna do'.

Later that day, I was sitting in a bar, watching these old blokes sitting watching baseball on the TV in the corner. It was almost like you'd stepped inside a telly. I felt I'd seen it all before, even though I'd never been to that bar before. Everywhere we were going, we knew what to expect. For instance, you walk into a bar and they put down the napkin and put the pretzels in front of you. You've seen it a million times and then, when it happens to you, it's like you've just stepped into the twilight zone. It's like you're on a set. You end up behaving like you're on a set as well.

The song is nothing deep and meaningful. It's a simple observation. I think it'll be a single though.

DANNY: In 'A Minute Longer' it seems the central character is being asked to do something against their will, but at the same time they don't want to confront the situation. Is that how you see it?

KELLY: That was written about a period of time when I moved out of my parents' house to live with my girlfriend Emma. It was about everybody adjusting to a new situation, a situation where the rules had changed. You don't like to offend people but sometimes you need your own space and sometimes they're not prepared to give you that space. The first half of the song is my memory of what my house was like when I was a kid. I suppose it ends up saying you want to stop living in the past and get back to reality, but sometimes, if that reality isn't great, it's nice to stay elsewhere for a while, even if it is in your mind.

DANNY: Well, if that one is based in reality, please tell me 'Stopped to Fill My Car Up' isn't. It seems to be part horror story and part crime caper, where you end up with an unexpected guest in the back of the car.

KELLY: I was coming back from the cinema in Cardiff one night, driving up the A470 at Abercynon, along the single carriageway. There are no lights on that stretch so it's always really dark. I got loads of ideas on that road really because I'd be bored of driving by that point.

I thought about this story a kid in college told me years ago. He said there was a petrol station right opposite his house and, as he got in his car one night, this boy got in and he had a bag of money. He apparently ordered him to drive him somewhere. That set my mind racing about similar situations. There's a pram in the middle of the road and you stop to move the pram and somebody jumps in the back of your car. Then someone's flashing you to tell you and you think the car is chasing you and you keep going faster. You know, all those type of shaggy dog stories.

So, I had this idea coming back from the cinema and I'd had this tune on the piano for weeks. It was the only one I can play because it's 'Imagine' backwards. When I got home I had three pages of words, but there was no real ending to the story, so I thought I'd just make it up.

I played it through and it all fitted neatly. I'd never written a song that quick before. Then the next day I wrote 'Bartender' and the next day I went into the studio.

DANNY: 'Half of the Lies You Tell Ain't True' would seem to be quite a cynical song. Do you agree?

KELLY: I wrote that after being on the graveyard tour in LA. They take you around and show you the sites where famous people died. People like River Phoenix, John Belushi and Janis Joplin. At the same time, the Princess Diana thing was dominating the media. The song's about how the papers make people believe in a certain life that never existed really.

DANNY: A few months ago, around the time of Cardiff Castle, there were rumours that 'Wouldn't Believe Your Radio' was going to be the first single. That was obviously nonsense, but will it see the light of day as a single yet?

KELLY: That's a possibility. There's a funny story behind that song. It came to me in a dream!

I'd bought a guitar that I later spotted George Harrison using in some old footage, so I dreamed that Ringo Starr and George Harrison were both sitting on my uncle's doorstep. Anyway, I dreamed this melody and woke up soon after. So I went downstairs in my pants, got the guitar out and recorded this melody. I remember Emma coming down and saying, 'Are you gone in the head?'

I remember writing in my book, 'Cheesy B-side, big brass section', because I didn't know what to do with it. I played it once on the tour bus as a joke and the next day I could hear everybody whistling it. They didn't know what they were whistling, but I recognised it because I knew what it was and I remember thinking that maybe it wasn't a B-side after all.

I wrote the words the first time we went through the Channel Tunnel. I'd had an argument with someone and I thought I'd write a song about it in a comical way. 'You can have it all if you like and you'll get paid in terracotta and white,' I think it was! It's about an argument about material things I suppose.

As time went on it became Richard's song because he split up with his girlfriend and she kept the car. We'd have a laugh about it and imagine that the car wasn't insured and maybe she'd prang it and have to pay for it. You make up all these stories about it then. That's what it's about really; it's nothing deep.

DANNY: Is 'Plastic California' the sister song of 'Pick A Part', except this is your ode to the west coast rather than the east?

KELLY: It was my first impression of Los Angeles I suppose. Typical clichés. All the waitresses want to be actresses. There's nothing else there but entertainment. Then you go up into the hills and it's a good-looking place and you think, it's so fake down there but up here it's quite good.

LA is an attractive place, but it's a bit disturbed. The first time you go there, there are all these kids who have borrowed their fathers' cars for the parties. It's like an episode of *Beverly Hills 90210*. Still the song doesn't make up its mind. At the end it just says, 'Pleased to meet you'. Some love it; some hate it. I probably love it more than I hate it.

[As Kelly's voice trails off, we can hear the support band, Feeder, kicking into their set. That's his cue that showtime is fast approaching. After tonight there's a week of arena shows supporting James before a big party at the Cardiff International Arena where they'll headline in their own right.]

DANNY: So, what of the imminent future?

KELLY: It's going to be a bit of an experience because we've never played places like Wembley Arena and the NEC. I remember seeing AC/DC play the NEC, so that should be a good *craic*. We've got used to the outdoor thing. The first year of festivals was strange and then the Castle gig helped a lot – doing the big one, you realise that people are really into you and you get a bit more confident.

We start touring the UK again after the album is released in April. That's going to be in places like the Brixton Academy. It would be nice if we could do venues like the NEC in a year's time ourselves. Every time we've come back to a tour we've gone up a size in venues, so that's the next step really after the April tour. If it happens, that's great. If it doesn't then we'll keep on going on the same level for a while. It'd be nice if it did happen because then we won't have to do so many gigs, we can just play bigger venues all over the place.

14 Spellbound

THERE'S AT LEAST FIVE MALE BODIES lying spreadeagled in the lobby of a Cannes hotel. At first glance it looks like they've been the victims of some indiscriminate shooting but on closer inspection it becomes obvious that they're all very much alive. In fact they're dripping wet and have collapsed laughing.

Beyond the lobby is a restaurant with a terrace, which in turn leads to a large outdoor swimming pool. It looks like several of the chairs from the terrace have gone for a dip in the irresistible pool with its deep-aqua-blue ripples and underwater lighting. The beautiful sunset is fading as night encroaches on the French Riviera, so it might be a trick of the light. Then again, maybe the aforementioned sodden souls had something to do with it. A disgruntled hotel manager is summoned and proceeds to survey the situation. By the time he returns to the reception area it's too late. A Trathens tour bus has collected the 'usual suspects' and has just pulled out into the street. Before he's had a chance to call after them the bus has been swallowed by the darkness. He'll never know. '*Merde!*'

It's 18 May 1999 and Stereophonics are busy touring their new album, *Performance and Cocktails*, in Europe. It's been quite a year already – 'Just Looking', the follow-up to 'Bartender', peaked at No. 4 in February. Its successor, 'Pick a Part That's New', is currently at No. 4 in the UK chart but, more importantly, the album is on its way to selling a million copies. Upon release at the beginning of March it went straight into the chart at No. 1 and has stayed in the upper echelons of the Top 20 ever since. Add to that a month-long sell-out UK tour and you find a band in particularly high spirits. Twelve hours before the 'great escape', the selfsame bus had pulled up on La Croisette, which is the main drag along the waterfront in Cannes.

Richard steps off the bus looking every inch the rock'n'roll star, complete with a cowboy hat, jeans and a sleeveless vest revealing his vast array of tattoos. Passing film fans don't know quite what to make of the sight before them. After all, it's only lunchtime and the stars don't usually come out until the day darkens. Is he? Isn't he? Who is he? Stuart follows suit. He's also sporting some Wild West millinery but has opted for a navy shirt with some dragons embroidered on it. Kelly, on the other hand, is in full uniform – black T-shirt and jeans.

The boys have travelled overnight from a gig in Milan at the Magazini Generali. Tomorrow they play the Theatre Du Moulin in Marseilles, but today is a day off, of sorts. They're in Cannes to meet up with a Radio One documentary crew which, to be honest, is made up of just one person – me. I am accompanied by Nicky Sussex, the woman responsible for the band's radio promotions. Nicky is in tow to make sure everything goes smoothly.

La Croisette is a colourful spectacle. Film fans line the walkways while various promotional people distribute information on new movies. They invariably have a gimmick to catch the eye. There are plenty of blondes on rollerblades but the real stand-out stunt is provided by a New Orleans-style brass band who march up and down the seafront blasting out the sounds of a traditional Louisiana funeral. Quite what they're advertising I have no idea but it sounds and looks great.

The really flash hotels are all plastered with film advertising. Billboards for *EDTV*, starring Woody Harrelson, hang above the Carlton Intercontinental as we wander off to check the place out.

Cannes is about thirty kilometres from Nice on the French Riviera. Apparently it was a poor fishing village until the mid-nineteenth century when wealthy British people adopted it as a holiday spot. It has since become a favourite Côte D'Azur playground for the rich and famous and now, by the end of the twentieth century, it bears little resemblance to its humble origins. The narrow winding labyrinth of European streets is still intact and the street markets hark back to a time when the place was a little less aspirational.

Cannes is tacky. It's littered with extortionate boutiques, cigar shops and cafés. The hotels are splendid, their prices even more so, but the place looks like one giant advertising bonanza. Everything looks cheap. There's litter everywhere and, despite amazing views, the thousands of people loitering around seem more interested in climbing all over each other than checking out the locale.

As you walk towards the end of La Croisette you can't miss Le Palais Des Festivals. It plays host to the film festival and during the day is home to thousands of business-types hammering out distribution deals, video rights and other such cinematic pursuits. By night, though, it's the location for the ultimate media scrum as hundreds of photographers jostle for *the* shot of the stars as they arrive for the various screenings.

This year the paparazzi have had a reasonable turn out. Matt Damon and Ben Affleck each made an appearance, as did Peter Fonda, John Malkovich, Ewan McGregor, Val Kilmer and Claudia Schiffer. Tonight we're expecting Susan Sarandon and her fella, Tim Robbins.

The film festival concludes each year with a major awards bash at Le Palais. In previous years the winners of the prestigious Palme D'Or have included David Lynch for *Wild at Heart* and Jane Campion for *The Piano*. This year all the talk is of a French film called *Humanity* and an equally obscure Belgian film, *Rosetta*.

The reason we've chosen to meet in Cannes is largely because of timing and geography, but the fact that Kelly is a big film fan has also been a deciding factor. However, without invites or schedules, we're a little stumped. There's a brief team talk and the plan is put into place.

Rumours abound that the Hollywood A-list stay at the Majestic. That's where Sue Sarandon and Robbo are expected this evening so, when we spot the palatial building in question, it's decided that this is well worth blagging. The plan involves me masquerading as 'a player' from BBC Films and it works perfectly: 'I simply must buy my friends a drink' – and suddenly the iron gates of the fortress open.

The Majestic is *the* spot. It's a huge white building in the shape of a half-open book standing on end. Within the shadow of the pages there are lush gardens with sculpted hedges and tropical plants. A winding driveway curls up to the main entrance from the security gates below on La Croisette. Le Palais is across the road and just beyond that is the sea. Just to the left of the small roundabout in front of the lobby is the swimming pool, which is truly luxurious. Up here the view is amazing – just clear blue ocean as far as the eye can see.

Given that it is the middle of May, the sun is beating down on the bedraggled star spotters down on the main drag. At the Majestic swimming pool L'Oréal are hosting an invite-only drinks party. Richard and Stuart ignore the PR people and wander over to a poolside table. No one bats an eye. If they do it's incredibly discreet, but as the wise old man once said, 'If you walk it like you talk it, you'll be fine.'

Drinks are ordered and we sit quietly eavesdropping on the conversations at the tables near to us. All around there are people pitching film ideas in an attempt to secure funding, there are aspiring actors talking shop with agents and several stunning actresses/models who seem to be doing a photo shoot.

The celeb count is disappointingly low until we spot Bernard Hill, or Yosser Hughes as he's better known. The English actor who made his name in the TV drama *The Boys from the Black Stuff* is entertaining a table of suits. Little did we know at this stage that he was the ship's captain in the Leonardo Di Caprio blockbuster *Titanic*.

After a while the conversation turns to Kelly's filmic leanings.

KELLY: I did graphic design in college and went on to doing a bit of scriptwriting. I started getting some support from BBC Wales to do a treatment for a script. It was based around the outdoor swimming pool across the road from where I grew up.

They gave me some money and then the band got signed, so it all fell through really.

It's interesting now to be sitting here listening to people pitching scripts behind us, producers and the like. It's something I'd love to come back to in the future. I'm in no rush to do that. It's great to experience what I'm experiencing, which will probably give me better script ideas for the future. I'm very happy with doing the band at the moment. To end up in this situation, I feel like the luckiest man in the world. My mum and dad still work in factories; my brothers still work in factories, and to be able to do something you love doing and get paid for it is incredible. There are not many people in the world who can do that. I feel happy that things are going the way they are. If they can stay this way, it will be brilliant. One day, I'll be able to buy this hotel and invite people like Michael Caine and Jack Nicholson down for a party. I would have invited Oliver Reed but unfortunately the main man passed away recently.

It's funny really to be sat here because when I think back to growing up, films were a major thing for me and I didn't really realise it at the time. I use to go down to the Ivy Bush and borrow the videos off Cliff Chips. Cliff used to pirate all these tapes. Not many people had videos at the time and he used to open all these drawers and say, 'Take your pick from all these films here but don't touch the top drawer because they're blue films'.

The films I remember include *The Odessa File*, which starred Jon Voight and was about the hunt for a Nazi war criminal, and *The Day of the Jackal*, which was also an adaptation of a Frederick Forsyth book. I remember *Apache* with Burt Lancaster. There was *A Fistful of Dollars* and *A Few Dollars More*. Clint Eastwood, as you know, was a bit of hero.

I've always been into films. It's probably because my old man was always watching them. I was probably watching films that were a bit too grown up because I had older brothers and my old man. There were more men in the house than women so it tended to be action films, Westerns and thrillers in the main.

Bruce Lee was probably my biggest idol as a kid. He was the one actor I had to watch everything he appeared in – *Fist of Fury*, *Big Boss* and so on. He was my first idol. *Star Wars* was probably the next phase, then it was football and boxing and then I came back to films when I was about sixteen I suppose.

At that stage I was into films like *Taxi Driver* and *Mean Streets*. You begin to get an idea of what you think looks good and I thought New York looked great. San Francisco was also impressive. I didn't realise it at the time, but now I've been to all these places it all adds up.

DANNY: Admittedly it's at least a year or so before either of us saw the film adaptation of Nick Hornby's *High Fidelity* but we spent the rest of the afternoon unknowingly playing the lead role. Is there a better way to talk films than to demand Top 5s?

Top five films, off the top of your head?

KELLY: *The Shining* became one of my favourite films when I was about nineteen but I remember watching it when I was a kid and not having a clue. Then, from nineteen onwards I've been going back to that film, trying to find something, and you always do find something different with it. The combination of Stanley Kubrick directing and Jack Nicholson in the lead role is too good to be true. The setting of it in a hotel in Middle America in the winter is cool. It's more than just a horror movie.

Pulp Fiction – Quentin Tarantino really made an impression upon me at a time when I was getting interested in scriptwriting. It wasn't really *Reservoir Dogs* – for me it was *Pulp Fiction*. The dialogue really fascinated me. The way that the film flitted back and forth, developing several stories at once – it's been done a lot since but then it seemed really fresh.

Raging Bull – the fight scenes are amazing and Scorsese really makes you think with this one. De Niro is brilliant as Jake La Motta, the boxer who loses the plot. It's a shame because then De Niro was *the* man. Since, though, he just seems to play the same character in everything, with the same mannerisms and way of talking.

Kes is a great British film. Ken Loach was, in a way, the Ray Davies of the film world. I think this was his first film and it really goes for that gritty 'real-life' feel. On the one hand, people might think this is just a story about a young lad who looks after a kestrel. On the other, you really get an impression of what life was like around him and that's why it's so good. Loach really conveys how shitty life was in parts of the north in the sixties.

Short Cuts has got to be in there. I like Robert Altman a lot. The casting in that series of short films is fantastic. Tim Robbins is hilarious as the motorbike cop. Tom Waits is great and so is Frances McDormand. It's genius really, the way all these individual stories slowly impact on each other.

DANNY: Top five actresses?

KELLY: Shirley MacLaine. Shirley's got to get a mention simply because of *Two Mules for Sister Sara*. That was the film that obsessed me when I was little. That was the one that was responsible for me cutting up the bedsheet and making a poncho. I just loved her character. She was a prostitute disguised as a nun and giving Clint the run-around.

Katherine Hepburn was great in early films with Bogart, like *The African Queen*. My favourite was a lot later: *Guess Who's Coming To Dinner* was made in the sixties and she stars alongside Spencer Tracy. It's all about a middle-class white couple dealing with the fact that their daughter has invited her fiancé to dinner at their home. The fact he's black was obviously a big deal in sixties America.

Madeleine Stowe also gets my vote. She is a good actress and to be honest I've always had a thing for her. There's also Ali McGraw, who was half the reason I started watching Steve McQueen films. There's a scene in *The Getaway* where they go swimming. Ali had great legs! Then Demi Moore took over. I was a big fan of the 'Brat Pack' films like *St Elmo's Fire*, basically because a lot of the girls at school were into them. It's good to have something to talk about. Anyway, after Demi, Madeleine Stowe appeared in films like *Blink* with Aidan Quinn and *Last of the Mohicans* with Daniel Day Lewis. She's at her best, though, in *Short Cuts*.

Gwyneth Paltrow is an emerging talent. Last year I really enjoyed *Great Expectations* and, while I've never really been into period dramas, I don't mind them every now and then. I first took notice of her when I saw her in *Seven*, so she's one for the future.

I also really like Nicole Kidman. She was great in both *Malice* and *To Die For*. She's convincing as a manipulative woman. We'll forget about *Far and Away* and *Days of Thunder*. Anyway, I hear she's working with Kubrick on *Eyes Wide Shut*, so that'll be interesting.

DANNY: Top five directors? Let me guess – Stanley Kubrick?

KELLY: Yep, if only for his cinematography. When you see a Kubrick film, it has a distinctive look. I really like the way he films things. I've already mentioned *The Shining* but people often overlook *Full Metal Jacket* and *2001: A Space Odyssey*.

I like the way Oliver Stone does things as well. He always seems to use bright lights over the top of people's heads. That is really evident in *JFK*. I like those conspiracy theory movies.

He's also not been shy about tackling current topics. Both *Wall Street* and *Talk Radio* were really relevant when they came out. Likewise, his 'Nam movies, *Born on the Fourth of July* and *Platoon* had an impact, certainly in the States.

Martin Scorsese, like Kubrick, has got a trademark look. It's like listening to certain singers on the radio. Some of them are distinctive. Others aren't. You only need to reel off his films – *Goodfellas*, *Mean Streets*, *Taxi Driver* – the list is endless quality.

In the same vein, Francis Ford Coppola is brilliant. *Apocalypse Now* is a film, like *The Shining*, that I keep revisiting. The first two *Godfather* movies seemed to go on forever when I first watched them as a kid. Now they're not long enough. *Rumblefish* was also a big film for me because it looked and felt like a James Dean film. The cast in that was interesting because it featured a young Matt Dillon, Nicholas Cage and Mickey Rourke.

As far as British directors go, I think Ken Loach is my favourite. I loved those grey, kitchen-sink dramas that he made in the sixties like *Kes* and *Poor Cow*. He's been consistent over a long period of time as well. *Raining Stones* and *Land and Freedom* were both released over the past few years. One tells the story of a drug-riddled council estate. The other's about a young Scouser who goes off to fight in the Spanish Civil War. Two wildly different subjects and yet they're both treated in a down-to-earth, no-frills way.

DANNY: Last but not least – top five actors?

KELLY: Since I haven't mentioned *Twin Town* yet, I'll start with Rhys Ifans. If you see Rhys in the *Trial and Retribution* TV drama, he's great. His character is accused of raping a girl, but he's drunk and he can't remember if he's done it or not and it's playing with his head. The acting in that is so good it's frightening. I think he's up there with people like John Hurt. He's one of those real actors. He isn't putting on a front. You watch John Hurt in so many films where you can just see it on his face. You believe him. It's the same with Rhys in certain films.

It's also the same with Al Pacino. I think Pacino and De Niro were on a par for so long but the key difference now is I still want to see Pacino, but De Niro is always just playing De Niro. Pacino seems to be more adaptable, whether it's as the great romantic in *Scent of a Woman* or *Sea of Love*, or the streetwise rogue in *Carlito's Way* or *Scarface*. The *Godfather* movies will take some beating.

I'm going to abuse the five choices and put Paul Newman and Robert Redford in together. When I was younger I couldn't tell the difference between them, but they've both made some classic films. Redford was great in *All the President's Men* and *Butch Cassidy and the Sundance Kid*. More recently he's proved he's still got it in films like *Indecent Proposal*. Newman, too, has aged well. He was funny as the lecherous governor in *Blaze*, but his peak was obviously around the time of *The Sting*, *Cool Hand Luke* and *A Cat on a Hot Tin Roof*.

So, since we've abandoned the rules – Brad Pitt and Tom Cruise get an equal vote as well. I remember first seeing Brad Pitt in *Thelma and Louise*. I thought *A River Runs Through It* was a good film, despite the fact that he was playing a young Robert Redford in it. It was no coincidence that Redford directed it. *Natural Born Killers* had an impact too and, although it's not the coolest thing to say, I like Brad Pitt.

I like Tom Cruise as well. People slate them but there's not many people that have got the presence on screen that they have. It's incredible. Just watch Tom Cruise when he flips out in something like *Rainman* or *Jerry McGuire*. I like him like that. I think he's a headbanger.

Last but not least, since we're dealing in doubles – Kevin Spacey and Johnny Depp. Depp because he's as cool as fuck and Spacey because he's a great actor – and I had dinner with him last year!

On that note we leave the poolside and wander over to the main reception area where the calm, 'too cool to be true' atmosphere is blown apart by news that Susan Sarandon and Tim Robbins' limo is coming up the driveway. We sneak a peak and then amble along the shore looking for a cab. Stuart turns 29 at midnight and a celebratory meal is planned in a nearby hotel.

The evening is balmy, almost idyllic. Out in the bay there are ten or so super yachts playing host to the glitterati. As we stroll past Le Palais, the press pack are in position and I spot a couple of familiar faces from the UK who proceed to fill us in with the day's gossip. Ronaldo, the Brazilian international footballer, is apparently in town and there's a party at the Hotel Martinez, which is 'unmissable!' Unimpressed, we jump in a car and head a couple of miles out of town to a hotel where the tour bus has parked up.

The hotel, which will remain nameless, is set on the coast. A large table has been erected outside on the rear terrace close to the swimming pool. The scene is like the Last Supper: a big long table with band and crew along either side. There's lots of wine and lots of chat. A couple of the lads were approached on the beach earlier by some crackpot with a TV crew. He was dressed in a fluorescent yellow shell suit and was asking them if they fancied being in his porn film. It was Ali G.

The rosé (or pink stuff, as it's become known) is going down well but soon the pool becomes far too tantalising for Kelly. He's on his second length as coffees are ordered. The caffeine is ignored as the pool begins to fill. Richard, meanwhile, is looking on with his customary shrug of the shoulders. He's on the mobile to his girlfriend, Gail, who's back in London. Stuart's birthday is toasted as Neil, the tour manager, begins to round everyone up. The bus is leaving in an hour for an overnight drive to Marseilles. His task is not an easy one because the spirit of Keith Moon has descended upon proceedings and there's all sorts of stuff, including furniture and human bodies, flying around. In among the madness everyone has forgotten that there is a woman in our midst, and she has a camera!

Nicky, the band's radio promotions woman and the sole female presence, has been keeping a low profile until now. The camera proves to be a reasonable incentive for most of the guilty parties to abandon any notion of drying off. Clothes are thrown on to dripping bodies and everyone tries to act like nothing untoward has gone on. However, the looks from the staff at reception are priceless as the drowned rats try to talk shop. The quizzical expressions soon become suspicious, but they're still dealing with Neil, who is the very picture of sobriety. He's paying the bill for dinner. As soon as that's sorted everyone's ushered on to the bus. Time for a sharp exit!

In the interim, the hotel manager has been out to the pool and is now at the door watching the bus headlights disappear. Myself and Nicky are heading back to London the following day. We've said our goodbyes but decide, in view of the situation, that it's a good idea to get out of the way. Luckily there's a cab at the rank outside. All's well that ends well.

The Radio One documentary was broadcast six weeks later, prior to the Morfa Stadium show and the interview with Kelly featured on a Radio One promotional CD, which was free with *Melody Maker* the same week.

Nicky was pleased. Job done. 'The whole day was just fantastic. It was a short caper film in itself. I can vividly picture Richard in his stetson, appearing out of nowhere, striding over towards us down the central reservation of La Croisette looking like Clint Eastwood.

'We crashed the Majestic Hotel and set up camp on the pool terrace. There were quite a few of us and we must have looked a right sight. Everyone else there was extremely well dressed, flashing money, doing deals and talking very loudly. The bar bill was extortionate but it was a lot of fun and kind of set the tone for the rest of the night.

'We ended up at a hotel just out of town where the band had a day room to use to get cleaned up. They aren't the most cosmopolitan bunch and I remember it was the first time they had come across rosé wine – very exotic! Stuart had a bit of an altercation with a waiter over a bread roll, the drinking continued and, inevitably, the swimming pool proved to be too much of a temptation. It ended up full of naked bodies, sun loungers and bottles of wine, and I've got the most interesting set of photos to prove it!'

15 Twin Town

Everybody came up to me after the show and said what a great day. At the end of the day that's what it's all about. You're giving people pleasure and that's what you're here to do really. They all came down there and got a great kick out of it. We probably got the biggest kick out of it. What a superb day! (Stuart Cable, August 2000)

I T'S TWO DAYS UNTIL Stereophonics play the biggest gig of their lives at Morfa Stadium in Swansea and the former landlord of their local boozer in Cwmaman, Graham Davies, is reminiscing about 'the boys' and their musical infancy 'over there just beside the pool table'.

The Ivy Bush is not unlike any other pub, with a main bar area and a walk-through games area on a raised floor to the left. It was here that Kelly cut his 12-year-old musical teeth playing old classic cover versions like 'Pretty Woman' by Roy Orbison and 'Proud Mary' by Creedence Clearwater Revival. He wasn't alone; the pool table was often moved to one side to make way for local bands to set up their gear. It's not such a long road though from Cwmaman to Swansea – it's a little further from an audience of fifty to fifty thousand!

'This I thought would have taken them ten years to do and they've done it in three.' Graham is warming to his subject. 'They were always confident; Stuart especially was confident. He'd always go around the pub talking to the boys saying, you know, this time next year we'll be there. We didn't know whether it was a joke but you could see he believed it.

'Kelly was always sort of the guy who was concentrating on the music. All he cared about was what it sounded like. How did that come across? What do you think of these lyrics? Richard was the sort of deep, quiet one who didn't say a word to nobody but Stuart was so confident that, one day, they were going to make it. To be fair, they did – and I think it's brilliant for them.'

Stuart's mother, Mabel, and Kelly's parents, Beryl and Oscar, have also joined us for a drink and one of the local characters is treating us to his party piece. Mervyn 'the Mop' Owen is standing at the bar casually chatting to the barmaid. What she can't see is that his trousers are around his ankles revealing a backside with two eyes tattooed on it. The place erupts laughing and she realises that he's 'at it again'. Incidentally, Mervyn's catchphrase, 'Keep the Village Alive', was adopted as the dedication on *Word Gets Around*.

In fact it's the huge leap from that album to the current offering that's the topic of conversation.

'I didn't think it'd go as well as it has, and I didn't think they'd have the response that they've had,' Oscar says. 'I was pleased they were signed but I didn't think that they would take off in the way that they took off, with all the airplay and press they've had.

'When they finished *Performance and Cocktails*, Kelly lent me one of the early copies and I took it on holiday with me. It was obvious he'd been looking around. There is a lot more experience on it. When I got back I phoned him and said, "Apart from *Talking Book* by Stevie Wonder, this is one of the best albums I've ever heard." I really felt that way about it. I was overwhelmed by it and when it went to number one, that was the icing on the cake. I just hope it continues and it doesn't go to their head.'

Mabel, for one, doesn't think that's a possibility. 'Stuart got married in March and he's got a lovely wife, Nicola, who is home here in Cwmaman. I think they've all got good roots here in Cwmaman – people who they care for and people who care for them, people who have raised them over the years and shown them the right and wrong way of doing things. When you come back to your roots like that, I don't think you can go far wrong, can you?

'I did think that one day they would make it because they were so determined. I did really believe in them, but of course it is on a large scale now and I'm so proud.'

The day of the Swansea concert, 31 July 1999, is blisteringly hot. Looking down from the surrounding hillsides at Morfa Stadium in the midday sun, the people below on all the approach roads seem to blend into one giant kaleidoscopic picture, shimmering in red, white and green. There is something magical about it all, like one of those displays before the Olympics that involve thousands of children holding coloured boards.

Initially it was thought that the athletics stadium would be rubbled immediately after the show to allow work to begin on a new-look 25,000-seater structure that would be home to both Swansea City Football Club and Swansea Rugby Club. However, there are ongoing wrangles to be resolved and a decision is expected later in the year. For the time being, then, Stadiwm Morfa is like a dying patient who has been given one last massive injection of life before bowing to the inevitable.

The place really has taken on the air of a carnival. There's a five-a-side football tournament, rugby sevens, a tug-of-war, a custom bike show and a funfair all taking place in and around the athletics track. In keeping with the venue, there's quite a turnout from the Welsh sporting world – Ian Rush, Ieuan Evans, Joe Calzaghe and Gareth Edwards to name a few.

The sole grandstand stands isolated along one side of the track at right angles to the stage. The pitch and the track are covered with pale bodies slowly getting scorched by the demon sun. The 2,000-capacity stand, meanwhile, is home to those with guest tickets.

There's a mix of celebrities and what seems like most of the population of Cwmaman milling around the record company-sponsored free bar. Oscar is talking rugby with Ieuan Evans while lots of the lads are forming an orderly queue for Melinda Messenger's autograph.

Kelly, Richard and Stuart, meanwhile, have got their own chill-out area right at the top of the stand in the executive suite. It's hard, though, to chill out when the air conditioning's broken and the temperatures are in the nineties. Still, they've had a fun-packed 24 hours.

Richard and Stuart went off into the city last night to check out a Manics tribute band. Richard describes events: 'It was a good laugh. Half the people in the club couldn't believe it was us, and half the people wouldn't believe it was us. There were people coming up to us and going, "Are you?" We were like, "Yeah, we're doing a show tomorrow," and they'd say, "No, you're not." I was like, "Yeah, we are. I am me!"'

'We went back to the hotel and talked about the madness of the situation and then had an early night. I didn't want a spinning head this morning. It was funny getting here in the people carriers with the blacked-out windows. On the approach to the stadium there were people running up to the vehicle. Crazy day!'

'We got a bit drunk last night.' Stuart is in fine form, despite a few shandies. 'I have never been so nervous in my life as I was earlier. I met Gareth Edwards! Nicola, my wife, set it up. Jeremy Pearce from V2 records is a big rugby fan as well and he got in touch with Gareth and invited him down to the show. So we're standing in the guest bar area and Nicola says to me, "Can you come here a minute. I've got someone you'd like to meet." I said, "No, I'm busy," and she immediately said, "Come here now," so I walked over and there he was!'

'The one thing I noticed on the way here,' Kelly pipes up, 'is that all the traffic signs have been changed and all the digital road signs are saying "Diverted traffic due to pop concert." I was thinking: we're doing all this. It's odd really. I'm making a serious effort to enjoy the day and not get wound up about it. I'm not going to worry about the equipment and all that. I'm going to just enjoy it because it may not happen ever again.'

After sets from the AC/DC tribute band ABCD, the Crocketts, Gay Dad and Reef, the crowd are primed and ready. The roar as Stuart, Kelly and Richard walk onstage is as loud as I've ever heard. After all, this event is five times bigger than Cardiff Castle.

Kelly is wearing that same white shirt that he wore at the Aberdare show just over three years ago when they didn't even have a management arrangement never mind a record deal. Now they're doing the biggest gig ever held in Wales.

The set eases in with 'Hurry Up and Wait'. Kelly is staring uneasily at the crowd but manages a smile about three quarters of the way through the song. Any concerns he had are discarded with the opening chords of 'Bartender'. Stuart gets rid of his flat cap and is shaking his head like a man possessed. It's hard to describe 50,000 people pogoing in unison. The Athletics Association of Wales, which used to be based here, would have been proud.

'T-Shirt Suntan' is next and Richard's overriding sense of calm has rubbed off on his colleagues as they settle into their new home. Just before 'A Thousand Trees', Kelly speaks to the audience – 'You all look very nice. It's nice to see you've made an effort.' The response is ecstatic and by the time they get to 'Not Up To Me' the skies are beginning to darken and the place takes on a visible glow. There's steam rising as the heaving mass of sweaty bodies picks up the pace.

The stadium is in a bowl and, as the lights come on in the houses on the surrounding hillsides, it's quite a sight. There's little time, though, to be gazing at the stars. 'Check My Eyelids' kicks like a tethered beast and the sensory attack doesn't stop there. The giant screens flicker with images from the recently completed video for the forthcoming single, 'Wouldn't Believe Your Radio'. It shows the band riding through desert terrain on motorbikes *à la Easy Rider*. The crowd are impressed, but not as impressed as they are with the lighting during 'Traffic'. The whole place is covered in swathes of red, white and green light and everyone is singing every syllable. Kelly affords himself a smile before launching into 'Last of the Big Time Drinkers'. Tonight this song is like getting a kicking. The drum beats are like punches and the vocal like someone trying to teach you a lesson. The crowd are gone, lost in the Catherine wheel of emotions lighting up the summer night. They'll be talking about this one for years to come.

Just when you think the crowd can't get any more animated they prove once and for all that this is no ordinary rock'n'roll show. The screens are showing a montage of famous sporting moments involving Welsh heroes. The place goes berserk and when the final clip, showing 'That Try' by Gareth Edwards against the All Blacks, runs to its end, there are scenes bordering on hysteria.

For ninety minutes the frustrations, the concerns, the reality of everyday life is forgotten and it's time for optimism and positivism. It's time to celebrate a new era, to toast an emerging nation, a nation with a new voice and identity, a nation that is no longer content with talk of mines, leeks or sheep, a nation that likes to congratulate itself every now and then.

The set boasts 25 songs covering both albums, with a few special touches thrown in. The cover of the Kinks' 'Sunny Afternoon' couldn't have been played on a more apt day. You can barely hear Kelly on 'Local Boy' or 'Just Looking', but it's the more mellow, contemplative tunes that steal the show. 'Nice to Be Out', the B-side from the 'Pick A Part' single, tells stories of their travels and brings a hush over proceedings before 'Billy Davey's Daughter' brings everyone together. There's just Kelly with an acoustic guitar singing a song about an untimely death and 50,000 people singing and meaning every word of it; 50,000 people literally lost in music, lost in a statement of who and what they are, lost in the afterglow of a glorious sunny day. It'll take some beating. Here, Kelly, Richard and Stuart have, in a way, achieved what Neil Armstrong and his cohorts did thirty years ago. They've conquered space! They made the massive tiny and the impersonal intimate.

Afterwards producer Steve Bush is beaming.

'You just simply cannot beat a quality voice and a good story well told – that's the bottom line. And it's a bit of a tonic I think to find that bands like Stereophonics are getting noticed, because I think people just love a good song and perhaps by the end of the nineties, some people are a little sick of "bleep, boom, tweek" dance-influenced pop and R'n'B.

'I remember being a kid and most of the best songs I ever heard – they always stay with you. And I think a band like Stereophonics coming along with a quality voice, a quality sound and a good song – with excellent storytelling, people will remember that – it stands out really. It's very rare that a Stereophonics song doesn't get me, as a punter. And that's important as a producer actually.'

A few weeks after the show Kelly, Richard and Stuart are still talking about it. In the interim there's been a minor media storm surrounding allegations in the *NME* that the band had whipped up the crowd into an anti-English fervour. It was started by an anonymous letter to the paper by one disgruntled punter who compared the event to a Nazi rally. His argument was based on Kelly's rendition of the song, 'As Long as We Beat the English' combined with the rugby footage and the general Welsh flavour of the day. Kelly is not impressed.

'That song was commissioned by an English guy at the BBC. He said, "Will you write a song called, 'As Long As We Beat The English?'" I said, "You've got to be joking, we'll be lynched!" He said, "It's for a rugby commercial to run ahead of the Wales–England Five Nations match." I said, "No, I don't think so." I went home and I left it at that. At the time I had this B-side tune on the go. I woke up one morning and eight lines just came on to this piece of paper, "As long as we beat the English". I wanted to make it a chant sort of thing. I thought, "Shall I? Shan't I?" So I ended up recording it.

'They said, "Can you come to Twickenham and sing it outside Twickenham and we'll film you for the advert?" I said, "I don't think so!" So they said, "Will you come outside and do it then?" So I was in the middle of Chiswick and these cockney boys across the road were going, "You've got some front, mate, doing that outside my garage!" I was singing this song and I was laughing. If you've seen the commercial, I'm looking around at people and I'm a little uneasy. That went on the telly and we did actually beat England for the first time in I don't know how long. I was in the working men's club and the advert came on after and I came on the screen singing this song and everybody just went mental. There was chips and pies and everything in the air! That was an unbelievable day because we scored in the last second.

'So then it comes to Morfa and Gareth Edwards was there and we were doing this celebration rugby thing at the end, not just Welsh people, it was the British Lions. There was English people too. It was a celebration of people that we felt had done something for the country because we hadn't had much to say, just to make people feel proud. I said, "We'll do that song just for the *craic*." Looking back now I shouldn't have done it really. I played the song and the crowd went barmy. There were probably 49,800 Welsh people!

'I'm still not convinced it wasn't the guy in the *NME* writing a letter to provoke an argument. We didn't want to respond to it because we didn't believe in the argument. We thought it was absolute bullshit.

'The only flag that was put up on stage was one that was thrown up and the song was for a TV commercial for a rugby match. The first line of the song is, "I don't want to be your enemy," so it's pretty clear. I don't see any difference in that to "Three lions on your chest". How do they think that makes Welsh people feel? It's not about Wales and England; half the people I bother with and work with and a lot of people I love as friends are English people. It's a *song*, for fuck's sake, but someone took it the wrong way. It did put a dampener on the ending really because it was in all the Welsh papers as well – especially the headline saying, "Nazis". That was a bit harsh.'

Neil McDonald is equally dismayed.

'To hear the cheering that was happening when they showed Gareth Edwards' try against the All Blacks, as an Englishman, was amazing. I'm English and I thought it was great. I think the pride they have in being Welsh is something to be admired and applauded rather than picked upon.'

The conversation soon turns to other more positive aspects of the day. Kelly has a grin from ear to ear as he recalls the moments prior to showtime.

'As we were waiting by the side of the stage to go on, this thought came into my head – everyone here knows my name.

That's a lot of people! Then I went, "Right, I need a vodka!" I went and had a vodka before I went on.'

'There was one arrest with 50,000 people in the middle of Swansea and that was for a guy climbing up a lamp-post,' Stuart says. 'It was a superb day and it was good for Wales really. I think that's why so many people came – because nothing like that has ever happened in Wales before. There were all the side attractions – custom bike show, tattooists, a funfair and all that, four other bands and us and all for under twenty quid.'

'When we walked on I was seriously thinking, what the hell are we doing here?' Richard says. 'There were people every-where, as far back as the light would take it. It was just amazing; you could fart into the mike and they would cheer!'

Kelly agrees. 'I couldn't believe how far back it went either. You can't think about it; if you think about it you're gone. When they started singing the words, that was great. For a while I just used to get really nervous about it because I was years on stage and nobody knew the words. I used to make the words up as I went along but now people know them, the pressure is on.

'It's an amazing feeling but it's just astounding – people from Japan came over to that show, and America. The Yanks were standing in that stand and they went back to America telling people they'd never ever seen a gig like that, because people don't react to gigs like that in the States. They couldn't believe people were reacting the way they were, just going mental and how loud they were singing!

'I just find it unbelievable how so many people can feel something from it. You write something and then you deliver it and they all feel something from it, so they're obviously all feeling a similar thing to what you're feeling yourself.'

16 Cinema Paradiso

K ELLY IS LYING ON AN OPERATING TABLE with blood everywhere. To make matters worse the band have just arrived in Australia and if ever he needed to be close to home it's now. The irony is he couldn't be further away. Stereophonics are due to spend the next month touring Oz but things aren't looking too good. The anaesthetist enters the room but, possibly as a result of the shock of what has just happened meddling with his mind, Kelly's convinced that the medic hovering over him is Richard. Elsewhere in the theatre six or seven people huddle in a group to discuss the predicament. Kelly's view is blurred but he's straining to hear what they're saying. The voice at the centre of the conversation sounds familiar too. Things must be bad – he's hearing broad Welsh accents. The medical team then gather around the operating table and begin the day's work. However, two of the esteemed professionals present seem to think it's more productive to pinch the patient in the nether regions, and everyone else is falling about laughing.

It's 14 September 1999. Stereophonics have set up camp on a stretch of coastline close to Botany Bay, Sydney, Australia. The place looks like the set from *M*A*S*H*, which is a relief because everyone is here to shoot the fifth and final video from *Performance and Cocktails*. 'Hurry Up and Wait' is getting the filmic once-over and this time the theme is based on Robert Altman's 1969 Vietnam War comedy, which portrayed the nutty activities of a mobile army hospital. Stuart and Richard have got their surgical kit on, conjuring up images of Donald Sutherland, Elliott Gould and Robert Duvall. Kelly is the hapless hero who has been stretchered in for immediate attention and, as with the four previous videos, the man at the helm is Pinko.

The landscape is breathtaking and a helicopter is hovering overhead. The props too are impressive. Everything is white, from the tents to the jeeps to everyone's uniforms. There's a signpost in the middle of the camp with directions and distances (I can't remember seeing 'Cwmaman 17,000 miles' in Altman's original version though). Fans of the ensuing TV series will doubtless recall the classic episode where Clinger decides to dress up as the Statue of Liberty and stand in the middle of the camp, much to everyone's amusement. Well, Pinko has persuaded John to abandon the world of contractual wrangling momentarily to re-create that very scene. Elsewhere in the video Stuart gets to show off his golfing prowess in one shot and Kelly has a lovely time lying on a stretcher being carried around by his bandmates. All in all a good day out!

Almost twelve months after the event, Richard, Stuart, Kelly, Pinko and myself are sitting in a West London pub on the eve of the release of *Call us what you want but don't call us in the morning: The Performance and Cocktails video collection*.

PINKO: When we did 'Hurry Up and Wait' we were nine months into the album's life, so by this point the record company have pretty much given me and Kelly carte blanche to go do what we want. The budgets were all around £75,000 I guess. I think 'Just Looking' peaked at £90,000 because of all the problems with the weather.

With 'Hurry Up and Wait', as with all the other videos, you have to fit in with the band's schedule and it turned out that the window of opportunity then was going to be in Australia, which was a place I'd never been to at that point. The idea I had for that one was always going to be a *M*A*S*H/Catch 22* military-based thing. We used certain specific things from *M*A*S*H*. There's an episode I remember where the General is due to visit and Clinger decides to dress up as the Statue of Liberty holding a burning torch.

The other thing I should mention, which has always been a running theme, is that in every video we try to put John, the manager, in some humiliating uniform. The only one he actually doesn't appear in is 'Bartender', though he was dressed as a General all day and in the end we didn't film him. He looked good as a big American General. He was the sheriff in 'Wouldn't Believe Your Radio'; in 'Pick a Part' he's the guy who's melting the gold down in the big leather apron, and in 'Hurry Up and Wait' we gave him the job of Clinger in a green dress. He was painted gold, standing in the middle of a field and he's holding this torch, which was a sort of emergency flare that gets really hot. It's so bright he couldn't open his eyes, so we let it run for about quarter of an hour after we cut and walked away. So, he's stood in the middle of this field, holding this torch up looking like a big tart on a podium, and we're all standing half a mile away laughing.

The basic idea of the video was that Kelly would be followed on this sort of linear movement of him being the patient lying on a stretcher. He went from point A to point B basically, being carried by Rich and Stewart, who played several roles. They were the paramedics bringing him into the operating theatre, the doctors operating on him, the drivers taking him out the other side, and then Richard was the helicopter pilot flying off with Kelly on the side in a ski run. They used to put the injured on these ski run things, which we built. Kelly's scared of cars never mind helicopters, especially after the 'Bartender' experience. So we carried him up, put him on the side and then swapped him over for a dummy. The scenes you see in the video, where he seems to be flying all over the place, we shot from the helicopter with a green screen and then had him imposed. It was the same with Richard. You see him pull a lever but there's a real pilot just out of shot next to him.

That was really good fun – two days out in Botany Bay. We were staying about a mile up the beach from where they were shooting *Mission: Impossible II*. They had really big helicopters and really big cranes and every time our little puny two-seater went up you'd hear this 'Get your fucking helicopter out of the sky; we're filming; Tom Cruise is going up,' and we were going, 'Fuck you.' It was great because all the crew I used there had just come off *The Matrix*, which had been shot in Australia, so they knew all the crew on *Mission*. The banter was very colourful. That was good fun and that did pretty well too. It was the conclusion of 'Let's rip off some films' or 'Let's pay homage to our favourite movies'.

KELLY: Yeah, that all started with the *Apocalypse Now* one in Thailand. We decided, since we've both got such a major love for film, that it made sense. Pinko's into *Get Carter* and *Alfie* and all the old Malcolm McDowell stuff. Every time we do a video, we always end up drinking a lot of Corona pop and talking about films.

PINKO: When I first met Kel he was very intense. He'd done a bit of scriptwriting at college so it's not surprising that there were loads of late-night phone calls ahead of the videos for *Performance*. I copied eighteen of my favourite movies on to VHS and sent them to him. He then watched them on tours around Europe. There were all the classics: *Georgie Girl*, *Apocalypse Now*, *The Italian Job*, all the Michael Caine stuff and all those gritty 'grim up north' sixties films like *Long Distance Runner*, *Poor Cow*, *Kes* and *Up The Junction*. All our meetings for the nine months before that record came out were just about films we liked – that and a combination of heavy drinking.

KELLY: Pinko actually said *The Italian Job* would be a good one because there are three Minis in it, which fitted perfectly. The one after, 'Wouldn't Believe Your Radio', I just wrote down a note when we were in Cannes to do *Easy Rider*. Richard and Stuart got the chance to ride Harley Davidsons and I got to be Jack Nicholson for the day, which was a good *craic*.

PINKO: Basically, at that time we had a list of about twenty films. When you get down to deciding what you can get across about that film in three minutes it has to almost always be an action movie. That's because other great films are built on tension and action and we're not acting. We don't have the capability to do that sort of stuff. *Easy Rider* was the next on our list. We worked out the scenes and who was going to be who. Kelly obviously wanted to be Jack Nicholson, so we got a very small white suit made for him. We all went out to Granada in Spain and found the location. Bizarrely, we all lived in a cave for that week. It did have fridges and cookers and showers, but they are built into the mountainside.

We had about three days of shooting and, again, I nearly topped myself on that one. I was on the back of a camera truck and, because we'd been filming for two days solidly and drinking each night solidly, I actually fell asleep on it and it went round a corner and I was just pulled back in by the producer. I was about to topple over the edge at fifty miles an hour. That was a good one because you could finish each day, come back to our cave, which had a swimming pool, get all the dirt and grime off you and chill. It was easy and comfortable compared to a lot of them.

DANNY: It was certainly easy and comfortable compared to 'Just Looking', which involved snowstorms, ever-changing storyboards and forty-eight hours without proper sleep. So what was the original idea?

KELLY: I was in a hotel in Scotland called the Devonshire – lovely hotel, a big house in Glasgow. I remember the week before we'd been talking about claustrophobia so I wrote this idea down about travelling in this car. The car crashes into a frozen pond and we all panic and try to get out. When we do get out, we get to the top and it's all ice. That's what I wanted the video to be about; really claustrophobic and a bit fucked up really. I was thinking about *The Dead Zone*, where the guy falls through the ice, and *The Omen*, when the camera falls and the kid is trying to get out from under the ice. That's what I wanted it to be – a video based on a couple of films.

Pinko liked the treatment but, by the time we got to the location, MTV had already hinted they wouldn't like showing that sort of stuff.

PINKO: Kelly had come up with this idea that was based on some obscure, tense, horror-type movie about people who get trapped under the ice in a lake. If you do that for real it's very, very dangerous and you can't get insurance for pop stars to go into frozen lakes. The only option is to re-create the scene in a studio like Shepperton, but that costs a fortune. I think we had about £60,000 (£65,000 for this video) so we were writing and faxing each other and gradually twisted it to another thing. In a way it was never related to a movie, although in my mind there's a little-known Roger Moore movie in which he plays a nice successful businessman. In one scene he's driving home in his nice Rover to his beautiful wife when suddenly he meets his doppelganger driving the same car in the opposite direction. The doppelganger drives him off the bridge, his car crashes and he dies. The new evil Roger Moore then goes off to wreak havoc on his wife and business and it all goes pear-shaped.

So there was this snow thing I kind of got tied into because of Kelly's thing, and the car crashing was my idea. The end result is I go to Scotland just before we're about to film. It's the most beautiful mountain location in Scotland and we're nearing the end of January and there's not one snowflake to be seen. All the locals are like, 'Don't you worry about it; it'll be snowing before long,' so I decide to stick it out and wait for the boys to arrive. Incidentally, the village is called Killin – should have read something into the title before we got there.

Anyway, the band have arrived and we're in the hotel bar when the producer walks in. He was driving the car with the sound equipment in it. He had his twelve-year-old daughter with him when he lost control and rolled the car. It hit a tree and catapulted all the stuff out of the back but thankfully no one was hurt. That was like, 'There's an omen here!'

That night, we wound up in the bar until about three in the morning (we had a 6 a.m. start so it's always good to get an early night). Anyway, I take a look out the door and there's been about two feet of snow landed while we've been drinking. Luckily the catering bus, the toilet bus and the changing bus had all gone to the top of our mountain location the day before.

KELLY: I just remember staying in the hotel and having these huge baths because it was freezing. We bought these woolly socks and long johns so we were well sorted for a trip to the North Pole. The cars wouldn't start and they were skidding all over the road because there was so much snow and everybody was freezing – but it was festive. It's great coming out of the cold into the warmth of the hotel.

PINKO: So, we all get up at six o'clock and we're told by the drivers, 'You can not get up the mountain, not without a snow plough, a bulldozer and a tractor.' Panic sets in. We have our Jags waiting by so we go off and try to find another field somewhere else. It's the one you see in the video, where the Jag flies down the hill. Again we're setting this up with two cameras. One of them's just below the ridge of the hill. The Jag is on a safety chain, so when it comes over the top it'll stop a few feet from the camera below the ridge. The safety chain snaps but luckily the car swerves to one side. Then, because it's out of control, it goes through a brick wall and ends up at the bottom of the loch – and this is all before breakfast!

By this point we hear that they've cleared a path to the mountain, so we get to the top of the mountain, where we're going to do a wedding scene outside a dummy church we'd built. However, the local electrical crew, who were doing the lighting, decide that, with a seventy-mile-an-hour blizzard coming in, enough is enough and walk off set. That then leaves the entire band and crew in total darkness, two thousand feet up a mountain with seventy-mile-an-hour blizzards, looking at this dummy church set up in the middle of nowhere.

So we reconvene in the bar and decide to admit defeat. The plan is to fly back to London and shoot the underwater tank sequence in which the boys swim out of the sinking car. We then realise we've missed the last planes back to London, so we drive to Edinburgh, get the night train back, don't sleep all night and get to London at 7 a.m. Then it's straight to the underwater tank, where we film all of the underwater stuff. That was very frightening because Stuart has about an inch to spare before his car runs out of oxygen.

STUART: The car's sinking down and the first person who gets out is Richard and he swims away. The second person to get out is Kelly, so muggins here is voted to stay in the longest. The idea was to let the water get up to my chin and then kick the door open. I didn't mind. I'm a good swimmer.

Then this diver comes over and he goes, 'Basically, if for any reason the door doesn't come open I'm going to ram this into your mouth. Just spit as hard as you can into the breathing apparatus and just start breathing normally and then we'll get you out.'

So, when the cameras started rolling, the car gets dropped and all the water rushes in and it's just that instant panic of, 'I've got to get out.' At the end of the day, what you've got to remember is, if you don't panic you'll get out – but tell yourself that when you're in a confined space with water rushing in at speed. Eventually I pushed the door open and made it to the surface. We only did one take on that!

PINKO: We finished there at 9 p.m. and then drove across London to this other studio, where they've beautifully re-created Scotland, complete with snow machines and a church. We then re-shot there until ten the next morning. At last the video's done! Not based on any one particular movie, I know.

KELLY: We kind of made it up as we went along then and I was a little bit disappointed that it wasn't going to be what I wanted it to be. I wanted it to be hard and it ended up with a Christmas feel to it, which is cool but it's not what I really had in mind. It looks all right though.

Actually, one of the highlights was meeting the girl who plays the pole dancer. She had just been working with Stanley Kubrick in *Eyes Wide Shut*. I was just asking her about Stanley Kubrick all the time. She told me that she had toothache on the set and he said, 'What's the matter?' because she kept holding her mouth in pain. Apparently, he then paid for her to go to the dentist and held back filming until she returned to the set. All the things you hear about Kubrick, and he paid for this girl to go to the dentist and get fixed up and come back.

I used to love doing the video shoots because to me it was like making a film for a couple of days, especially if you get involved in the treatment and stuff like that as well. I used to like doing it and I got on really well with Pinko and Cameron. It's like making a record or touring. It's different people; it's not just all the boys in a bus. You can try to do something different each time. I just used to like making little films every couple of months and being in a different country. Scotland's always a good *craic*. It all went tits up: the weather was awful and we ended up staying up for days. I think we flew to Japan directly afterwards, so we were well and truly fucked, but then that's the way every video went. It wasn't very glamorous but it was a laugh.

PINKO: After 'Just Looking' we learned from there on only to make videos in warm places. *The Italian Job* was definitely next on our list, so we went out to shoot in Turin, which is where the original was shot. Turin is pretty much a company town, and that company is Fiat. You look at a map of Turin and all the areas that are painted blue are owned by Fiat, and that's about sixty per cent of the town.

Obviously, all those famous locations in the movie had changed after thirty years, like the weird angular-roofed church. There are now sixty-foot oak trees all around it, so you can't actually see it, and it's rotting. You couldn't walk on it, never mind drive a car on it. The chase sequence on the rooftop was actually filmed at a test track on the Fiat building. However, that was being renovated in time for the millennium, so we had to find a multi-storey car park and shoot on that. We went as close as we could to all the locations and, again, that was fantastic. We had three brilliant stuntmen. The lead stunt guy had been a stand-in for *The Saint* TV series and he had all these stories. Stuntmen always have the best stories. That was a pretty good shoot to do. Just chasing Minis round with buggies and stuff.

The Minis, though, had no footbrakes, but they were such good stuntmen they could stop things with handbrakes. There was one good Mini, the green one. When I asked about the other two they told me not to ask too many questions. I found out later that they'd nicked them off the streets of Rome the day before, put them in the back of a removal truck, driven them overnight to Turin and changed number plates! So, somewhere in Italy, there are a couple of Italian families wondering where the hell their Minis are.

4

Jukejoints, Exploits, Encores and aPplause

You asked me so where have you been
Let me think now let me see
I stood once where Hitler's feet
Had stood when he made his speech
In Nuremburg in thirty eight
When he tried to build the perfect race
He said black man ain't gonna run
Alongside our perfect sons

There was Dallas too, the library
The place they ended Kennedy
We stood where Oswald took his shot
In my opinion there's a bigger plot
Costner's back and to the left
The picket fence the better bet
Paris came and summer went
The tunnel's now a flower bed

The famous turf that made Jeff Hurst
The vodka stops to quench my thirst
The Golden Gate stroke Alcatraz
And the fat man failed to get us passes
Jimmy's corner in Raging Bull
De Niro's jokes and bottled pills
Elvis tales from Mr Woodward
Any Richard Burton if you could

Tourists stare at tourist stops
One more picture one more God
Another top up for a change
It makes you think, it makes you sane
Talking more about yourself
There's a mirror too, have a check
Cheques are always passing through
Some depart but a lot come too

Restaurant talk or pick your teeth
You bite your tongue or chew your meat
Sleep or drink or drink to sleep
And one more week and we will meet
We'll talk of what we haven't done
Since we departed back a month
We argue why we have to shout
All in all it's nice to be out

17 The Blues Brothers

A YEAR OR SO LATER the focus is very much on the future. The news-stands all along Broadway are emblazoned with the latest headlines from the race for the White House. George W. Bush seems to be faring better than his Democratic rival, Al Gore, but in New York City it's the First Lady, Hilary Clinton, who is the talk of the town. It's looking increasingly likely that she will become Senator for the Big Apple when America goes to the ballot box in just over a month's time. There is, after all, nothing more showbiz than a US election, and Hilary has cut a colourful dash on the campaign trail so far. Quite what she's about politically is, as ever, secondary to her celebrity status.

Kelly has stopped off at a bar near Madison Avenue for a chat en route to the studio where Stereophonics are mixing their third album, *Just Enough Education to Perform*. There are two guys close by talking about Bill's missus. The older of the two, who bears an uncanny resemblance to Jack Lemmon, is recounting his favourite Hilary anecdote:

'Hilary and Bill are driving through Little Rock in Arkansas when Bill spots one of Hilary's old boyfriends pumping gas. The guy waves from the forecourt of the gas station. The President and the First Lady wave back before Bill muses that Hilary's life could have been so different: "If you'd stayed with him, you'd now be the wife of a gas pump attendant." Hilary shakes her head slowly and replies, "You're right I'd be his wife, but he wouldn't be pumping gas – he'd be the President of the United States."'

Stereophonics' third album is going well and is on schedule for release at the beginning of April 2001. It was recorded during the summer and now the 'Phonics party has decamped to New York for a few weeks to oversee the final mix. They've chosen the legendary Andy Wallace to provide the Midas touch. He's perhaps best known for his work on Nirvana's *Nevermind* and Jeff Buckley's *Grace*. Andy is currently holed up in the soundtrack studio on 21st and Broadway where he's working with Marshall and Steve, the producers of all three Stereophonics albums.

Kelly is due to pop in to see what fine-tuning has been going on but for now his mind is on other things. He's been hanging out with one of his heroes, Chris Robinson from the Black Crowes.

'He's got this unbelievable pad and a few days ago he invited me and Stuart round. When we went up in the elevator it actually opened into the apartment. It was a bit mad when we got there. Chris's girlfriend, the actress Kate Hudson, was lying on the couch eating a box of cereal. She's Goldie Hawn's daughter.

'Anyway I had a CD on me of four tracks which we'd mixed. Chris asked for it, so I gave it to him and said, "You're probably going to want to sue me after the first track ('Vegas Two Times') because its influences are quite obvious!" So he put it on and he was into it. I played him "Vegas" and "Mr Writer", "Lying in the Sun" and "Size Nines". They're probably going to be the four singles.

'They were both just sat on the couch getting into it. It was weird. Me and Stuart were sat there with Chris and Goldie Hawn's daughter and you could see Gramercy Park out of the window. I was like, "I've had approval now off Chris Robinson! We're doing all right with this then!" '

Kelly was right. Chris Robinson would later give the new material the thumbs up:

'The Vegas song – that's like a whole other thing they have going, which again I think goes to prove that bands are only worth what they believe in. Those guys are moving along and I think they're letting their experiences influence their music and they're not limited. Creativity is nothing to be limited by – it's something to be celebrated – and I think whatever kind of music you're into you should let it loose when you get to make records. The similarities between us and them aren't guitars and vocals or their arrangement but their spirit and the reason why they want to be making music.'

The Black Crowes have established themselves over the last decade as one of America's most consistent and successful rock bands. Formed by brothers Chris and Rich Robinson in Atlanta, Georgia, the Crowes burst out of the Deep South with their debut album *Shake Your Money Maker* in 1990. It featured tracks like 'Hard to Handle' and went on to sell 3 million copies. The follow-up in 1992, *The Southern Harmony and Musical Companion*, hit the top of the Billboard Album Chart immediately and consolidated their position as one of America's premier live bands.

The Crowes soon developed a reputation for hard living, which was to be expected for a band moulded in the great old bar-room blues/rock tradition that produced a host of hell-raisers from the Stones to Zeppelin and Lynyrd Skynyrd. Chris and Rich also 'enjoyed' one of those explosive fraternal relationships that had plagued the Kinks and would launch Oasis.

The mid to late 90s saw three more albums, which enjoyed varying degrees of success, but the decade ended on a career-defining high. *Live at the Greek* featured the Crowes performing with Led Zeppelin's legendary lead guitarist Jimmy Page and signalled the start of a new chapter for the band.

By October 2000 the Crowes are holed up in an old Yiddish theatre on New York's Lower East Side. The theatre's been converted into a studio and work is under way on a new album. They've signed a new record deal with V2 records, home of course to their friends from Stereophonics. In fact, about a week after Kelly and Stuart were at Chris Robinson's apartment, the band received an invitation down to the studio.

'Me, Richard and Bushy went down. It was in this theatre in this dodgy-as-hell area.' Kelly's face lights up in the dimly lit bar as he describes the scene. 'You walk in and it was all candles and lamps and Christmas lights and rags. It was an old theatre basically and the Crowes were playing on the stage. The control desk had been installed where a small audience would once have been. We sat there and watched them play and then Chris turned round and said, "Can you do a melody for this part?" We were sober as judges because it was three in the afternoon, and I was thinking, oh no! It was a new song so I didn't have a clue what it was. We sat on the couch and they went back to the control room, listening to stuff. He shouted down from the control room and called me up. I thought, number one, this is brilliant; number two, I'm fucking out of my depth here!

'He got a lyric sheet out and he says, "Can you try singing parts of this?" So I was working on harmonies and his brother started playing piano. All that was in my mind was that I had to be back to our studio by six to listen to this mix. It was half-five and I thought, if I blow this now, it's not on. They had to put a guitar down and by that time it was sixish and I said, "Look, I'm going to have to go." Thank God, though, he said, "Can you come back later tonight or tomorrow?" The next day I had a phone call about twelve and went back down.

'Don Was was producing. He was a really nice guy. So Don set the mike up in the control booth and they all sat behind me on the couch and they said, "There's the lyrics; there's the song!" I was shitting myself. I did a couple of different versions. The track's called "Lay It All On Me". Whether it'll be kept or not, I don't know. There was a boy filming the whole thing – I don't know who he is but he was filming the making of the album. How much of it they'll keep, I don't know, but I sang the whole thing, so if they keep any of it – great!

'Afterwards, when I was on my way out, Don Was chased me and said, "We should be paying you for this. We've got a budget." I said, "I don't want money. I should be paying you more like."'

As we leave the bar Jack Lemmon and his pal are still swapping Hilary anecdotes. Outside the steam is rising out of manholes in the road as we rejoin the merry-go-round on

Madison Avenue. The noise of the beeping traffic is over-whelming and it's difficult to immediately adjust to the pace of the sidewalks. People are running by in all directions. We say our goodbyes and Kelly jumps a cab to the studio, disappearing beyond the horizon into the vastness of it all. New York City in the Fall – it plays tricks on you.

Stereophonics first met the Black Crowes when they were both part of the supporting bill at the Toxic Twin Towers Ball at Wembley Stadium on 26 June 1999. The headliners were Aerosmith and the line-up also included Lenny Kravitz and Three Colours Red.

Four years previous, Kelly, Richard and Stuart had been playing cover versions by the Crowes, Aerosmith and Lenny Kravitz in the pubs and clubs around Cwmaman. By June 1999 they were a month away from headlining Morfa Stadium, so a support slot at Wembley Stadium seemed like the perfect baptism of fire. Understandably they were nervous but, looking back, Kelly admits he lost the plot that day:

'I watched the Crowes from the side of the stage. We were on after them. That was weird enough to start with. They were amazing. I was wondering to myself how we were going to follow that. I was standing with Emma and my Uncle Mike and Auntie Linda. I was really into it. It was the most excited I'd been for a long time watching a band. Noel Gallagher and Meg Mathews walked towards me and Noel shook my hand and we watched the Crowes.

'When it came to our turn, I've never felt so uncomfortable at a gig in my life. It was like we shouldn't have been there, even though we'd probably sold more records in the UK that year than anyone else on the bill. It didn't feel right. I thought we played bad. Dave, our front of house sound guy, had a lot of problems. The desk went down at one point, I think. I hated it. My old man was at the gig and I overheard him complaining to John Brand about the sound. It was horrible. It was Wembley but I fucking hated it. Scott Thomas, our agent, said afterwards that he had never seen me look that way.'

Scott Thomas takes up the story. 'I just think it was more of a personal thing for Kelly and the band than anything else.

Suddenly they were in the middle of something they'd been looking at from the outside for ten years.

'I saw Kelly beforehand and I can normally sit down with him and talk about anything and it's quite relaxed, but I'd been chatting for a while and I realised he didn't need it. I just said to him, "I'm not doing any good here, am I?" and I walked out and left because it was a case of his head being somewhere else. He was the same afterwards.

'I wouldn't be surprised if it all suddenly just hit him. We said maybe it's a year or two years hitting him in one gig and in one day. Maybe other people would take off and get a quarter of Jack Daniels and do something else. He actually reacted to it in a very quiet way. Perhaps that has informed his actions since then.'

Scarlet Page also noticed that Kelly wasn't his usual self: 'He was in a state of shock. I've never seen him quite so nervous. He had Black Crowes vinyls with him that he wanted to get signed, but he was too nervous to ask them. He was almost sort of gesturing that he was going to be sick and I've never seen him like that. He really was like, "God, we've got to go on after them."'

Kelly continues: 'We watched Aerosmith from the side of the stage, then we left. The car was silent on the way back. I didn't go to the bar; me and Emma went to bed. I remember ordering a huge fuck-off garden burger and going to bed. That day I felt a bit off and lost with it all. It was all very strange.

'Things picked up the next day though. The day after Wembley, we did the charity thing that Pat Cash organises at the Café de Paris in Central London. The bill featured Jimmy Page and the Crowes, Aerosmith, Roger Taylor and Pat Cash, and, er, us. We opened.

'I remember Billy Duffy coming up the day before to say good luck. I bumped into him again on the way in to the Café de Paris. He said, "Are we gonna do something together?" I said, "Er, don't know." I told him we used to do "Wild Flower" by the Cult. I can see it now – Billy Duffy and Stuart backstage trying to remember Ian Astbury's lyrics and us lot laughing at them. When we gave Duffy the Les Paul guitar it was great – slung down as low as it could go. It was hysterical. It was really cool to have jammed with Billy Duffy. He's one of the nicest guys I've met.

'I remember the Crowes watching us at the side of the stage at the Café de Paris. We were out to impress. We'd been sending tapes through our agent for years for support tours and nothing ever happened, so it was time for results.

'Scarlet Page was photographing us and because we knew Scarlet, we kind of had an "in" with Jimmy. I got talking to him and told him that we felt a bit weird playing Wembley. He told me that we needed a few of those types of gigs under our belt before we'd feel comfortable with them. He said, "You probably felt better there than I did playing here." I watched their whole set standing next to Jimmy's tech.'

According to John Brand, 'It was £10,000 a table. I met David Coulthard, which was a big treat for me. Alice Cooper was there, and Roger Taylor and John McEnroe. I just remember Kelly standing there watching Jimmy Page and the Black Crowes. It was extraordinary; it was an absolute trip. They got on really well; they stayed in the same hotel and a lot of serious bonding went on.'

It was also an interesting night for Scarlet Page: 'Actually, I was thinking on the night about this time we shot some pictures in Cwmaman [NB including the one on the front of this book]. We were taking a photo by some posters on a crumbling wall and this biker went past and Stuart called him over. He had this massive ginger beard and ginger hair and he's in that song, "Goldfish Bowl". He's the guy referred to as "red head gingerbread". Apparently he's a huge Led Zeppelin fan, and they were like, "Do you know who this is?" I don't think he believed them.

'The fact my dad is who he is has been a frequent topic of conversation. They like to bring it up, but not in a bad or silly way. They just seem to call me "Jimmy's little girl" at every available occasion. It doesn't bother me because they're so enthusiastic and funny about it. It's not like they're asking things like, "What amp does your dad use?"

'Anyway, Dad told me that night at the Café de Paris that he thought they were great. He met them later that summer at the *Kerrang!* Awards. He was getting some sort of Lifetime Achievement award and they picked up Best Band. As he was walking up to the stage, Stuart got up, with a cigar in his mouth, and gave him a really strong handshake and went, "Well done, Jim!" All those little things – he can tell they're good people.'

Chris Robinson from the Black Crowes was also paying close attention at the Café de Paris: 'I remember watching them at Wembley Stadium and I remember meeting them and digging it, but it wasn't until I saw them play at that club, the Café de Paris, that I really got to hear the songs and see that they were a band. I had more time, and I was closer, and I could see in more detail what they were doing – and I really liked it. You can tell instantly with something like that when it's a real band.

'Besides being talented guys and talented songwriters and having those great songs, I think Kelly has a phenomenal voice, a very identifiable voice. I think it's the dynamic of being in a band and being with these people that you started out with – and no one knows what it's like except those other two people.

'Being in a band to us always meant being free and music always represented that, so when you share that with someone, which I think they do, that's when it gets its dimension. That's what gives it that vibe and that's what a real band is – it's not a project someone puts together; you have more things committed in there.'

The Aerosmith tour left the UK with both Stereophonics and the Black Crowes in tow for a handful of European dates throughout July 1999. First stop was the Njimegan Amphitheatre in Belgium, where Kelly finally had a chance to have a decent chat with Steven Tyler for the first time.

'I bumped into him in the toilets at the Café de Paris gig. I told him that I'd seen him at the Birmingham NEC in 89 and that I'd played on his bill at Wembley just yesterday. He looked up at me and then, in his amazing husky voice, he said, "Stereophonics? Yeah – great band, man, great bill: you, the Crowes, Lenny. It's good to meet you. So, you're doing a couple of shows in Europe with us too, right?" (We were booked to do Belgium and Berlin.) We did our "see you laters" and he left. When I followed some time later, Emma was stood outside, grinning. She said she asked Steven Tyler if she could shake his hand and he said, "No, but you can give me a kiss instead," and he stuck his tongue in Emma's mouth. She was shaking.

'So, in Belgium I was backstage and Steven Tyler was comparing rings and stuff with Chris Robinson of the Black Crowes. I thought, I've got to say more to you than "I saw you at the NEC," so when we saw him outside his dressing room later on, Stuart and me walked over to him and asked if he'd known Bon Scott from AC/DC. He said, "Yeah, we shared a bus with AC/DC in 77 – or was it 78?" He looked over at Joey Kramer, the drummer. He was as confused as Tyler. He said he'd kicked himself for the fact that he'd been so out of it at that time that he didn't have the chance to get to know Bon, but added that *Highway to Hell* was *the* album. Then he started screaming the lyrics from "Touch too Much".

'It was great that night. We all walked to the stage together and I stood back, watching Tyler. The Black Crowes and us watched the show from the side of the stage. At one point, Tyler looked over to me and said, "This one's for Bon." I nearly died. It was unbelievable.

'The next gig was at the Waldebuhne in Berlin, a couple of days later. We arranged to meet the Crowes in a downtown Irish bar. We got to the bar and there was this German band doing Creedence songs. We had a few more beers and decided we'd ask them if we could do a few songs. Richard wasn't with us so me and Stuart sang, Swampy (drum tech) played drums, Simon (guitar-tec) played guitar and Rooster (bass tech) was on bass. We did "Ain't No Fun Waiting Around to be a Millionaire". The Crowes had arrived by now. We were all over the shop – Swampy couldn't play the tune, even though there's the same beat throughout. It was a good *craic* but it sounded awful.

'Then the Crowes got up and Chris said, "Take the second verse; just sing anything – it's OK – it's the blues." They started playing an Allman Brothers song. Audley, the Crowes' guitarist, was playing slide with his lighter and I babbled some nonsense during my verse about Stuart drinking and being blitzed. It was top jamming with the Crowes.'

Chris Robinson takes up the story: 'I have no idea if anyone realised who we were at all. We were there hanging out and having a good time and we just sort of did it to play. All I really remember is the house band that was like a rock cover band – they were like, "Give us our stuff back!" They weren't impressed because that was their gig and they thought we were going to stay up there all night, which we weren't. I think somebody said, "Do you want to do one more?" and they were like, "No, man, we want to finish our set." Anyway, we all retired to the bar.'

Kelly was on a roll: 'We all started ordering slammers – peach things – and I sat at the bar talking with Steve Goram, Audley and Chris. I was a big fan, so I knew a lot about the band. I remember at one point Chris smiled at a girl who was just leaving. When she turned away, he mumbled in a sarcastic Southern tone, "Obviously I didn't sing good enough tonight." We talked about Motown and Otis, about living in Atlanta and having barbecues at Don Duck's house. We talked until the bar closed.'

Stereophonics might well have been impressed with the Black Crowes, but the feeling was mutual. Chris Robinson was thrilled to hear that they were fans.

'It's very flattering. We're always really surprised when someone's heard our records or when someone listens to records the way we listen to records. When you make music it comes from a different place than just being a celebrity or something. When someone else's music has made an impact on you, that's what it's all about, so they were influenced by us. At the same time, we're really into what they do so it's all reciprocal, good vibes.'

Kelly continues: 'Next day we were in this Amphitheatre in Berlin where Hitler used to hold rallies. We bumped into Skunk Anansie that day. They played on the bill too.

'During the Crowes set, Joe Perry from Aerosmith came to the side of the stage. He had his cane and his cigar and gave us the nod. Earlier he stood and watched the Crowes with us. During the Aerosmith show the Crowes came and said goodbye. It was good; it was like we'd bonded with a band we'd admired for so long.'

The summer of 1999 was nothing short of momentous. After the Aerosmith dates, Stereophonics played a massive home-coming show at Morfa. There was V99 where they appeared alongside Suede and Gomez with Kelly sporting a particularly fetching Afro wig. Slane Castle with Robbie Williams followed and soon after that they decamped to New York for the NetAid press conference and MTV awards. While they were there they also played on the Conan O'Brien television programme.

'Karen Dirkot was our friend in common with the Crowes,' Kelly says. 'She works at V2 now but worked with the Crowes when they were on Def Jam.

'When we did the Conan O'Brien show Chris Robinson came down with Karen. Afterwards, myself, Stuart and Swampy went to the theatre at Madison Square Garden to see the VH1 divas. Tom Jones was singing. After Madison we went to a bar but Stuart and Swampy were feeling a bit tired. I didn't want to go back to the hotel; the less time in hotel rooms, the better.

'Chris had given me his number earlier on and said to give him a call. He's not too far from Madison so I called him up. He was watching TV and told me to bring some beers – he'd not got many left. I went to a nearby deli with Matt Pollack from V2, bought some beer and walked round the corner to Chris's place. Inside, it looked like a Black Crowes gig – candles and rugs, wooden floors with paintings and a lot of books, records, CDs and videos. There were a few old guitars, including a sixties Martin. I had a go, acoustic. I put the beers in the fridge and I laughed when I saw a bottle of HP brown sauce. He likes Britain, Chris. He has a lot of British comedy – *Black Adder* and *The Young Ones*, that kind of thing.

'The Conan O'Brien show, our very first time on American TV, was to be aired in about an hour. Matt called his wife and

said he was going to be late. We drank beer. Matt and Chris
talked about drugs and why certain people do or did things. I
gave my opinions about being brought up in a small community with not much of a drug culture due to everyone being
skint, but everyone got pissed out of their brains at the
weekend. I'd never had any interest in drugs. In fact they sort
of scare me. Every man has his poison. Chris showed me
around the apartment and told me if I was ever in town I could
use his place to stay.

'I couldn't believe I was there. It's difficult meeting someone
you've looked up to and they don't know who you are when
they meet you. The conversation can only go one way, but
when the person you look up to, or has influenced you, has
respect for you also, then it's more of a friendship thing than
just gushing over someone. Chris told me many times that I
was his favourite singer and, to me, that was great, and odd.
He was the guy everyone in my town wanted to sound like –
it's like Tom Jones and Elvis. When Tom first met Elvis, he told
us Elvis was walking towards him singing Tom's latest single.

'A few other people called at Chris's place. An English girl
and her boyfriend. She'd been to the premier of *American
Psycho*. She was in the film, I think.

'Conan O'Brien came on. The song sounded good. It was
"Roll Up and Shine". It was weird to hear Chris singing along
and saying the middle eight was his favourite part. The couple
left. We started messing with the guitars. Matt asked what the
new stuff I'd written was like. I remember playing them "Lying
in the Sun". It was difficult 'cos I was really pissed, but Matt
liked the song and Chris was asking me the words and singing
the bridge. Then, somehow, we started writing a tune. There's
a riff I'd been playing about with for a while and me and Chris
started playing about with melodies. We made a deal that night
that we will one day make a record together. I'd go to New
York for a week and Chris'd come to Wales for a week and
we'd write a record. It was a big thing for me.

'I left and got back to the Corla Court on Lexington about
6 a.m. I ordered a cheeseburger and then woke up to Neil's call
at 10.30 a.m. The burger was still there by the bed. Still a bit

pissed and fully dressed, I ate half the burger and left for Orlando, flying at 12.30 p.m.'

As Kelly flew off into the sunshine, Chris Robinson was left to deal with his neighbours. 'I was living in an apartment in Chelsea. I've since moved to a new place but the old place had really thin floors. It was an old industrial building with big lofts. Kelly had these boots on and he was singing really loud and stomping on the floor. It sounded great but it was like three in the morning and I was like, "Fucking hell, I'm going to hear about this!"

'The best thing was, a couple of days later I got a letter in the mail from the neighbours. They never came to say anything to me personally of course. Anyway, it was such a good evening: we sang some songs; he played me some new songs; I played him some new songs; we sang together and stuff. We just had a great time, and then these people left me a letter chronicling the whole evening from how it sounded below – and our stories corroborated perfectly. I was like, "Sorry about that."

'One thing I thought was funny was that they wrote, "Mr Robinson, you seem to believe that no one lives beneath you," and I was like, "I'm a lead singer! What do you expect?" That was an excellent evening; we had a great time at the expense of my neighbours. I've moved since so the curse has gone.'

18 North by Northwest

TWO THOUSAND MILES in a day and a half! The metallic-silver Stereophonics tour bus has cut a lonely figure, speeding through the heart of America from Washington State on the north-west coast, inland through Idaho, Montana, North Dakota and finally arriving in Minneapolis, Minnesota, thirty-odd hours later. Tonight the band will play a place called the Quest on North 5th Street but then, a few hours after the show, it's back on the bus for the 450-mile overnight drive to Chicago.

Tempers are getting frayed and tiredness is turning to madness. By anyone's standards, Stereophonics are touring veterans with four years' solid gigging under their belts, but the irritability level has never been this high before. Kelly admits he's bored with the set at times and hints that the band have taken their eye off the ball. Stuart, meanwhile, is doing what he does best. He's trying to remain buoyant and boisterous. What he doesn't realise is that it's beginning to piss people off. Looking back on that pivotal day, keyboard player Tony Kirkham, for one, admits he couldn't cope.

'It was one of those days where I just felt like I was on the edge of the planet and I didn't know what was going to happen next, and then these two kids came on to me. They didn't know I was working with the boys or anything. I just started talking to these two lads who were coked out their faces, two young American lads, unstable sort of characters. So I got rid of them and they went away and I went on and played. After we came off, these guys were hunting me down because they saw I was in the band and I got really paranoid.

'They'd told me this story about how they'd got rich parents and I could see they were coked off their heads. I started thinking that they could be carrying a gun; that they might get upset that I'm not talking to them. I just lost it completely.

'Tommy Lee was playing down the road in a club and Stuart wanted to go see his band, so we were all going to go down there, but I was losing it a bit. Stuart had gone back to the hotel to get a shower and when he got back he announced, "We're going to the club." I said, "No, I'm not going to the club. I'm going to stay in the bar across the road until the bus comes. I know where I'm at; I don't feel up to it." He called me a cunt or something like that, very glib. I lost it. I said, "I'm not taking this shit any more; you don't have to call me names."

'So I went into this bar and I started drinking and Kelly comes in. Now, up to this point, Stuart had been getting a bit laddish, a bit out of order; he was getting a bit out of control. I love the guy to death. I think he's so important to the whole thing, but he just can be larger than life sometimes. With Stuart, 99.9 per cent of the time you spend laughing. He's a lovely guy but I think he's a bit insecure. So anyway, this night I goes into this bar and gets absolutely wasted. I don't care at this point. I just want to unleash all this stuff. I don't care that I'm letting it all out. So, Kelly was there, Neil was there and they were having these political chats about this and that.

'For the first time ever, I was completely out of order as an employee of the band and I unleashed all this stuff on everybody that night – all these little things that I thought were the reasons why things were starting to get a bit heavy and going wrong. Thing is, everybody's very reasonable and everyone's nice and nobody's got any agendas, but for some reason there was all this stuff building up.

'The first thing I said to Kelly was, "You're the boss, and the reason this is falling apart is because you're not stamping your authority on it, so people don't know where they stand." He was trying to act a bit like, "Well am I the boss? I didn't know that." I was like, "You know you're the boss, now take the responsibility; they need leadership right now. It's falling apart. You've always been the driving force; you've got to get the boys back together."

'I was on a self-destruction course so, when Stuart came on the bus, I didn't care – I was a maniac. I told him how he gets a bit overpowering and he has to sort of bang you down a bit. I just launched into this whole thing about how insecure he was and how he's always having a crack at everybody because he's so insecure.

'It was a really bad moment for everyone and I was pissed out of my mind, but I think the others thought I was going to get my lights kicked out by everybody – but I just didn't care. I was at that point where I was just like, "Send me home 'cos this is it. If this is where it's going to end up, boys, I don't want anything to do with it; this is not what it's supposed to be."

'Oddly enough, after that it was great. I just got up the following day and laughed and did what I did every other morning. There'd been the odd night before where I'd taken a slamming off other people. You know you've got to get up and have a laugh. The funny thing was, I've had many nicknames but the one from that night stuck: Fruity Boy. They all think I'm a schizophrenic now.

'That was the ugliest thing that ever happened without a shadow of a doubt. It needed to be done – it was just very frustrating to see. Stuart was probably the strongest of the lot because of his sense of humour and his constant energy. I love all that. Richard's just as funny as everyone else but he spends a lot of time on his own, thinking.

'There was a real divide developing and, because I didn't belong to one clique or another, I'd be chatting to everyone at different times. I'd be having a conversation with Stuart and he'd be telling me all this stuff and then I'd be talking to Kelly and he'd be unloading his stuff and that night I exploded I thought, Boys! Are you on the same fucking bus?'

Tony Kirkham joined the band as live keyboard player in the summer of 1998. Now, almost two years later, he's very much part of the 'Phonics family.

Tony started out in a pop band called JJ, who released two albums between 1987 and 1995, *Intro* and *Naked But For Lilies*. When they split he picked up bits and pieces of session work, most notably with fellow Mancunian Ian Brown. When John Brand invited him to T in the Park in 98 he readily admitted he didn't know one Stereophonics song but, after watching them sidestage that day, he was blown away: 'It was proper energy. I thought, this is the real thing.'

An audition was hastily arranged in the Oxford studio where the band were working on *Performance and Cocktails*. Tony pulled a quick one:

'John Brand phoned me up and said, "What gear have you got at the moment?" I knew exactly what they'd need and I just reeled off this list of gear, which I knew was the gear that they'd want and, sure enough, he turned round and said, "That's perfect!" I didn't own a scrap of the stuff I'd mentioned so I went out and borrowed £4,000 off my brother and I bought all this gear and hired a van. I was banned from driving at the time so . . . anyway, I hired this van and drove down to do this audition.

'It was pretty nerve-wracking because they were a band at this point and they knew exactly what they were up to and I was thinking, can I cut this? I'm not really a keyboard player and he looks a bit moody, that Kelly guy.

'I got down the night before and I was rehearsing the parts throughout the evening. I woke up early in the morning and rehearsed the parts again and I remember this guy giving me a really hard time. It turned out to be the monitor guy, Darren. He was just not making me feel comfortable at all. Fortunately, Kelly walks in wearing his undies and a pair of black socks, all rough, rubbing his eyes. I was worried they might think I was coming on a bit Jean Michel Jarre, but Kelly just told me not to worry. He turns round, scratches his arse and walks out.

'So, next thing we're in the rehearsal room, which was quite funny. They were throwing these samples at me and I was pretending I knew where they went and off we went, making error after error. I was playing this Hammond bit on "Traffic" so I was overdoing it a bit, but I didn't think anyone particularly cared. I was trying to be authentic, and Kelly stopped the song and said, "Can we have less of that Nicholas Parsons bit, please!"

'Anyway, over the next couple of days I just had my head on keeping the whole thing together, trying to stay one step ahead, trying to stay professional. They were being quite professional and then, two days in, they had to go and see a band who were going to support them on the road. They said, "We'll go out and have a beer tonight," and I said, "Great." Secretly I like a drink, although they didn't know that at that point. So, we went to this club and we had a great night. Halfway through the night I went to the toilet and Stuart staggers in behind me. I hadn't really talked to Stuart at all at that point. So, Stuart comes in and he staggers against the wall and he goes, "You're going to be all right you. I didn't like you when I first saw you but you're going to be all right!" '

On 30 January 2000, seventeen months after Tony joined the band, Stereophonics embarked on their biggest ever tour of North America. Since that first promotional jaunt at the end of 1997, Kelly, Richard and Stuart returned for a month in March 98. Broadly speaking, America had taken a back seat because of the workload in Europe. Then there was a handful of US dates in October 99 on the way back from Australia, but this was their first proper assault on the Land of the Free.

Things got under way in Los Angeles with 48 hours of madness around the making of the 'Mama Told Me Not To Come' video with Tom Jones. Immediately afterwards they flew to Chicago for a one-off date before joining Canadian outfit Our Lady Peace for a two-week tour of their home country. Our Lady Peace had supported the 'Phonics during their Christmas tour of the UK a month previous, which culminated with those memorable shows at the Cardiff International Arena. Now the roles were reversed and the fourteen-strong Stereophonics entourage wound their way through the arenas of Canada. It wasn't an inspiring tour but it was worthwhile nonetheless. The real stretch, however, started a month later, when they embarked on a thirteen-date tour with the Charlatans.

Tuesday, 28 March 2000

The Warfield Theatre is situated on Market Street, which is basically San Francisco's equivalent of Oxford Street except longer, a lot longer. As you would expect, the venue is a fair distance from the luxurious department stores and a lifetime away from the financial district, a mile or so in the opposite direction. The Warfield is very definitely in one of the more down market parts of town where a community of hookers and dealers ply their trade in amongst the fast food vendors and the touts. It smacks of Kerouac's prose, combining an impulsive energy and colourful chic with an addiction to all things seedy. After all, this is the spiritual home of the beat generation, which later made way for the hippie movement, who colonised the West Coast and declared Frisco their capital. Ironic really that one of the key local bands in the late 60s were called the Charlatans and they have since forced Tim Burgess and his mates to change their name in the States to the Charlatans UK.

I arrived in San Francisco about three hours ago. Despite the fact it's March and it's 6 p.m. the temperatures are still in the 60s. Any notion of jet lag is soon forgotten because tonight Stereophonics and the Charlatans play the third date of their North American tour, which started at the weekend in Los Angeles.

At 8.30 p.m. local time (4.30 a.m. body-clock time), Kelly, Stuart and Richard try and blast any notions of peace, love and understanding into orbit with an opening barrage, comprising 'Roll Up and Shine', 'T-Shirt Suntan' and 'Pick A Part That's New'. There are a fair number of ex-pats in the audience and they make their presence known, but the audience is predominantly local and characteristically bohemian. They too know their 'shit'. Kelly's voice is in good shape and the band are as tight as the proverbial. Highlights include 'Bartender', 'Just Looking' and a dusted down 'Goldfish Bowl'. After the gig the guys head for Dylan's, a Welsh bar, but the jet lag has finally won. It's 7 a.m. body-clock time and I can just about make it through the Charlatans, who are equally impressive. Afterwards they talk about sharing the bill, concluding that it inspires and intimidates them to go on after a band of the 'Phonics' calibre.

Wednesday, 29 March 2000

The boat out to Alcatraz is blowing away the cobwebs quite convincingly. There are, as ever, a few hangovers kicking about, not to mention one particularly serious case of sleep deprivation. Jet lag is a monster. The Stereo-bus will hit the road for Seattle later this afternoon but everyone has struggled out of bed for the trip to Devil's Island. The last time the band were here they couldn't get tickets (as detailed in 'Nice to be Out'), such is the demand to see 'the Rock' in all its macabre glory.

Alcatraz is set on a small island just off the coast of San Francisco. As the boat pulls out of Pier 39, to the left the Golden Gate Bridge is shining in the early morning sunshine. Behind us, on the pier, hundreds of souvenir shop owners rub their hands in grubby anticipation of another day selling crappy Al Capone fridge magnets and Machine Gun Kelly mugs. Only in America! Where else would a prison and its inmates be so celebrated?

Alcatraz is a mass of contradictions. In the space of thirty years it's made the giant leap from the nation's premier maximum-security prison to one of the key tourist attractions on the West Coast with an estimated one million visitors each year.

The naturally uninviting building lying ahead looks for all the world like an unwanted blister on the otherwise idyllic Pacific coastal waters which make San Francisco Bay such a dramatic and beautiful sight.

Originally colonised by the Spanish, it was named La Isla De Los Alcatraces (Pelican Island), after its first inhabitants. A century or so later, in the late 1800s, a military fortress was built here. It was modified in 1934 to create America's most infamous prison. At the time, the country was struggling to cope with the depression and the crime wave it inspired. Prohibition added to the problems, as did the emergence in most major cities of racketeering. The gangster era was in full swing and the government needed to make some sort of statement that it was getting tough. That statement was Alcatraz.

Its first inmates included Al Capone, George 'Machine Gun' Kelly and Robert 'Birdman of Alcatraz' Stroud. These were among America's most violent and brutal prisoners and the authorities decided to treat them to years of rigid discipline, hardline routine and basic living conditions.

Mass murderers are slowly becoming a theme of the trip. Later, Kelly will buy a series of videos detailing the life and times of such 'inspiring' loons as Jeffrey Dahmer and the Boston Strangler. For now, though, it's headsets and spoken-word stories about the thirty years in which Alcatraz etched itself on the American psyche. The inmates, who were incarcerated in tiny cramped cells, called the main corridor through the prison Broadway.

In 29 years there were 14 escape attempts, which is incredible when you look at the layout of the place and bear in mind the frequency of the routine inspections. The most famous of these was in 1962, a year before Bobby Kennedy decided to close Alcatraz. Frank Lee Morris and brothers Clarence and John Anglin managed to get into the water with homemade inflatable rafts. They launched themselves out into the freezing darkness and have never been seen since. Kelly is particularly interested. This is the basis of the Clint Eastwood film *Escape from Alcatraz*. There is, of course, a very thin line between truth and fiction.

A few hours later and we're in the Maxwell Hotel on Geary Street for lunch. Kelly and Richard have been shopping down on the more respectable end of Market Street. Richard has bought some sort of computer game based around a recording studio. Kelly has opted for the entire Stanley Kubrick collection on DVD, plus the aforementioned videos about celebrated basket cases. Not surprisingly, the conversation is still focused on Alcatraz. It is definitely the kind of place that leaves a lasting impression. We conclude that the worst thing for anyone who was imprisoned there must have been the views through the small windows in certain parts of the place. Just crouching down momentarily to snatch a glimpse of San Francisco stretching up the hilly shoreline, with its cable cars just visible, must have been unbearable. The thought of this great, colourful city unashamedly continuing to shout and sigh, continuing to laugh and cry while you waste away in this pitiful hell obviously did, understandably, consign quite a few of the inmates to the nuthouse.

Kelly hands me a four-page document entitled 'Hangman'. It's dated February 2000 and is the first draft of a treatment idea he's put together for a film. The paragraph at the top reads: 'NOTE: Most public executioners had everyday jobs until they were called up for a hanging. Some were publicans; others were ice cream men. The story will be a study of the double life of the main character. Facts based on the memoirs of a public executioner: The Hangman's Tale.'

The story is set in 1948 and centres on Charlie Tucker, who works as a pit storeman, providing miners with equipment and supplies. Charlie secures a part-time number as the Assistant Executioner at HM Prison Lincoln. This coincides with complications in his private life, when he becomes embroiled in a love triangle. Charlie isn't the most sophisticated individual and can't cope with the sense of remorse brought about by his new job. He also can't deal with his growing jealousy and soon begins to lose his mind.

He ends up killing his rival and inadvertently incriminating his lover. In a brutal twist of fate he's subsequently summoned to then take part in her execution, which in turn prompts him to commit suicide. End of story.

The bus pulls out of Union Square and heads out of the city for the highway north, to Seattle. The talk is dark; the day is bright but the jet lag is still winning. The mind is dumbing down but the body is sleepless . . . How very apt!

Thursday, 30 March

Seattle is beautiful. Again, like San Francisco, it's built on the hilly shoreline of the North West coast. It's slightly less marine and more industrial but downtown is pristine and spectacular. No wonder grunge came crawling from the gutters of this place. It's so bloody clean! I've never seen so many coffee shops – they're everywhere.

The big bonus today is that we're all checked into the W Hotel on Fourth Avenue, which is very lovely indeed. As ever, the venue is in the 'lived-in' part of town. It's called the Showbox and has played host to them all – Tad, Mudhoney, Dinosaur Jr, Nirvana, Pearl Jam and, perhaps most significantly, Mother Love Bone. It's not that long ago that Tragic Love Company were tipping their caps in tribute. Even more spooky is the fact that the Melvins are playing in a couple of days. They are credited with being one of the founding fathers of the whole grunge phenomenon. Kurt Cobain was a good friend and a big fan.

The Showbox pulls a more discerning crowd than San Francisco. You get the sense that these people are waiting to be impressed. Stereophonics play pretty much the same set, but at sound check they debut a new tune based on the recent shenanigans in Las Vegas with Tom Jones. Highlights tonight centre on the big songs – 'Traffic', 'Hurry Up and Wait' and the closing tune – a heart-rendering version of 'Stopped to Fill My Car Up'.

Back at the W Hotel, Kelly is trying to sum up his feelings towards America.

'I've never been to Seattle before. Tonight was significant in a way because we used to do cover versions by Pearl Jam and Nirvana. It would have been nice to have been here in 92 when all that was at its peak.

'We've been coming here, to America, since the first album. Most of the lyrics for *Performance and Cocktails* were written across America. We're not going to neglect the rest of the world for America but I feel that we have got an audience here. It just takes a long time to find it.

'The Charlatans have been coming here for years. Obviously they've been around a lot longer than us so we don't feel that we deserve to be on top or anything. It's quite nice to be the underdog opening up for another band. You can become quite complacent being a headline act and playing to ten thousand people every night. It's nice to have that challenge of winning over new people.

'If we're playing to two hundred people in a club and it's full, that's just as exciting as playing to fifty thousand people in a field. It wasn't that long ago we were playing in the Duchess of York in Leeds or the Alleycat in Reading. It's all happened very quickly in Britain. Here in the States I don't think many British bands or decent American bands are getting radio play. It's all Limp Bizkit, Offspring or Blink 182. All those bands should be put in a field and bombed. There's nothing there to listen to. They think they're punk bands and they're not. Exploited was a punk band. The Sex Pistols was a punk band. All they are is Wham with a fucking hard guitar. I think the videos are quite funny but I'm not really into the music.'

Friday, 31 March

Liverpool's 2–1 victory over Newcastle is the chosen viewing on the Stereo-bus en route northwards from Seattle to Canada. By the wonders of satellite, there's pre-recorded footy available now whereas twenty years ago all there was to do was drink yourselves round in circles. We get through the Canadian border with precious few problems. The landscape remains the same but the radio is very different. Welcome to the land of Alanis, Celine and Bryan Adams. Still, before we get too clever for our own good, Canada has been good to Stereophonics and they too have been known to enjoy a Tragically Hip tune or two. It's only six weeks since they were here last with Our Lady Peace, so it's no surprise that tonight's show at the Commodore in Vancouver sold out within minutes of going on sale.

As we're speeding through southern Canada, Kelly plays me some of the rough demos for the new album, which, even through a small mini-disc player with an even smaller speaker, sound powerful. The band are due to start rehearsals back in Wales on 5 June before starting work proper on the album on 25 June. For now, though, Kelly is more animated than I've seen him for some time.

'We're out here until the end of April. We've got a bit of May off in order to finish writing and then it's time to rehearse and record. We're looking forward to that. We've got ten songs written and I'm very happy with the way the writing's going. So that's what we're excited about now – doing a new record.'

The first tune that comes through the mini-speaker is called 'Caravan Holiday'.

'It's called "Caravan Holiday" right now but I've also been calling it "Seven Day Holiday". It is basically about being stuck in a caravan for seven days with someone and it's raining for the whole time. I want to put the word caravan in a song but trying to sing the word caravan isn't easy, so it's not actually in there.

'It's about being in a relationship. There's something romantic about being in a caravan with someone. If it's raining, you can't go anywhere.

'This line's like, "Saturday watched the game, you fried our food, nothing busy, nothing easy but something you . . ." It's just stuff like that. Just respecting each other for having nothing. Going back to basics, I suppose.'

A crackly voice comes on at the end of the track and mentions 17 June 1999, which was the day before the Hultsfred Festival in Sweden and the day, it would seem, that 'Caravan Holiday' was written. Next up is 'Lying in the Sun', which takes a while to find. Kelly admits that one of the great dangers of small kit is the ability to lose things. He maintains the main guitar line for 'Bartender' went missing until the eleventh hour. Thankfully though, 'Lying in the Sun' turns up quite quickly.

'The music was written in the house just as I was about to go out. That always happens. I've got all day to write and then a song comes to me just as the taxi is at the door. So then I have to record it before I forget it. The taxi man's outside waving his card, and I have to leave it and come back to it at a later date. I wrote the lyrics during a holiday with Richard, his girlfriend Gail and Emma. I couldn't go out because I had a rash on my neck and the sun irritated it, so the others were down by the pool and I was sat in the room on my own. I was feeling sorry for myself and then I thought, count yourself lucky, you stupid dick, it's only a rash on your neck. Then I thought about this bloke we saw on the street in Lisbon, Portugal. We'd played the Superock festival there last July and we were wandering about the following day when we saw this poor guy who looked like the Elephant Man.

'So the song starts: "Wish I could lie in the sun, the same as everyone." And then goes on to say, "I'm lucky I can see and I've got a good heart," and all that sort of stuff. But in the last verse, it kind of asks why he is this way. Is he being punished for something he did in his past life? Or is he just that way to make us think we are really lucky? Whenever you see somebody less fortunate, you think you are lucky and maybe they're put on earth to make us realise there are different people and we are better off. I don't know. It's just questions like that.'

Once again the tape crackles and plays what sounds like the noise from a TV. Kelly apparently dropped the mini-disc and it started taping the telly. 'Lying in the Sun' followed 'Caravan Holiday'. It came along about a month later on 26 July 1999 during the week prior to Morfa. 'Caravan Holiday' was the second song written for the new album. The first was 'Nice to be Out', which is on the B-side to 'Pick a Part'.

'I bracketed it as a demo 'cos I really knew it was going to be a song for the album. That was written on a train on a promo trip in Germany. It was only me and Richard so that must have been when Stuart was on a week off prior to his wedding. It was February 99. We recorded the Tom Jones vocal in March and did that song at the same time.

'To be honest with you, that's pretty much a summary of what happened in that year. You know, going to Wembley, talking about being on the famous turf, me and Geoff Hurst and stuff like that. Just a summary of all the things we did. "Nice To Be Out" is something people say when you're in a pub back home.'

Vancouver is quite easy on the eye. It's surrounded by snow-capped mountains and is situated in a basin. The layout is very American – symmetrical streets and fast food places lining the way into town. However, downtown is actually quite European. The roads are closely knit and very busy. In most US cities there aren't too many people on the sidewalks. Standing outside the 1,200-capacity Commodore on Granville Street, you could be in Cardiff, or Glasgow for that matter, as the Friday night post-work crowd hit the local bars and shops. What's even more noticeable is that there's a long queue already forming outside the venue, much to Richard's delight:

'It's not a bad bill really, is it? I'm a big fan of the Charlatans. I've watched them about three times now. I got into them over the last year 'cos Gail, my girlfriend, she really likes them and she plays them a lot in the house. Nice people as well. Good bunch of boys.

'We've only been here once before but I think we've got more of a following in Canada than in the US. They tend to listen more here. The Americans tend to watch more TV. The good thing about Canada is that they read magazines and they make their own minds up about music they want to listen to and want to watch.

'I like touring but then I'm looking forward to getting back into the studio as well. It's really good getting an idea from Kelly and seeing what we can do with it, then seeing what everybody thinks of what we've done as well.'

'Roll Up and Shine' kicks things off again and the crowd in the Commodore goes nuts. They're noticeably more animated than the San Francisco and Seattle gigs. There are Welsh flags in view tonight and it feels more akin to a UK gig. Kelly charms the crowd with tales of when you meet all those relatives who you can't stand at a family wedding. All in all it's a roaring success. The audience down the front is singing every word of every song, which would suggest that *Word* is as big as *Performance* in these parts.

Saturday, 1 April

Burrard Street, Vancouver, 1 p.m. The upstairs of the Virgin Megastore has been closed and a huge crowd has gathered downstairs, in between the racks of records. Stereophonics are due to play a four-song acoustic set but for now we're pinned in the book section out of sight. Fateful. The credit cards take another pummelling. Among today's purchases: *Head On* by Julian Cope, *Don't Look Back*, the Bob Dylan documentary, and *Angel Headed Hipster*, a Jack Kerouac biography.

The in-store gig is a bit of a shambles. Richard's bass is out to lunch but everyone laughs it off. Stuart's wife Nicola is leaving to catch her flight home and so there's a touching farewell. The old romantic even manages to wave and blow kisses mid-tune.

After a mammoth signing session it's back to the bus and time to hit the road for Minneapolis. It's only a 36-hour drive! I say my goodbyes and watch the AC/DC-fuelled Welsh wagon pull into the distance. Little did I know that a storm was brewing out on the lonely plains of Middle America. While it wasn't quite *Twister*, Minneapolis would witness some very cold fronts indeed, and a band teetering on the edge.

19 Reality Bites

K ELLY, STUART AND RICHARD ARE WORKING OUT an arrangement
to the classic 1978 Who track, 'Who are you?' They've
joined producers Marshall Bird and Steve Bush at
Westside Studios in West London. Nick Cave is next
door in the recreation area playing pool. It's a bright but nippy
October afternoon and the mood in the camp is relaxed.
Stereophonics will spend the next week or so working on
B-sides but for now they're concentrating on completing the
Who track for an imminent tribute album. Noel Gallagher,
who has become a good friend over the past couple of months,
is expected tomorrow to add some backing vocals.

It's an interesting choice of track in the light of the identity
crisis the band have suffered over the past twelve months. The
lyric reveals a tormented and confused narrator who is losing
the battle against indulgence. Little did Pete Townshend know
when he wrote it that, ironically, it would be the last Who
release featuring their legendary drummer, Keith Moon. Less
than two months after it charted at No. 18 in the UK, Moon
was found dead in a rented Mayfair flat. He'd accidentally
overdosed on pills he had been taking to combat alcoholism.

Six months earlier, Stereophonics had returned from their US
tour and were on the verge of splitting up. After four years, life
on the road had almost broken them. Relationships were
fractured; tempers were frayed and, most importantly, they
seemed disillusioned and directionless. Kelly had written some

great new songs but he was unsure what he would do with them. In his mind music had taken a back seat, but it was Tony Kirkham's wake-up call that perversely had hit home. On that fateful night in Minneapolis Tony had urged Kelly to stamp his authority on things. The diminutive frontman spent the remaining three weeks of the tour trying to figure out what to do. He'd always called the shots creatively. Everyone else respected him as the leader but he'd never had to assert his authority before. Stuart and Richard were two of his best friends and didn't need a talking to from him, or at least that's what he thought. However, by the time the Stereo-bus reached the Embassy venue in London, Ontario, on 22 April for the final date of the North American tour, Kelly had decided he would issue an ultimatum.

'After we came back from America in April, I wrote a letter to Richard and Stuart saying, "Look, we've got to get our arses into gear. People are already suggesting we can't top the last album. You've got to get your heads down now. We can't just go to sleep on it. We've got to make a better record." I was concerned because, when we left America, it seemed that nobody gave a fuck about music any more. We'd been touring for two years and during the last three or four weeks we all went off the rails and everybody was just counting down the days. I really didn't want that because I had nine songs that I knew were going to make the record. It got to the point where the gig was the least important thing of the day and I didn't want that.

'I wanted us to be like Beck or Macy Gray, who were doing proper shows. I wanted us to be a proper band, like the Black Crowes. We weren't a proper band. We'd been bluffing for a long time and I wanted us to turn into a proper band and move up a level. Otherwise we might as well call it quits. I didn't want us to be complacent, assuming that we'd do stadiums in the summer and arenas in December and that's it. The money's in the bank. Thank you. Goodnight.'

Richard immediately got in touch and told Kelly that he understood completely and was behind the new material 100 per cent. Stuart too was into developing the band's sound but he couldn't understand the drama:

'I was surprised in getting the letter because we had spoken about its contents beforehand anyway. We'd all listened to Neil Young records and decided that's the way we wanted to go. The whole situation came about because we'd been on the road for four years. It had come to a head coming home from Canada. Everybody was knackered and everybody just wanted to get home and spend some time at home. It was like cabin fever. Everybody was climbing the walls. We'd been on a tour bus together for almost two years solid. I felt I just wanted to come home and just relax and get off the road and get out of the routine of getting up every day and doing the same thing: wake up, go do interviews until five, then go do sound check, have some food, go on stage, have a couple of beers, then go to bed. That was my side of it and then everyone else had their side of it, so we just had a few tiffs. It had to come at some time.

'In Minneapolis it was more me and Tony I suppose, me and him arguing. The two of us were pissed and he says one thing and it starts off as a joke and then it gets serious. He said something that he wanted to get off his chest and we just end up arguing all night and I think it pissed everybody off. I didn't really read into it as it being a big thing, but that's the way it goes really.

'I understood exactly where Kelly was coming from before the letter because, musically, that was the kind of stuff that I wanted to do. I wanted to go in and make something that sounded on the kind of vibe of Neil Young's *Harvest*. Anyway, everybody's sorted their differences out so we can put all that behind us and just get on with it.'

It's 8 August 2000 and Stereophonics are holed up in Peter Gabriel's Real World Studios in a small village called Box, near Bath. Box is a traditional Wiltshire village complete with ornate stone cottages, flower boxes and a cutesy post office. The signposts en route suggest an area that is maybe not quite as twee as it seems. I didn't fancy turning off the A4 and checking out Thickwood – or Slaughterford for that matter – but to all intents and purposes this is a genuine slice of little

England in all her ancient glory. We are in the land of crop circles, standing stones and burial mounds.

The studio complex is buried out of sight of the main road and is housed around a converted mill. The old buildings have been restored to provide luxury accommodation and the newer ones are home to the studios and their state of the art gear.

Real World was built in the late 80s by the former Genesis frontman who had huge solo success with tracks like 'Sledgehammer'. It's since become a thriving business with clients such as James, the Beautiful South, Kylie, Placebo and the Propellerheads, to name but a few.

Stereophonics finished *Performance* here in one of the smaller studios, but this time around they're in the 'Big Room'. It's a lavish, comfortable space – like an arc-shaped atrium looking out on to a pond. There's a vague sense of the Starship Enterprise about the layout. Huge floor-to-ceiling windows form a giant windscreen, while the semicircular console points forward into the unknown. To the rear of the room is where equipment is set up and there are performance booths annexed to the side.

It's the first time the band have actually spent any considered time in a studio. Both the previous albums were recorded in bits and pieces in between touring, but Kelly, Marshall and Steve have been here for the best part of the last month. Richard too has been around and Stuart pops in as and when he's needed (his wife Nicola is pregnant with their first child so he's busy balancing his responsibilities at home with those 'at the office').

By the side of the console there's a whiteboard with a progress chart detailing which song is at what stage. At the bottom it says: 'Album title: *Just Enough Education to Perform*, meaning a subtle dig at the music industry and journalists and us and everyone; we learn just enough to get by in life.'

There are sixteen songs currently under scrutiny. The ones most likely to make it on to the album include 'Vegas Two Times', 'Lying in the Sun', 'Nice to be Out', 'Rooftop', 'Caravan Holiday', 'Every Day I Think of Money', 'Have a

Nice Day' and 'Watch Them Fly Sundays'. That's not forgetting the two tracks they're working on at the moment, 'Mr Writer' and 'Step on My Old Size Nines'. Those sitting by the touchline have working titles of 'Stripper', 'Mr Nice', 'Blues Driver', 'Outside', 'Maybe' and 'Shoeshine Boy'.

The morning sun is glinting through the window of the communal living room in the old main house, which forms the focal point of the studio complex. The room is cosy; the sofas are sumptuous and, in true rock'n'roll fashion, we're hitting the coffee hard. Richard is off racing around the Wiltshire countryside on his monster of a motorbike; Stuart is missing and, bizarrely, one of the other artists in residence, Natalie Imbruglia, is walking her dog on the vast lawn outside. Elsewhere, Marshall and Steve are busy getting everything sorted for another day's work but, for the time being, Kelly is having a chat about the new album.

'Before we started I gave everybody a CD with about fifteen acoustic songs on it, nine of which I wanted to use on the album. Another two have been written since. We rehearsed and put together demo versions over a fortnight at Monnow Valley Studios in Wales. Then we came here to record them properly. As happened before, a couple of the demo versions end up on the record. This time it's "Every Day I Think of Money".

'It's been all right; so far it's been pretty laid back, the parts are going down and there is no stress about anything really. People are all going off and doing their own thing. Working hard and playing hard. We haven't been restricting ourselves. If we fancy going out for a pint then we do, but the real focus is on the record. We've been here over a month and I think we'll be done in a fortnight or so.'

In just under three weeks, Stereophonics will play some of the biggest gigs of their lives. They've been asked to headline the Reading, Leeds and Glasgow Green festivals on consecutive nights over the August bank holiday weekend. Also on the bill are controversial US outfit Slipknot, Rage Against the Machine and Placebo. That is the least of Stuart's problems. He thinks Slipknot are a cabaret band but says he's looking forward to seeing Rage. The charismatic drummer is holding court in the

communal dining room where most of the studio's residents
will eventually turn up to savour today's delights – salmon en
croute, garlic potatoes and a wide selection of fresh vegetables.
Stuart, though, is more concerned with the proximity of the
London to Bristol mainline to the studio:

'I went to bed last night at about half past twelve and the
first train comes past about half past five and I jumped out of
bed because it sounds like it's literally just there, just on top of
the brambles. It is very, very noisy indeed!

'Apart from that, though, this is a great place. The food's
great; everybody's laid back; the accommodation is great. It's
quite nice that everyone sits around and has dinner together.
The Super Furries were here when we did *Performance and
Cocktails*, so we had dinner with them. It's a good atmosphere
here, a good vibe – a nice place to work.

'I've got nothing to complain about. Today I finished my last
track more or less, apart from some bits of tambourine and
overdubbing. I didn't come up last week and Kelly did a load
of stuff last week 'cos he was here just doing vocals and
guitars. It's very awkward 'cos Kelly gets all the pressures of
doing two things 'cos he sings and plays guitar. He had to be
a clever arse, didn't he!

'Every time we go in the studio to record anything I try and
take it slowly because, if I lay down six or seven drum parts,
Kelly's there going, "Shit, I'm falling behind." He had a bit of
work to do last week, so me and Richard had a bit of a week
off, which was quite nice 'cos I'm moving into my new house.

'It's a very different-sounding album in a way, but it's still
got its rock songs and its still got it's acoustic-sounding songs.
The one key difference is that the guitars are more elaborate,
so I think we're going to have to take another guitar player on
the road with us. There's going to be a lot of stuff on here that
is going to be fairly hard to reproduce as a three-piece. The
song we're working on today, "Mr Writer", needs another
guitar player when we play live. It needs someone who can sing
a bit of backing vocals, so we're looking for someone who can
play guitar *and* sing! Tony's still going to be there playing
keyboards but we want to get another guitar player. It's a tall

order for whoever comes in. You've got to have the right personality; you've got to have the right temperament and you've got to be able to take the piss big time because that's what happens on the road with us. We were very lucky with Tony.'

'It's been really relaxed so far.' Richard is pouring the orange juice and offers his take on the new stuff. 'It goes to show in the songs. They're nice and laid back and more mature. There's a couple of different sounds for the instruments but nothing special. Stuart's had a lot of time off because he's been sorting out his move. Kelly's not been stuck in here 24/7; he's been going home at weekends.

'The songs are strong, even the ones which won't make the album. There's one called "Mr Nice" which I like because it's about Howard Marks and how he gave Kelly a ring to go and see him down at a show. It's about Kelly going down and seeing him. It's a song that I can relate to because I know the fella and he's a nice chap.

'I'm looking forward to doing the Reading weekend. We didn't want to do any British shows this year because we thought we'd have a year off to relax and get our heads together and record a new album. Then the Mean Fiddler came to us and said they've grabbed Oasis for Reading and offered us a lot of money to do it. It'll be great to just be in good company and have a beer or two before and after and relax. Festivals are usually rush on and rush off, but because we're topping the bill, we can pretty much relax all day and let the boys get the gear on and then go on and do as long as we need to do.'

The evening is spent recording several vocal takes for 'Step on My Old Size Nines'. It's all been very civilised and the mood is almost tranquil – a far cry from Minneapolis. The sense of calm is further enhanced by a beautiful midsummer sunset. The sky is idyllic with huge dashes of pink strewn across a pale blue backdrop. Outside by the pond you can hear the birds in the trees and there's a balmy feel to it all. Marshall and Steve have stepped out for a breather and a smoke. I mention that it must seem like a lifetime ago when they were en route to the

Stereophonics

Borderline in Central London that fateful winter night when they met Stereophonics for the first time. Steve agrees and then concludes that their success is due in the main to the sheer volume of ideas, which Kelly brings to the table.

STEVE: It's a weird thing. There are always ideas in progress with Stereophonics. On the first album there were ideas that we put down that became songs for the second and, subsequently, the same thing happened for this album.

There were a couple of songs that we knew already and a whole load that Kel had recorded acoustically either on the bus or in the house. I remember we had about eight on a cassette. A lot of them were very hard to get into because, essentially, they were just vocal and acoustic with not very much indication of where they were going to go.

MARSHALL: There's twelve now that are very much alive, and they'll all survive either as album tracks or B-sides. There's twelve that we've been concentrating on for the last two weeks and we only got to that point three weeks ago. Up until then we had to think of the shape of the record – some of the rock songs weren't as good as some of the slow songs – that whole album dynamic that you need to think about. But I think we've got it right.

It's the most cohesive Stereophonics album by some way and not necessarily because we've done it in one block. The ideas that are going on are more adventurous, using other instruments and even backing singers. The embellishments that come naturally with a band as they get older and realise the limitations of being a three-piece are interesting. For all the excitement, you do need to branch out. Kel's been out on tour with bands like Aerosmith – the big boys, the players with backing musos and different ideas going on. He's gradually warmed to it and this record definitely is the first chance we've really had to throw what we wanted to hear all along into the pot.

STEVE: The band have done it pretty well in terms of sounding like who they are at various stages in their career. The first album, give or take one or two songs, is about Cwmaman. The second album was a little more verse/chorus accessible and a little less with the words carrying the song. They've always insisted on doing nothing that they couldn't reproduce live.

MARSHALL: Which is a natural by-product of being just signed, a three-piece without the experience of touring, without seeing other bands – but third album in, it's a whole different prospect.

To Kelly's credit, the songwriting itself has taken a massive step forward. That's all the influences that have been absorbed and there's a real maturity to the songwriting now – it's impressive stuff.

Ten days later, Kelly is sorting out guest passes for his family and friends for Reading. Envelopes are methodically laid out on his kitchen table as he sticks the kettle on. His home, a modest semi tucked away on a back street in Aberaman, is a couple of miles away from where he grew up. It's tastefully decorated, extremely tidy and very quiet. He shows me one room full of memorabilia. There are photos on the wall with various rock stars plus an impressive array of gold and platinum discs. Lloyd Grossman wouldn't have a problem here – jukebox, guitars, piano and hundreds of CDs – could it be that a musician lives here?

Exile on Main Street by the Stones is playing in the background as we sit down to talk through the new songs in some detail.

DANNY: We spoke in Canada about two or three of the new songs, so let's just start with them. 'Nice to be Out' was a B-side to 'Pick a Part' and was written while you were on a train in Germany if I remember correctly.

KELLY: I was just thinking about all the places we'd been to really: this stadium in Berlin, where the Olympics were held. Hitler apparently used to address mass rallies there and we were actually stood where he once stood. When we played Wembley you think of the Geoff Hurst thing. There was Jamie's bar in New York where De Niro did *Raging Bull*. We've just been to all these different places and then there was Tom Jones telling stories about Elvis and Richard Burton, but in the song we call him Mr Woodward, not Tom Jones, because that's his real name. It's like a musical postcard casting us back into the past with scenes of JFK. You stand there in Dallas and you see all these different buildings around you and when you go to that site you can't stop thinking about it for hours. Then of course there's Alcatraz. So that's all that song is – a musical postcard.

DANNY: Is 'Vegas Two Times' about the lunacy in January surrounding the video with Tom Jones?

KELLY: Yeah, the words came when we were in Canada in March. It was just about getting there, not necessarily about the Tom thing. The title refers simply to when we were leaving Vegas, going to meet up with everyone in Los Angeles. We drove out and we got lost and we had to come back in and leave again because we couldn't find our way out. I couldn't call it 'Leaving Las Vegas'. I wanted to but I couldn't because Sheryl Crow had a song called that.

The line 'Vietnam vet taxi drive' is about this taxi driver who was like that bloke in *Falling Down*: 'You and me, we're the same!' John's in the back and Pinko and me only got in there for a lift and he's telling us all this stuff about all these dirty bars and stuff – well, that's Vegas, innit! The song starts with 'immigration, information' and then it goes to the gambling floor and Studio 54, where Tom took us. It's more about the music than the words really and I just wanted some lines which were about nothing more than getting a bit messed up with weird people I suppose, nothing deep.

DANNY: You mentioned that 'Lying in the Sun' was inspired by a beggar in Portugal.

KELLY: We'd been to the HMV in Lisbon, buying some posters or something, and we'd seen this bloke. I thought he had a mask on because we were about 150 yards from him. As we got closer we all stopped and had a look and the bloke was holding up a medical card. He looked like the Elephant Man. His face was all red, like a kind of birthmark, and you could see only one eye, no other features.

So then I had this rash on holiday and started thinking about this guy and tried to write from his perspective, wishing he could be a normal person doing normal things. He's trying to think why he looks the way he does, why he's been so unfortunate. I don't know if there's past lives or future lives. I don't know, but I suppose he says maybe he was there to make you feel better, and that was his sacrifice.

DANNY: 'Mr Writer' is going to get you in a lot of trouble. You'll be accused of not being able to take criticism and of unfairly criticising people who feel that they're presenting a version of the truth.

KELLY: Don't get me wrong, I respect good journalists. 'Mr Writer' is not about these people, it's about bad journalists and bad journalism. Those people who misrepresent the truth. They have limited musical knowledge and are unable to see how trends begin because they can't place music within a context of time. It's frustrating talking to some little dick who thinks he knows everything about you. At the end of the day he will always have the last word; no matter what you have said he will twist it to suit his own agenda.

I find journalists in Europe and Japan are more interested in discussing the music rather than the lifestyle. In this country the press are only interested in the drugs you're taking and who you are seeing, and although it is very British and I love all that George Best stuff with musicians there's often a lot more going on which is never written about.

DANNY: 'Step on My Old Size Nines' is as close as you've come to a love song, or is it?

KELLY: Again it's one of those 'What's it all about songs', isn't it? A 'What are you here for? What are you supposed to be doing? Where are you at?' kind of song. Then you see an old couple doing their thing and you wonder if all this analysing is worth it because it'll happen despite you. They've been through it all and at the end of it if you're with someone that you want to be with then all that stuff in between is kind of irrelevant.

The title line is quite sentimental but in another kind of way . . . it's quite laddish. It's something that a geezer would say to an old bird. He's too afraid to say, 'Would you like to dance with me?' 'cos it's a bit too Fred Astaire. It is sentimental, and it's got the word love in it.

DANNY: 'Caravan Holiday' was one of the tunes you talked about in Canada. More romance?

KELLY: The song is written in a way where you're spending time with someone that you want to be with and it doesn't matter what's going on around you. Again it's quite sentimental.

In the same way, a lot of it comes back to my old girl I suppose. When you're a kid, if you had a terrible holiday because of the weather or something, your parents had to make it into something that you'd remember. It's inspired by that.

DANNY: 'Rooftop' would seem to be another of your mini-plays in the same way that 'Stopped to Fill My Car Up' was on the last record.

KELLY: I had this idea driving home one night about this bloke. He's working in this office, goes up for a fag, top of the building, and he's only up there trying to clear his head, and then all these people underneath think he's a jumper, that he's a suicide guy. Anyway, he starts really liking the attention and then, in the end, he stands on the highest place and gets that feeling. He likes the attention so much that he thinks, maybe I should. It can be taken as a metaphor for what we do now really. However, I only did it a couple of weeks ago so I don't really know what it's about.

DANNY: 'Every Day I Think of Money' is in a similar vein, although I expect it isn't a metaphor for your own experience. You're not thinking of running off with the takings are you?

KELLY: No, not yet! It's a fictional thing. I got the seed of the idea off a film. It tells the story of a guy driving a bank truck full of cash. I thought, if you were driving that and you were in a dead-end situation and you had all that behind you every day, it must play with your head a little bit. You'd be thinking that all your problems could be sorted and you'd start daydreaming about what you could do with the money if you stole it.

It says in the second verse, 'ditch the truck and tie up his right-hand man and buy a new face, plastic surgery'. At the end, he's in a truck and he's with convicts, so whether he's been caught or he was just dreaming all along, I don't know. Again that can be taken in a few different ways. It's a fictional story about people thinking that money can solve all your problems, next to the Beatles saying it can't buy you love. It can't give you soul but it can drag you out of the hole. A lot of the time it magnifies your problems in the same way that drugs do. It takes you out for ten minutes and you think it's all over, but then you wake up and it's the same as it was before. It's like being famous or not being famous; if you're an arsehole before, you'll just become a bigger arsehole.

20 A Hard Day's Night

THERE'S A DEAFENING SILENCE ONSTAGE. 'A Thousand Trees' has been abandoned midflow and Kelly is staring helplessly at the biggest crowd he's ever played to. The Stereophonics frontman seems at a loss for words, prompting fears of a rock star tantrum. The reality of the situation couldn't be further removed.

There are 60,000 people, minimum, on site at the Reading Festival 2000 and Stereophonics are closing the final night. It's 9.30 p.m. The vast area stretching back from the stage to the horizon is a sea of faces but some of those faces towards the front are contorted in pain. The frenzied atmosphere has inadvertently caused a crush and the organisers have called a halt to proceedings. Security men are trying to pull some of the people at the front over the barriers and Kelly is now urging everyone to take a step back.

Only two months previous, nine young men were crushed to death during Pearl Jam's set at the Roskilde festival in Denmark. Understandably it's a tense moment at Reading but thankfully order is restored and no one is badly hurt.

The Sunday at Reading has, over the years, become known as 'rock day' and, in keeping, today has already featured sets from Supersuckers, Blink 182, Rage Against the Machine, Placebo and Slipknot. In previous years the Sunday night headliners have included Metallica, the Red Hot Chili Peppers and Nirvana. The admission of Stereophonics to this hall of fame is as confusing as it is flattering. They consider themselves rock fans rather than an out and out heavy rock band. Whatever!

There was speculation in some sections of the media that Slipknot's so-called 'harder edge' and circus-like stage show would prove to be the highlight of the day. They were sadly mistaken. Despite the fact that Kelly, Stuart, Richard and Tony are playing no new songs whatsoever, the now familiar anthems get a wild response and ensure that Reading 2000 will be remembered as a benchmark gig for Stereophonics. This is it. Official confirmation, if it were needed, that they are now premiership material.

The final encore arrives and just when you think the crowd can't get any more frenetic, they do. 'Ladies and gentlemen, Mr Tom Jones.' Mr Woodward takes to the stage in front of the biggest crowd he's ever played to. It goes without saying – Vegas this ain't. Tom laps it up and the assembled cast play 'Mama Told Me Not To Come' to the delight of the 60,000 people singing along. It's quite a spectacle, and on the wrong side of the Severn Bridge too!

Back at the hotel afterwards, the Stereo-family plays host to Tom Jones. The Dom Perignon is ordered and, of course, Tom's beloved Cuban cigars aren't far behind. However, as Kelly explains, three years ago things were very different.

'The last time we played the Reading festival was 97 and we opened up on the main stage. I think the Manics were headlining and I think we were paid about £250. I think we were going to Germany the next day and we were probably in the back of the Mercedes splitter van. It was a good van but not quite as nice as this hotel. They pay you more than £250 now, you see. [Rumours abound that the fee for the weekend is in seven figures!]

'It's great. My family turned up earlier with packed lunches and Welsh cakes. I was glad to see the flasks and sandwiches turning up. It's like a family outing, which is great. It's very normal, it's very down to earth . . . in some ways.

'I was nervous earlier on because before this weekend we hadn't been in front of an audience for a while. You always worry at festivals as to who's there for who, especially because the bill was a bit weird. There was Slipknot and Rage Against the Machine, so when we went on I was a little bit dubious about the crowd. Then, as soon as you start playing, it's great. They all knew the songs and stuff so I was only anxious until about the second song. I can't believe that we're in this position to be honest. I probably won't even think about it until next week.'

Stuart joins us: 'I'm hoping today will be one of those "I was there" days for people. The fact that Tom came on made it even more special. I'm sure there are a lot of people who will remember this one. Then again, there are a lot of people up in Glasgow today who will remember that Celtic–Rangers match. [Celtic beat their arch-enemies 6–2 earlier in the day.] That's it – I hope this goes down as an Old Firm gig. History in the making, hopefully.'

So, it's only six months since Stereophonics had been close to breaking point, vowing that they would steer clear of playing live for the foreseeable. Tour manager Neil McDonald explains:

'After the American tour everybody had had enough. It's no secret. Most bands talk about the pressures of touring but, if you'd been stuck on a bus or a plane with people for 26 months, you just want to go home and see the cat and the missus. I'm sure everybody was the same. So the line was that after the last tour there would be no more dates after that.

'However, offers kept coming in. There was a show in Costa Rica that was offered, some kind of charity show, and the fee would have been a small section of rainforest, which seemed quite an original way to be paid. I think Kelly's line was, "What the hell am I going to do with a piece of rainforest in Costa Rica?" It's not really a holiday destination, so that one was knocked on the head.

'I remember the Reading call coming in. We were in a hotel in Toronto, waiting to leave. John called me and asked me to put the offer to the band. I went up to see Kelly and said, "You've just been offered X amount to do Reading." Maybe there was a couple of seconds gap but the nod of the head came pretty quickly. I think they thought the offer was too good to refuse.

'I think it's worked well for them as well. They were worthy headliners and I think it put them up alongside the Oasis' of this world. I'm absolutely sure that shows like that have a lasting impact on people's lives, just like Deep Purple at Knebworth did on mine.'

Keyboard player Tony Kirkham is in a buoyant but reflective mood: 'I think tonight was the end of an era, definitely. I think everybody has now heard the first two records. That growing phase in the Stereophonics career has kind of peaked. I think there's a different phase coming. They've made a new record that is a bit more organic.

'For the first time in a long time I felt they really revelled in the old songs; they really enjoyed the old songs and they really wanted to play the old songs, and play them like they played them the first time around.

'Standing onstage, it's a funny perspective for me anyway. I'm obviously a bit further back and I'm a bit detached anyway, but the size of the gig didn't really hit me. I've been doing this for two years and I was playing all the same parts, doing all the same things, but for some reason I really felt a real energy off the crowd. It's funny for me because, being a sort of outsider, I get to feel what the boys are up to within themselves on the stage and there's just nights when they light a fuse between the three of them and it goes. It just seems really special when they do that because they let all their inhibitions go and they get passionate about the music.'

The August Bank Holiday weekend 2000 kicked off with a headlining show on Glasgow Green. The bill at 'Glasgow Festival in the City' also featured Paul Weller, Beck and Elastica.

Upon arrival in Glasgow I'm confronted with a Stereo-camp slightly the worse for wear. They've been here for a day or two and last night Kelly's girlfriend Emma led them all on a tequila frenzy.

As the bus pulls away from the plush Malmaison Hotel in the city centre, the mood is regular. The usual anecdotes about who made a fool of themselves the night before are the order of the day as we head for the festival site. Everyone is keen to check out Beck, who's on about five-ish, so we're getting there good and early. Their headlining slot isn't for another six hours at least.

Backstage, the dressing rooms are arranged in a village green style, so everyone is pointing on to the same communal area. Kelly is chatting with Paul Weller, who has been a great fan and supporter of the band over the years. There was talk at one stage of him doing some production work with them but that has yet to materialise. Richard, meanwhile, is chilling out in the portakabin/dressing room.

'We've all got hangovers. We were in and out of bars down Sauchiehall Street last night and we ended up bumping into a bunch of Welsh lads. So we had a bit of a late night and then an early morning, doing a sound check.

'I'm looking forward to tonight because we've got quite a big following up here in Scotland. They've been with us since the beginning. We started touring up here as soon as we had a record deal and they've never forgotten us, so it's been excellent. I think that's the reason why we're headlining tonight, because they just embraced us and supported us fully.

'I'm looking forward to seeing Beck and Weller as well. The only other two bands I'd like to see are the Crocketts and "A". There's a lot of hard rock bands on and there's a lot of American bands which fit into that category. They're not my favourites at the moment.'

Beck is great, as are Stereophonics who play a headlining set to a 30,000-strong crowd in the pouring rain. The set is made up of almost everything from the first two albums and you get the impression that a lot of these tunes won't be getting an outing for a long time. Stand-out moments include a raucous 'Thousand Trees', where the line 'wake up and smell the rain' takes on a life of its own, and 'Bartender', which sounds for all the world like a call to arms. The crowd responds and the weather takes a backseat. Stereos 4, Crappy Scottish Weather 1.

Leeds is like *Groundhog Day*: alarm call in the Malmaison in Glasgow, on to the bus, into the Malmaison in Leeds, back on to the bus and down to the site. The weather is even the same:

it's bucketing down. There is, however, one key difference – the bill is slightly different. Today there's no Paul Weller, no Beck. Instead there's Slipknot, the US noise band who dress up in overalls and slightly disturbing masks. There are eight of them and they all have a name and a number, hence No. 6 – the Clown and so on. Slipknot are a phenomenon and they revel in their controversial image. They like to sniff jars with dead birds in and throw up on their audience. Maybe it's because they're the first ever successful band from the American state of Idaho, which is often referred to as the 'lonely state'. No bloody wonder!

Anyway, when we arrive on site in Leeds, security informs us that they're not allowing anyone through because 'the Knot' are about to take to the stage. Richard's brother Terry is acting as Stereophonics' minder for the weekend. He's not impressed. Terry is an absolute gentleman but one would imagine, given his army experience, a rather tasty gentleman. He informs the site security guy, who obviously hasn't twigged who he's dealing with, that this is not the ideal way to treat your headlining turn. The guy still doesn't get it so Terry quietly asks him if he would prefer 'local or general'. This confuses him even further until Terry whispers, 'I'm talking about anaesthetic.' A split second later everything is sorted and we're ushered through.

No wonder Slipknot didn't want anyone backstage. These 'psychotic, dangerous' creatures are rolling around in the mud. Their overalls are white and the whole scene resembles a Persil ad. They obviously feel the dirty look makes them even more menacing. The pre-gig preparation doesn't end there. They all line up and take turns at running into the door of their dressing room!

Three hours later, Stereophonics take to the stage. Oddly there's no rolling around in the mud or throwing themselves into doors beforehand. The gig is bigger than Glasgow, with an estimated crowd of 45,000. There are dozens of people on shoulders and the noise is deafening. 'Traffic' provides *the* moment when Kelly pauses and 45,000 voices sing the song for him.

Back at the hotel, Kelly is trying to articulate the experience.
'The crowd tonight stretched all the way back up this hill.
It's a bit weird because the last shows we did were in these
poxy little clubs in America. I don't really get frightened of the
amount of people but I just find it a lot more difficult to talk
to them. What do you say to 60,000 people? Some of them
might not be listening and nobody can understand me when I
talk anyway, so I don't bother saying much any more. I just
play the song. That's the hardest part for me – knowing what
to say. I'm not really big on talking in between songs. That's
what I find most difficult.'

Stuart interjects: 'It was superb up in Scotland. Obviously
the rain didn't dampen spirits and today in Leeds it was great
too. We listened to a tape of some of it on the bus on the way
back to the hotel. Listening to "Traffic" when they're singing
the words is amazing. They were in time; you can tell they've
listened to the record. One song that will stick in my mind for
a long time is "Local Boy". The whole place, from the front to
the back, was just going up and down. It must have been mad
if you were actually on the ground because whether you
wanted to jump or not it was tough shit! It was, you're going
up, you're going down!'

A fortnight after Reading, Stereophonics are in London for
Shine On, a John Lennon tribute show. They'll perform
alongside Sharleen Spiteri from Texas, Moloko, Paul Weller
and Oasis, among others.

Kelly is picking at a tuna salad in a North London café close
to George Martin's famous Air Studios. It's fitting really that
the former Beatles producer is, ultimately, the host for today's
event. Had he lived, John Lennon would have been about to
celebrate his sixtieth birthday, so a whole new generation of
musicians are turning up to pay their dues including perhaps
the Beatles' most celebrated fans, Oasis. Noel and Liam are
also Kelly's new best pals.

'I first met Noel over a year ago at the Kosovo benefit gig at
the Forum here in North London. I was in France just before
that and Weller phoned up to see if we would do it because his

sister was organising it. He said, "I'm really into the band. No one's writing lyrics like that any more. Power to you." Then he started quoting bits from *Twin Town* down the phone to me. "Buy your own fucking glue" – he was doing all that. I was thinking, this is Paul Weller on the phone!

'Anyway, on the day of the gig, we were just sitting around all day waiting for the sound check. I was watching Ray Davies and I was thinking, one of the reasons I'm doing this is because of bands like the Kinks and the Jam. Later in the day we were back in the dressing room and we heard this big riot coming up the stairs. It turned out to be Liam, Noel, Goldie and a couple of other boys. They'd all been to see Man City, who had won promotion to the Premiership by winning the play-off final at Wembley in extra time.

'Liam was on one. He just burst in the room and took over. He grabbed a guitar and started playing "Little James". He was talking about their new album, saying it sounded like "Punk Floyd". That was funny because the press had got hold of that quote and thought he was talking about Pink Floyd.

'This was the second time I'd met Liam. I met him once before when we were celebrating *Performance* going to No. 1. The party was at V2, which is next door to the Halcyon Hotel. Liam was in there on his own, so we joined him. At the Kosovo show we were about to go on when he grabbed my arm and thanked me for my company that night. That was really weird – here was the life and soul whispering his thanks to *me*.

'I'd said hello to Noel earlier in the day but when we came offstage I remember him coming up to me and rubbing my head like he was my old man. He said, "Good show, kid. Don't ever lose that voice." He then promised to take us on tour in America, but he took Travis instead, the bastard! I just remember him being really nice. I didn't know him from Adam but he knew what we were about at that time 'cos it was probably our year that year.

'From that day we've been in loose contact. He sometimes gets me footy tickets but it wasn't until recently that we had a really good chat. I went back up to Leeds on the Monday after we did Reading. Oasis were headlining. That was weird because I walked on to the same stage we'd headlined forty-eight hours before, but this time I'm stood at the side.

'We saw Noel later and he asked if we were doing "the Lennon thing". "We should do something together," he said, and I agreed. We arranged that he would come down to Real World to try some songs. I'd said I would prefer to play acoustic guitar. A few days later he turned up with Jason, his right-hand man, and Gem from the band.

'We were all like steaming the night before, so I thought I might as well keep drinking this morning 'cos I didn't know if I could get through the day if I wasn't slightly in a daze. So I carried on drinking a little bit. When we started in the rehearsal it was still all a bit polite, so I said, "My head's banging," and he said, "Mine is too. I could do with a pint. Why don't we have one?" So we put the guitars down and we went to the Queens in Box. We all spent about ten hours in the beer garden, exchanging stories about what we'd done over the last five years.

'On the way back from the pub me and Noel were walking behind. We were steaming. I remember us just ranting in the street. We sat on the kerb for forty minutes talking nonsense and this bloke walks by with his dog and does a double take. When we got back to the studio we played our latest tracks to each other. It was a great night.'

The main room in Air Studios is decorated with Lennon memorabilia. The guests present include film stars Jude Law, Sadie Frost and Johnny Lee Miller. Kate Moss is wandering around but, oddly, there are no Beatles. There are precious few musicians other than those who are performing or taking part in some other way. Liam has done an interview for the programme and is taking advantage of the free bar. There's a few of Lennon's contemporaries – Donovan, Ronnie Wood and Lonnie Donnegan – but the general idea is a bunch of contemporary musicians reworking Lennon's material.

Richard and Kelly perform a version of 'How' before Stuart, Noel and Gem join them for the Lennon-penned Beatles tune 'I'm Only Sleeping'. Kelly also takes the vocal on 'Revolution'.

The music is supplied by the Jools Holland Orchestra. By 11 p.m. it's all over and the Stereo-gang retires to a nearby hotel for drinks. Kelly leaves the studio with Liam Gallagher to face the waiting paparazzi outside. As the shutters click, Liam looks every bit the rock'n'roll star, complete with shades and vintage jeans and denim jacket. Kelly, on the other hand, is sporting a hooped jumper and looks understandably uncomfortable if not a little thrilled by the situation. Later he explains:

'Earlier in the day, while I was rehearsing "Revolution", Liam walks in with his sunglasses on, Clint Eastwood style, and sat down in front of the stage going, "Proper, man, Proper!" He was pointing at his throat. I thanked him and carried on trying to be cool. When I'd finished rehearsing I went down and said hello. He's always on about the voice. We were all waiting for Noel to do the sound check. He was late and Liam says, "You know what's going to happen, don't you? When I walk out, he's going to walk in." And he walked out and Noel did walk in.

'I remember at one point Liam said, "Another stripy jumper? Is your grandma knitting them for you? They're fucking top. Where do you get them from?" There's no reply to that really.

'At the end of the night we were talking outside and I said, "We're off down the hotel. You coming?" So he grabbed my hand and pulled me out of the door and we all walked down the street hand in hand and the photographers were everywhere. I was thinking, what's going on here? It was a strange day!'

Epilogue – Don't Look Back

THE ST DAVID'S HOTEL stands centre stage in the heart of the Cardiff Bay area, towering like a monument to a new world. Sound familiar? It should do. It's almost a year since that fateful night when we decided to commit the Stereophonics story to paper. Tonight we're back in the same place, but a lot has changed. The area has been further developed and the winter chill doesn't seem quite so wind-swept and romantic. The horizontal hail doesn't help.

This time around there's no foot stomping or ruthless abandon. There's no CIA, no Christmas arena tour. Still, there are certain parallels. There is a sell-out show, albeit at the smaller Cardiff Coal Exchange and Stereophonics are still plastered all over the front page of the *South Wales Echo*.

It's Friday, 24 November 2000 and the Kelly Jones solo acoustic tour has just wound up back on home turf. For the past eleven days Kelly and his gang of merry men have traversed the country from Brighton to Glasgow and back. It's a back-to-basics opportunity to try out some of the new material and a deliberate step to get out of the album–tour–album–tour cycle that so many bands fall foul of. Kelly has decided to hit the road for the *craic*, and for the first time in a long time he's doing it at a loss. In tow is his new onstage compadre and esteemed Stereos co-producer Marshall Bird. There's a stripped-down crew comprising most of the usual suspects but the people most notable by their absence are Stuart and Richard. Richard got married a few weeks ago and has just returned from his honeymoon. Stuart, on the other hand, has been surveying building work at his new country pile.

Understandably, the decision to embark on this project has fuelled speculation over the band's future and Kelly has deliberately started every gig by publicly denying any possibility of them calling it a day. He's also been working on his onstage communication skills. There's a lot of banter with the audience and a fair bit of insight into where the new album has come from. He tells the story about the deformed guy in Portugal; there's a tirade about lazy journalists and there's much talk about laddish love songs.

The crowd at the Coal Exchange justifiably feel they're witnessing something special. Earlier in the afternoon the 'Phonics held a press conference and announced two huge shows for next summer, under the banner 'A Day at the Races'. They'll play Donington Racetrack on Saturday, 14 July 2001 and Chepstow Racecourse a week later. It goes without saying that tonight is a rare opportunity to hear the songs at close range. It's up close and personal all right. In fact, the toilets are just to the rear left of the stage so there's a constant procession of people wandering under Kelly's nose throughout.

The stage is Crowes-esque, with candles and fairy lights creating an intimate atmosphere. Kelly is perched on a stool for the duration with only Marshall to his left on keyboards. Highlights include the Motown-like 'Have a Nice Day' and a frightening rendition of 'Handbags and Gladrags', a song he tells everyone that he heard on a Rod Stewart CD recently. There are reworked versions of 'Just Looking' and 'Hurry Up and Wait' but the real stand-out moments come at the end when he's joined by Richard and Stuart for the encores. They do a cover of Neil Young's 'Heart of Gold' (with support turn and all-round top friend Davey Crockett on harmonica), before a mellow rendition of 'Local Boy in the Photograph'. The show ends with lots of smiles, onstage hugs and general good vibes!

Back at the hotel, Stuart is talking about the last six months.

'It was nice to get back on stage and play – the three of us again. It was good. I went to watch Kelly in Birmingham on

Wednesday and it was strange being at the front and him being on stage, but it was good. The songs sounded great and he sang really well.

'He mentioned doing this tonight to me last week. He said, "When Richard comes home do you fancy doing a couple of songs with me?" and I said, "Yeah, great." It was great. The crowd went mental and it was the appropriate place to do it as well – Cardiff. We can put all the rumours to bed that we were going to split up and everything.'

Ten days previous, Noel Gallagher and Gem from Oasis are drinking tea in the bar of the U2-owned Clarence Hotel in Dublin. Everyone once again is nursing hangovers and Noel is suitably attired in leather jacket and shades. Last night was the opening date of Kelly's acoustic tour and the two lads turned up to guest on a couple of tunes and, of course, to party afterwards. Noel is ribbing Gem, who sneaked off to bed at about 2 a.m. – part-timer! He, on the other hand, decided to 'give it the lash' and is now paying for it.

The gig was a riotous celebration. When Kelly took to the stage the crowd didn't stop cheering for about five minutes, and from that moment on it was obvious it was going to be one of *those* nights. The heckling was good-humoured and frequent and the onstage retorts were equally amusing. The set featured a mix of old and new material with seven songs from the new album. 'Mr Writer', 'Nice to be Out' and 'Lying in the Sun' seemed to go down particularly well. Oscar's prophetic words about his son's vocal abilities improving with age seemed particularly poignant.

Noel and Gem's appearance was the worst-kept secret of the night and when they appeared the place went crazy. They started with a version of 'Live Forever', with Kelly on lead vocal, rounding off with 'I Wouldn't Believe Your Radio'.

It's obvious Noel and Gem enjoyed it. Otherwise they'd be at Dublin Airport catching a plane home. Instead they're happy to chat.

Gem takes up the story: 'I seriously had goose pimples. I went right to the back at the beginning and he couldn't even start for five minutes. When he eventually started playing I thought it was phenomenal. I saw one girl with her mobile phone held up. Everybody was so anticipatory and they just seem to have found their feet. I don't know if the new songs are deeper or whatever, but they definitely worked last night. It was magical really.'

Noel continues: 'He was very, very good. I'm not a massive fan of Stereophonics but the main thing about the new stuff is, for me, it sounds a little bit slower and a little more introspective.

'We've become good friends since that John Lennon programme, *Shine On*. We all went to do "I'm Only Sleeping" and me and Gem had learned it in E Minor and Richard had learned it in F. So we sort of busked our way through it a couple of times in rehearsal. Then we went, "Fuck it, let's go to the pub for an hour." Twelve hours later we were still in the pub. It just went from there really. Kelly's a good lad; I like him a lot.

'He was petrified before he went on. He wasn't looking his best and we were saying, "It'll be all right. They're your fans; you sold the tickets on the Internet from your fan club. Once you go on it'll be all right." Of course, as soon as he went on, he hit the first note and away he went. No problem at all.

'There was a lot of shouting going on between the songs but you expect that in Dublin anyway. They weren't as rowdy as they could be. He didn't get stuff thrown at him. They were all very polite. It was polite rowdiness really.

'Everyone was coming up to us last night in the hotel bar afterwards and congratulating us on a great gig. I kept telling them, "Don't tell me, go and tell him because it was his gig." We only came on at the end but it was good. We were going to do that Beatles song and then one of mine followed by one of his but we still can't get this Beatles song right. We thought we'd ditch that and do one of mine and one of his. He picked his and I picked mine, so that was that. I thought that mine would be poignant as it's a song about friendship. His choice, "Wouldn't Believe Your Radio" has got some strange lyrics: Got himself a flying giraffe and had it in a box by the window? And they reckon my lyrics are daft!'

Gem concludes: 'It was like that last day of term vibe really. There was really no reason to do it; it was just for the *craic* – no pun intended.

'I met Kelly at the John Lennon tribute night. Noel's known him for a while and they definitely hit it off. All of Stereophonics – they're just full of stories and it's just like a mad *craic* really. I think they're totally in it for what I'm in it for. It's not about the nonsense that's out there really. It's about the music.'

It's a fortnight after that Dublin show and Kelly is sitting in the bar of the Halcyon Hotel in West London. Since the end of the solo tour a few days ago he's guested with the Who at the Albert Hall and is now in the throes of sorting out some of the creative decisions that surround the release of the new material. He's spent the afternoon next door at V2 talking about artwork and video treatments but now we're safely holed up in familiar surroundings – the hotel bar. Coffee is the order of the day as Kelly casts an eye back over the past couple of weeks, not to mention the six months that preceded them and, indeed, the four years that in turn preceded them.

DANNY: You said on stage at the end of the Cardiff show that you came close to splitting up. Let's just put the record straight. How close?

KELLY: There were no bad feelings about me doing this acoustic tour. Everybody just knows that I like playing and that's what I do. When we started it, the *NME* wanted to do an interview and obviously they asked if the band was splitting up. So then the whole issue is brought back up again about what sparked all those rumours.

When we came back from America we knew stuff had gone on and it took a while to sort out. When we did Reading it would have probably been the end of it. The Tuesday after Reading we all sat down and said, 'What the fuck is going on?' It was a weird vibe around Reading. There was a lot of shit going on, a lot of stuff had been boiling up to that point and nobody had ever said anything. It wasn't even that big a deal when we got round to it. Basically everybody was telling their problems to various members of the crew and by the time they get back to you they get magnified, so the only way to sort it was the three of us to say, 'Well, what's the matter then?'

I just think that we forgot about the music and just thought it was about getting blitzed every day – which it can be. You go on tour with the Chili Peppers, for example, and they've got their drums and amps and everything downstairs and they do a mini gig before they do the proper gig. All we were doing was eating tortilla chips and stretching our trousers to make sure they still fit before you walk on. I was like, 'This ain't right.' That last tour of the States was terrible. Everyone was complaining so much that the boys and everyone in the crew were counting down the tour by the hour for when we would return home. I was like, 'This is not right, touring is supposed to be a good thing; we could be in a factory!'

I think it's all sorted now. We went to America to mix the album in September and we rehearsed during the days and we were mixing it at nights. It was the first time the three of us had been together for a long time. We spent time in an apartment together and we sat up talking all night and it just got back to how it was.

You find your own little clique on the bus and you end up doing this and doing that. You forget why you got into it in the first place.

DANNY: Was it weird playing without the two boys?

KELLY: All the solo gigs were great. I've never enjoyed gigs so much for years because everything had become routine. This was not part of a routine because we were learning new songs in sound checks and just improvising on stage.

Last Friday, when Richard and Stuart turned up for the sound check, everything clicked again. It was like we were doing a reunion gig or something and everyone was close to tears. Everyone was just being really nice to each other. Something happened when the three of us got on stage together and then at the gig itself – when they came on at the end the crowd went mental.

I loved doing the acoustic thing and I will do it again because it's a completely different thing and it just takes it back to when you wrote the song in the first place, without all the bullshit. The band thing is a completely different thing again. I was watching a video of Reading the other day and it gets you excited again because you want to go and play again. I just think we need to do what we do, just to keep us all happy because otherwise it gets stale.

DANNY: Was Dublin the highlight of the tour?

KELLY: It was hard to beat Dublin; it had it all really. It was all the anticipation 'cos nobody had a clue. I didn't know how loud or quiet the audience was going to be. I didn't know if I could play the songs and, to add to it all, Noel Gallagher was coming on to do the encore. During the show, when we'd done something wrong, I could hear him shouting from behind the curtain: 'Fucking Rubbish!'

When we started it was just an amazing feeling to do the songs in such a stripped-down way. People were there to listen to them for what they are, without the big lights and screens and amplification, just the dynamic of one man and a guitar.

The crowd were great and there was a lot of funny banter. It just became really relaxed. There were people shouting and I was shouting back. I suddenly thought, this is what it's about.

Noel came on for the encore and we're doing 'Live Forever'. Basically, I was Liam Gallagher for three minutes. I wanted to be Liam Gallagher three years ago. Two years before that I was Eddie Vedder. Dreams can come true. Dublin was quite a night.

DANNY: So how did the gig with the Who come about?

KELLY: We got asked a while ago to contribute to a tribute album for some charity, so we did 'Who Are You'. Soon after, John phoned me up and said, 'Do you want to do a song with the Who at the Albert Hall?' John was like, 'We've got to phone Roger Daltrey, tonight.' I said OK and we ended up doing 'Substitute'.

Anyway, the day came and Noel had called and said he'd pick me up. I was like, 'This life is getting weirder!' So, when we arrive at the Albert Hall we walk up on to the front of the stage and the Who are sound-checking. I've got my bag over my shoulder and my parka on like a schoolkid. I was just grinning. Roger Daltrey said, 'Kelly, how do you want to sing this then? Do you want to bounce a few lines back and forward or just sing it all?' I said, 'I don't mind, whatever!'

At the end of the night I'm sitting in the green room having a pint with the boys and Harvey Goldsmith walks in with Mick Jagger. Jagger points at me and says, 'I remember seeing you at NetAid.' We had our photo taken and then he was gone. Next Jimmy Page comes in, gives me a hug and we have a chat and then I'm introduced to Eddie Vedder, who was also guesting. It was surreal.

When we decided to leave I bumped into Daltrey and I've had a few by now so I was like, 'Roger, any chance of a lift in the car?' He looks outside at all the people and he goes, 'Come on, Kelly, you go out first,' and then he looks at my parka and he goes, 'Nice parka that, son! I used to be a mod too. Thanks for coming. It made a lot of kids happy tonight. Be lucky!' I walk out and there's sixteen Mercs outside but no car for me. It's pissing rain and I'm signing autographs and trying to flag a cab! Straight back down to earth with a bump!

DANNY: It seems appropriate that you have the last word, so how would you sum up the road from the Tragic Love Company playing the Ivy Bush to hanging out with Jagger, the Who and Oasis?

KELLY: Every year's got odder and this year's been the oddest. We've worked our bollocks off throughout and achieved a huge amount. All along we've been getting recognition and respect from some of our heroes. It's not so much from the critics but from people who we've really looked up to.

This year the people we've met and worked with have been incredible. That's the fun about it really – those small rewards that remind you why you got into it in the first place. The music press might not think that doing the Albert Hall with the Who or doing a duet with Tom Jones is cool. I don't care. To me it is!